Globalization, Export-oriented Employment
and Social Policy

Globalization, Export-oriented Employment and Social Policy

Gendered Connections

Edited by

Shahra Razavi
UNRISD

Ruth Pearson
University of Leeds, UK

and

Caroline Danloy
UNRISD

First published 2004 by
PALGRAVE MACMILLAN
Houndmills, Basingstoke, Hampshire RG21 6XS and
175 Fifth Avenue, New York, N.Y. 10010
Companies and representatives throughout the world

PALGRAVE MACMILLAN is the global academic imprint of the Palgrave
Macmillan division of St. Martin's Press, LLC and of Palgrave Macmillan Ltd.
Macmillan® is a registered trademark in the United States, United Kingdom
and other countries. Palgrave is a registered trademark in the European
Union and other countries.

ISBN 1–4039–3485–1 hardback

This book is printed on paper suitable for recycling and made from fully
managed and sustained forest sources.

A catalogue record for this book is available from the British Library.

Library of Congress Cataloging-in-Publication Data
    Globalization, export-oriented employment and social policy : gendered
    connections / edited by Shahra Razavi, Ruth Pearson and Caroline Danloy.
        p. cm.
    Includes bibliographical references and index.
    ISBN 1–4039–3485–1 (hardback)
      1. Women – Employment – Case studies. 2. Foreign trade and employment –
    Case studies. 3. Globalization – Economic aspects – Case studies.
    4. Globalization – Social aspects – Case studies. I. Pearson, Ruth, 1945–
    II. Razavi, Shahrashoub. III. Danloy, Caroline.

HD6053.G57 2004
331.4—dc22   2003070199

10 9 8 7 6 5 4 3 2 1
13 12 11 10 09 08 07 06 05 04

Printed and bound in Great Britain by
Antony Rowe Ltd, Chippenham and Eastbourne

Contents

Acknowledgements

The editors would like to extend their appreciation to the chapter contributors who responded positively to the numerous rounds of revision requested. We would also like to thank those who contributed to the Workshop that UNRISD organized in Bangkok (October 2000) to initiate the research project on which this volume is based.

Preface

A central preoccupation in both developed and developing countries is the impact of globalization on social policy. Globalization affects social policy both at the normative level and in a more practical way, by setting constraints that social policy must be attentive to. Adhesion to international conventions and responses to an international discourse of 'social rights' permeate domestic politics and affect social policy – or at least the thinking about it. At the more practical level, it is often feared that globalization is not only reversing the social gains made in the developed countries in the 'golden era' of capitalism and the welfare state, but that it makes it highly improbable that developing countries will have the policy autonomy to nurture interventions in the labour market without losing international competitiveness and scaring away domestic and foreign investors. Furthermore, the erosion of the fiscal capacity of the state (partly due to 'exit' possibilities for capital) is likely to undermine the domestic capacity to finance social policy. In sharp contrast to this view, is the argument that there is no simple relationship between globalization and social policies. National political arrangements and resolution of social conflicts mediate the pressures of globalization. The frequently cited argument shows that openness to trade has often been associated with increased social expenditure, and that there is no uniform pattern of response among the developed countries to globalization. In other words, generous welfare states have been, and continue to be, compatible with open trading regimes.

These questions form the backdrop to the present volume. Women's entry into paid labour – not least in the context of global factories and export production – has been a subject of long-standing interest. However, much of the analysis to date has focused on women's individual experiences of export employment: the extent to which it represents a positive opportunity or gross exploitation. In spite of the extended discussion of social rights in the global economy, little attention has hitherto been paid to the implications for women's entitlements arising out of their pivotal role in export sectors. Two opposing sets of assumptions have fuelled this neglect: for some, participation in global markets is inherently inimical to the achievement of social rights, while for others, women's presence in key economic sectors will automatically be reflected in the ways in which social policies are formulated. As a result there has been up to now little empirical and analytical engagement with this question. This volume attempts to fill this gap.

The conclusion of the volume, namely that in six of the countries included as case studies, a combination of factors – gender segmentation of labour markets as well as the global and local pressures for welfare retrenchment – have denied women industrial workers the opportunity to attain welfare entitlements, is sobering. Even in South Korea, a developmental state nurturing globally competitive industries women workers had much less access to the significant welfare entitlements obtained by permanent male workers, particularly those employed by large corporations. Although there are opportunities of combining an orientation towards export markets with an emphasis on social rights – as recent developments in Korea seem to indicate – the gendered segmentation of labour markets and the architecture of social policies need considerable policy attention before this can become a reality.

Financial assistance for the preparation of this manuscript was provided by the Rockefeller Foundation and the Swedish International Development Agency (Sida) and UNRISD's core funders, the governments of Denmark, Finland, Mexico, the Netherlands, Norway, Sweden, Switzerland and the United Kingdom.

Thandika Mkandawire, Director, UNRISD

List of Contributors

Viviane Brachet-Márquez Centro des Estudios Sociolólogicos, El Colegio de Mexico, Mexico.

Sheila Bunwaree Department of Sociology, University of Mauritius, Mauritius.

Hyoung Cho Department of Sociology, Ewha Womans University, Sudaemun-gu, Seoul, Korea.

Jinjoo Chung Institute for Occupational and Environmental Health, Kuri, Kyunggido, Korea.

Delia Davin Professor of Chinese Social Studies, Department of East Asian Studies, University of Leeds, UK.

Caroline Danloy Research Assistant, UNRISD, Geneva, Switzerland.

Jayati Ghosh Centre for Economic Studies and Planning, School of Social Sciences, Jawaharlal Nehru University, New Delhi, India.

Gillian Hart Department of Geography, Chair, Center for African Studies, University of California at Berkeley, San Francisco, USA.

Insoon Kang Division of Social Science, University of Kyungnam, Masan-City, Kyungsangnamdo, Korea.

Orlandina de Oliveira Centro des Estudios Sociolólogicos, El Colegio de Mexico, Mexico.

Ruth Pearson Professor of Development Studies and Director of the Centre for Development Studies, Institute for Politics and International Studies, University of Leeds, UK.

Shahra Razavi Research Coordinator, UNRISD, Geneva, Switzerland.

Ann Zammit Independent Consultant, Geneva, Switzerland.

1
Globalization, Export-oriented Employment and Social Policy: Gendered Connections[1]

Shahra Razavi and Ruth Pearson

If in an earlier era citizenship was bound up with the capacity to bear arms and defend the nation, in more modern times it has been associated – both symbolically and programmatically – with a person's capacity to 'labour', or perform paid work.[2] One of the key questions confronting feminists is whether the capacity to 'labour' – a criterion that is inscribed at the heart of social policy arrangements across diverse contexts – works as an exclusionary principle, denying large numbers of women social rights of citizenship. In the case of advanced industrialized countries, as Orloff (2002) observes, historically men gained social rights (to pensions, unemployment insurance and the like) on the basis of their paid work, while women's access to benefits was usually mediated by their relationships to men. She further argues that this set of arrangements has been fundamentally challenged by the movement of women into the realm of paid work: women have gained symbolic and material resources for citizenship as well as access to benefits initially created with male workers in mind. Their increasing presence in the workforce has also spurred the development of new forms of income security, such as parental leave, with some countries extending this to paid or unpaid leave for a wider range of 'domestic' responsibilities including the care of elderly or disabled dependants, or family illnesses and crises.

But does work as a route to economic and welfare entitlements have any resonance, or even relevance, in developing countries? Evidence suggests that women in many of these countries have significantly increased their labour force participation (UNIFEM, 2000). To some extent the increase in women's labour force participation rates is a

1

statistical artefact – it reflects better ways of recording seasonal, unpaid, and casual wage labour, although it should be acknowledged that much of women's work still goes un-recorded (Charmes, 1998). But it also reflects a number of real changes. More women must now work to ensure family survival – in the face of declining real wages and the increased monetary cost of subsistence resulting from cutbacks in public services and subsidies (Pearson, 1999). But a further reason, particularly regarding the increase in women's labour force participation, is that there has been greater demand for women workers in particular sectors of the economy, particularly in export sectors that have in some countries experienced considerable growth. Much of this has been in low-skilled manufacturing – notably in garments, footwear and electronic products. This increase in demand for women's work has been extensively analysed in terms of the comparative advantage of women's 'nimble fingers', the docility and productivity of women's work and the resulting lower unit costs attainable with the employment of 'cheap' female labour (Pearson, 1998). But has women's growing presence in the realm of paid work, and particularly in high profile factory work, been translated into more secure access to social rights, along the lines suggested for the advanced industrialized countries?

What spurred our interest in this question was the curious absence of social policy concerns in the extensive and diverse feminist literature that devoted itself to understanding different facets of women's employment in export-oriented industries (Razavi, 1999). Some strands of this literature, by both neo-classical and heterodox economists, focused on wages and gender-based wage gaps in the context of export-orientation (Tzannatos, 1995; Seguino, 1997; Bhattacharya and Rahman, 2002). Other strands, more sociological or anthropological in outlook and approach, explored processes of gender subordination, empowerment and agency in households, communities and factories where women workers lived and worked (Wolf, 1992; Kabeer, 1995; Hsiung, 1996). Other writings, some of it by trade unions and women's organizations, were concerned with working conditions in the so-called global factories (Edgren, 1982; Heyzer and Kean, 1988). This third cluster came closest to asking questions that related to 'social policy' in the narrow sense of concern for the rights and security of the work force, highlighting the absence of health and safety provisions, the ban on workers' rights to organize and so on, but little attempt was made to link these findings to broader social policy trajectories and their gendered constructs.

We were struck that there had not been any serious attempt to problematize the possible connections (or lack thereof) between female employment in the highly feminized export-oriented industrial processes and broader social policy arrangements. The implicit assumption seemed to be that women's work in export-oriented industries was taking place in a social policy vacuum. This, in turn, could have been attributed to three possible factors. First, that employment in globally competitive low-wage export-oriented industries could not possibly generate anything but a very low wage. Second, that coinciding with the neo-liberal turn in state policies and the constraints imposed by 'globalization', women's emergence on the labour scene had taken place alongside labour market 'flexibility', welfare retrenchment, and the rollback of the regulatory state. And finally, that 'footloose' foreign capital, considered as the main employer in these export-oriented industries, enjoyed special privileges in developing countries which effectively absolved it of all responsibility for workers' welfare. But although these factors seemed to offer at first glance plausible explanations as to why women's overwhelming numerical presence in export-oriented industries in the South had failed to translate into more secure entitlements or social rights, on closer scrutiny they were far from convincing.

For a start there was no theoretically derived *a priori* argument that we knew of to suggest that employment in export-oriented industries in open economies must be devoid of all social rights or social wage subsidies.[3] Nor did the historical evidence point to such an inevitability. After all, precisely the opposite argument had been convincingly made by political economists to explain how small open economies of Europe had responded to external vulnerability (Katzenstein, 1985).[4] The vulnerabilities that more open economies were exposed to, these analysts argued, required greater social protection, social cohesion and solidarity, and the welfare state was a response to the challenges of economic integration (Gough, 2000). Furthermore, despite the initial fears and hype that 'globalization' would lead to the demise of the welfare state, by the late 1990s the evidence seemed to point to the continued dominance of national institutional traditions of interest representation and political consensus-building as important parameters shaping growth, employment and welfare objectives in the advanced industrialized countries as they sought to adapt to the pressures of globalization (Esping-Andersen, 1996).[5] In other words, the gloomy prognoses of the lack of viability of European welfare states in a globalized world did not seem to hold up to scrutiny; generous welfare states have been, and continue to be, compatible with open trading regimes.

In developing countries export-oriented industries had taken root in national economies marked by different political economies and industrial strategies – from the more *dirigiste* or interventionist Northeast Asia states that gave temporary effective protection to infant industries conditional upon export promotion, to the more 'market friendly' approaches that seemed to underpin the emergence of *maquiladoras* in the Mexico/US border. Foreign direct investment (FDI) was not always the prime mover; in many countries it was national capital rather than FDI that nurtured export-oriented production processes.

Nor was the growth of female employment always taking place in a social policy vacuum. Some of the most celebrated cases, like the Export Processing Zones (EPZ) in Mauritius and even the *maquiladoras* in Mexico, took hold in the context of national development projects which had fashioned nascent welfare states (which may or may *not* have been inclusive of women who laboured in the EPZs). Much the same could be said of the East Asian 'success stories'. These states may not have nurtured European style welfare states, but they underwrote the low money wages paid to industrial workers with a range of implicit or 'surrogate' social policies (Chang, 2001) or 'social wage subsidies' (Hart, this volume). As Chang puts it: 'there were a lot more social policies in East Asia than it is typically believed, if we define social policy more broadly than what is the custom (which equates it with "welfare-state" type of policies)' (p. 12). These implicit social policies included extensive land reforms, some protection of labour, public housing programmes, inter-ethnic income redistribution and welfare provisioning by the corporate sector. The 1997–98 crisis may have marked the end of an era in East Asia, forcing widespread structural revamping in the conduct of politics and management of the economy along more 'liberal' lines (Woo-Cumings, forthcoming), but it has also prompted a keen debate on 'social policies'. Some observers argue that 'globalization' far from marking the demise of social policy in East Asia, has in fact given a new lease of life to policy interest in this area (Kwon, 2001).

A key question, it seemed to us, which was not being asked, was the extent to which these explicit, implicit or surrogate social policies were inclusive of women workers. As already noted, the analyses of women in export-oriented industries have tended to focus on women's working conditions and remuneration rather than on the wider economic and social entitlements available to the workforce. Hence the nature of the interface between female employment in export-oriented industries and social policy remained an open, and in our view under-researched, topic. There are significant differences among developing countries that have nurtured export-oriented industries, both in terms of their economic/industrial policy traditions as well as social policy arrangements (however embryonic they may be). We felt that it was important to highlight these policy differences in order to show that there was more than one way of nurturing employment in export-oriented industries, and with potentially different implications for women workers.

The challenges facing developing countries in the present era in sustaining viable social policies are legion. Putting in place inclusive social policies requires both financial wherewithal and strong state administrative structures. These are enormous challenges for many developing countries that are struggling to raise public finance domestically while being burdened with weak state administrative capacity after having undergone more than two decades of state 'restructuring' and 'reform'. Hence the second question we wanted to explore was the extent to which *access* to social policies – explicit, implicit or surrogate – is being extended beyond its initial narrow base to include the new cohort of women workers, or whether access has become more restrictive and exclusionary in the current era.

The chapters that follow this introduction cover a range of countries with different histories and in different stages of industrialization. They attempt, in their different ways, to tackle the questions raised above. In this article we contextualize some of their findings. But first a few words on social policy, since our discussion so far has already pointed to some ambiguities in how this concept is understood.

Implicit and explicit social policies

In the 1990s social policy became prominent on the agendas of a wide range of development actors. This re-discovery of 'the social' (Mkandawire, 2001) came in the wake of more than two decades of stabilization and adjustment policies that had monopolized the development agenda, and generated a sharp rise in income inequalities as well as persistent poverty in many countries. The apparent consensus on the importance of social policy, however, masks diverse, and often conflicting, conceptions of what social policy is, of the goals and values that underpin it and of the nature and extent of state responsibility for social provision and delivery.

Organizations like the World Bank now argue for some forms of 'social policy' so as to reverse the worse excesses of economic policies, contain social unrest and enable the neo-liberal project to move forward. Here social policy takes the form of safety nets designed to capture those who fall through the cracks in the process of economic reform, together with public provision of basic health and education services, grafted on to an essentially unchanged macroeconomic policy agenda with a focus on market-based criteria (World Bank, 2000).[6] For others, however, the dismal social and economic record of the past two decades underscores the unsustainability of the neo-liberal project on its own terms. These critics argue that an alternative approach to considering social policies as an afterthought to macroeconomic policies would start with the idea of 'mainstreaming social issues into macroeconomic policy by means of a rethinking of macroeconomics and of the organization of macroeconomic policy processes' (Cornia, 2000; Elson, 2000, 2002).

Two important, though obvious, implications follow from the latter perspective. First, the distinction between 'economic' and 'social' becomes highly ambiguous – a position that has long been maintained by political economists and sociologists who see 'the economy' and its institutions, especially markets, as socially and politically constructed (Polanyi, 1957). Second, and following from the above, it underlines the fact that all policies (including macro-economic policies) have a social content and/or social effect, and are thus *social* policies in the broad sense of the term. Deflationary policies which have been in vogue over the past two decades in both developed and developing countries, and which prioritize low rates of inflation, tend to benefit financiers while they denote stagnant employment opportunities. This stands in some contrast to Keynesian economic thinking, which underpinned policy debates for much of the post-Second World War period: social development – expressed in terms of *full employment* – was embedded within Keynesian macro-economic policy.[7] At a substantive level then the distinction between 'economic' and 'social' policy is no more than an abstract dualism, and an effective way of pursuing social policy is to make explicit the social biases of economic policy, adapting both economic as well as welfare policies to achieve social ends.[8]

Informed by such a vision, UNRISD, for example, defines social policy broadly as 'state policies, practices and institutions that directly influence the welfare and security of various groups within a particular society' (UNRISD, 2000: 9). The advantage of such a comprehensive definition is that it embraces a wide range of policies that shape the welfare and security of different social groups. The UNRISD document makes a further distinction between implicit and explicit social policies. Not all elements of social policy, it argues, need to be explicitly addressed. 'For example, social policy may be embedded in economic policy, when the latter has intended welfare consequences or reflects implicit or explicit socio-economic priorities, such as reducing politically unacceptable levels of unemployment' (ibid.). Macro-economic policies belong to this category. Nevertheless some elements of social policy, it asserts, are more explicit, such as direct government provision of social welfare, in part through broad-based public services and subsidies. Social policy in this more explicit or narrow sense also covers income policy and social security systems, including pension schemes.

Yet, among those who want to see social concerns re-inscribed into macro-economic thinking, there are different perspectives on how this should be done, and the conditions under which social forces can demand policy responsiveness. For some it is imperative to reinstate the Keynesian development vision, thereby legitimizing the pursuit of the twin goals of national industrialization and full employment. This agenda would require bringing both the developmental state and national trade unions back into the picture. It would provide the opportunity to build essential institutions for regulating aggregate demand and cross-border flows, and provide the basis for an inclusive social dialogue in pursuit of security and prosperity for the majority.

Others, among them many feminists, argue that macro-economic policy approaches that rely solely or principally on full employment to achieve socially desirable outcomes are severely limited because they fail to recognize different forms of unpaid 'care' work that are just as much at the heart of provisioning human needs and ensuring well-being as paid work (Elson and Cagatay, 2000). The failure of the twentieth century, they argue, was to legitimize *labour* but not *work* – like caring work, voluntary work and community work (Standing, 1999). If social policy is to be re-embedded, then all forms of work will have to be legitimized in that process. The idea of constructing systems of mutual assurance around recognizing the different kinds of contributions that people make to society – and not only their contributions to paid work – is considered to be vital for devising systems that are inclusive (especially of women) and citizenship-based.

But this takes us ahead of our story. We will return to this debate once we have set out the main findings from our case studies elaborated in the following chapters of this book.

Findings from the case studies

The gendered construction of developmentalist social policies in East Asia

The two East Asian countries in our cluster – South Korea (thereafter Korea) and China – despite having different levels of income and being in different stages of industrialization, share a number of historical and institutional characteristics that are important to bear in mind. Emerging from decades of colonialism, war, conflict and insecurity, both countries built strong state structures ('developmental states') in order to survive their tumultuous geopolitical predicaments, to develop, and to 'catch up'. In this process of compressed development, markets were strongly 'governed' (in the case of Korea) and suppressed (in pre-reform China) and the direction and pace of development was strongly guided by the state. Despite their divergent political ideologies, both countries implemented radical land redistribution programmes that left behind an egalitarian legacy in terms of wealth and income distribution (between social classes). It could also be argued that radical land reforms and a range of explicit or 'surrogate' social policies, including the provisioning of social welfare by enterprises, have effectively subsidized industrial wages (rendering them globally competitive), dampened labour conflicts and provided a certain degree of legitimacy for the state and its developmental project. However, less widely appreciated in the mainstream literature, is the fact that these rather egalitarian societies also harbour starkly unequal and rigid gender hierarchies – reflected in their highly masculine population sex ratios (Greenhalgh and Li, 1995; Park and Cho, 1995) that are carried over into the social construction of labour markets as well as the social arrangements and institutions for welfare provisioning.

The case study on Korea, by Hyoung Cho, Ann Zammit, Jinjoo Chung and In-Soon Kang provides, to the best of our knowledge, a unique analysis available in the English language of the female employment/ social policy nexus in Korea spanning two different policy regimes that have marked the country's post-Second World War political economy. As is well known, Korea's early developmentalist era of compressed capitalist industrialization with spectacular economic growth and structural transformation was followed from the late 1980s by a gradual shift towards a less interventionist approach – a trend that was reinforced by further liberalization and deregulation under the aegis of the IMF to deal with the severe economic and financial crisis of 1997–98. Government intervention to force the pace of industrialization had been achieved through its close association with big business (the *chaebols*) on the one hand, and the banking sector on the other – the very structural ties that came in for sharp criticism by the Bretton Woods institutions after the crisis. The aim of industrial policy until the mid-1970s was to promote light industry, the output of which was increasingly destined for export markets. Thereafter and until the late 1980s, for strategic reasons, the focus turned to promoting more capital- and technology-intensive 'heavy' industries and petrochemicals.

What is important to retain for our analysis is that from the early 1960s and until the 1997 crisis, Korea maintained an annual rate of growth of real GDP of about 8 per cent that generated what was tantamount to full employment for men, *increasing* levels of employment for women and overall growth in real wages averaging about 7 per cent a year. However, the extent to which industrialization, structural transformation and rapid economic growth reduced gender hierarchies in employment and gender gaps in wages has been limited (Seguino, 1997). Our case study draws attention to a number of persistent gender hierarchies that mark Korean labour markets.

First, while from 1970 to 1997 women's labour force participation rose by almost two and a half times, with manufacturing and services absorbing the greatest numbers from the growing female labour force, after 1990 (i.e. even *prior* to the crisis) both the absolute numbers of women workers in manufacturing and the share of women in total manufacturing employment declined. This points to the 'de-feminization' of manufacturing employment, which has been observed in a number of other export-oriented Asian economies as well (Ghosh, this volume, 1999; UNDESA, 1999). In the case of Korea, despite the changing industrial structure resulting from the government's promotion of heavy industry and petrochemicals, women were mainly employed in light industries (which were experiencing relative decline) while the new capital- and technology-intensive industries principally employed men. In other words, the shift from the so-called 'low road' to 'high road' industrialization has been marked by the gradual displacement of women workers.

Second, after several decades of industrial development and high growth about 40 per cent of female workers had regular full-time jobs, while more than 60 per cent had temporary or daily work. The bulk of employed women therefore faced considerable insecurity and instability regarding their employment and income (with implications for their welfare entitlements, as we will see later). However, contrary to the common belief that all Korean males had 'life-long employment', Hyoung *et al.*, report that only about two-thirds of male workers had regular contracts. Nevertheless, the relative share of men and women within each category of employment displays the familiar pattern whereby men take the lion's share of regular jobs, while women constitute a higher proportion of employees on temporary and daily contracts.

Third, despite gradual improvements in women's wages, the gender wage gap was far from closed and gender wage inequality in Korea was one of the largest among the OECD countries for which data is available.

Finally, the case study confirms that the 1997–98 crisis had disastrous consequences for gender equality. The earlier introduction of labour market flexibility allowed enterprises to rid themselves of regular workers during the crisis. This interrupted the slow progress that women in particular had made in accessing the more secure jobs so that by the end of 1999 women had a *lower share* of such jobs than in 1990.

The Korean welfare regime has been described as 'productavist welfare capitalism' (Holliday, 2000): heavy emphasis was placed on social policies which bolstered the regime's developmental efforts and its attempts at nation-building, with considerable investment going into education, health and housing. Employment policies until the 1980s provided 'life time' job security and thus a certain protection for many male workers and their families. The case study also underlines the importance of corporate welfare throughout the period, especially for workers in the core firms (the *chaebols*), while noting that the pressures for corporate restructuring after the 1997–98 crisis pose a critical challenge to this particular style of welfarism.[9] Finally, over the past four decades four social insurance schemes – for Industrial Accident, Pensions, Employment Insurance and Health Insurance – have formed the core of social welfare provision (together with a minimal public safety net). From a very narrow base their scope was gradually extended and reinforced in a substantial way in the wake of the financial crisis.

What the case study adds to the existing body of research on social policy in Korea is a detailed analysis of how far Korean welfarism has been inclusive/exclusive of women. The short answer to this question is that the limited provision of social welfare in Korea, even in the more expanded form which was implemented in the post-crisis period, has not delivered equitable access to women. To be more precise, the sectoral distribution of women's employment, the size of the firms in which they were employed, the occupations in which they were clustered and the nature of their contracts combined to ensure that both the direct benefits of employment (remuneration, non-wage benefits, stability of employment, career enhancement, accumulation of savings) and indirect outcomes (access to social welfare insurance, and security in old age) were generally less advantageous for women workers than they were for male workers. For example more generous corporate non-wage benefits were provided by large firms, whereas the bulk of women workers were concentrated in the small- and medium-sized firms which could ill-afford the same level of benefits. Moreover, even the key employment-related social insurance schemes were only extended to small- and medium-sized firms with considerable delay, and in any case could only benefit a small number of working women due to the high proportion on temporary and daily contracts. Even though small firms (of under five employees) where women were concentrated were legally able to subscribe to social insurance schemes, implementation of this law has been weak.

Whether the greater emphasis that is now being placed on social insurance and social assistance can be considered a step forward as far as women workers are concerned is also debatable. The chapter argues that the gap in welfare between large and medium- and small-sized firms may have narrowed in recent years as a result of two parallel developments: first, the post-crisis corporate governance reforms causing large firms to scale back fringe benefits, and second, the fact that large numbers of workers in small- and medium-sized firms have become eligible for membership in the social insurance schemes. Whether this will indeed have an equalizing affect on gender disparities in access to welfare entitlements is an open question. Much depends on how thoroughly the extension of the social insurance schemes to employees in the small- and medium-sized firms is implemented. If benefits are strictly calculated on the basis of employment-based contributions, then the implicit bias against women workers is likely to remain. If, on the other hand, the government steps in with financial subsidies to compensate those who make lower contributions, then the potential for a more egalitarian welfare system will be greater.

In sum, Korean women workers have been at a disadvantage in terms of welfare entitlements under both the developmentalist era and in the more 'liberal' (if not *neo*-liberal) period of welfare expansion, largely due to the gendering of labour markets and the way in which welfare entitlements have been, and continue to be, linked to employment-based contributions. As Hyoung *et al.*, point out, greater job insecurity and cut-backs in corporate benefits have provoked a keen debate in Korea on whether the country should proceed towards a full-fledged redistributive welfare state that embodies citizen rights and is financed by general taxation, or whether it should continue to rely on a system of social insurance that is largely tied to employment. Ironically, despite the deep gender interests that are implicated in this question, to date the debate on the future of welfarism appears to have been un-gendered.

Korean developmentalism was driven by strong nationalist sentiments. Feminists have often been critical of nationalism for the way it subordinates women's interests to the larger goals of national struggle and nation-building. Communist regimes, however, often make an ethical commitment to the 'emancipation of women' based on women's juridical equality, their entry into paid work and the provision of social rights to health and education, even though the 'real socialisms' that took hold in the twentieth century used the political mobilization of women in highly instrumentalist ways to consolidate the power of the Party (Molyneux, 1996). The chapter on China by Delia Davin is interesting because it illustrates both the considerable extent to which communism in China enhanced the project of gender equality, as well as the persistent gender hierarchies and biases that proved difficult to dislodge. The Chinese style of economic and social restructuring – whatever its merits and divergences from the orthodox liberalization policies advocated by the 'Washington Consensus'[10] – is, however, fast eroding some of the hard-won gains that an older generation of women workers made under socialism, even though Davin is not too dismissive of the prospects that have opened up for a younger generation of largely rural women in China's booming export-oriented industries.

A number of pertinent findings emerge from this case study. First, the chapter draws attention to the subtle ways in which welfare entitlements in pre-reform China were gendered. In addition to significant cleavages in welfare entitlements between rural and urban populations, it draws attention to disparities among the urban population, largely due to occupational status. In pre-reform China social welfare was largely distributed through the enterprise: state employees in government offices, state-owned enterprises (SOE) and schools enjoyed the greatest job security and the most generous welfare entitlements, while those who worked in enterprises operated by local governments and by collectives had far less generous entitlements. This stratification had a distinct gender subtext since men greatly outnumbered women in the formal state sector and also predominated in senior grades.

Second, in the context of economic reform the private sector has proliferated while the state-owned enterprises have come under pressure to become more 'competitive'. The latter have laid-off workers in large numbers, job security for life has come under attack for making workers complacent and enterprise-based responsibility for social welfare has been trimmed. It has been widely reported that a disproportionate number of workers who have been laid off, and who remain among the long-term unemployed, are women (Cook and Jolly, 2000). As Davin observes, for a generation that was brought up to believe that women should be in the labour force and to draw their self-esteem from the contribution their work made to their society (and families), the impact of economic reform has been hugely negative.

These developments have posed serious questions about the future direction of social policy in China. The state has indicated an interest in developing social insurance mechanisms. However, in practice these systems still cover only a limited number of employees, while enterprises, even newly established ones in the private sector, continue to play an important welfare function. Needless to say, the ability of enterprises to perform welfare functions depends largely on their profitability *and* the extent to which non-wage benefits are perceived to be necessary and/or beneficial for recruiting labour – requirements that may be considered superfluous in the case of abundant and 'cheap' female labour that is willing to make itself available even for a low wage and little or no welfare benefits.

In fact as Davin demonstrates there has been rapid growth of demand for women workers both in the export-oriented factories of the Special Economic Zones (SEZs) in the coastal provinces of the Eastern seaboard, as well as in the town and village enterprises (TVEs), reflecting significant transformation in the structure of the labour market since China reoriented its economy to global markets and undertook extensive economic reforms in the 1980s. It could also be argued that that the foreign-owned, export-oriented industries located in the coastal provinces of China profit directly from the social investments made during the communist era, while running these investments down (Hart, 1995). The extent to which China can continue to capitalize on the benefits of earlier redistributions and investments in human capabilities, however, may be eroding very fast as the impacts of domestic liberalization (of both land and welfare) lead to increasing inequalities and the erosion of human capabilities (Croll, 1999).

In the SEZs there is a multi-faceted labour hierarchy: most technical and managerial posts are held by foreigners, though some Chinese middle-class men also attain these positions, while the semi-skilled workers are predominantly female. Most of the permanent workers are local inhabitants who have worked for some time in the new industries. But the majority of the work force is recruited from rural areas with temporary status and no entitlement to social protection or welfare benefits in their place of work. Migrant women suffer a whole series of discriminatory practices, including the impossibility of achieving permanent or settled status even on marriage. Most migrant workers are single women and those who are married have problems finding accommodation. Unlike permanent workers they have to pay for healthcare and their children are either excluded from urban schools or have to pay high fees.

Davin argues that the majority of women who work in the export-oriented industries come from villages where they had little or no entitlement to social welfare so that their lack of non-wage benefits in their new employment does not represent a loss of previously enjoyed benefits. However, whereas in earlier phases of the country's industrialization women as well as men recruited to the industrial workforce were awarded the status of permanent workers and offered a level of job security and social welfare (though unequally), this is not the case in the current phase of export-led industrialization. Wages and conditions are poor from the perspective of international standards and there is little or no union advocacy or representation for temporary migrant workers in export factories. Many young women migrants are well aware of these conditions and see employment in export factories as a temporary phase in their life cycle.

What path is Chinese social policy likely to take in the years to come? Davin argues that while the state may try to control the worst forms of labour abuse in the export-oriented factories, it is bound to make China's competitiveness in the struggle for foreign investment its first priority, and is thus unlikely to force investors to fund an expensive system of social security. The government will try to attract more high-tech industries that require a more skilled and educated workforce, which may mean greater willingness on the part of employers to invest in the welfare and training of their workers in order to reduce labour turnover and retain workers. Whether this will entail a gradual displacement of women workers by male workers is a possibility. At the same time, Davin doubts that the state can – or rather, will – take the burden of social provisioning on itself. The Chinese reformers, like their Korean counterparts, have shown a clear preference for contribution-based social insurance that is linked to employment – an institutional arrangement that follows in the path of enterprise-based welfare system. This development, as we have argued in the case of Korea, is likely to prejudice many, if not most, women whether as paid workers or as unpaid carers.

Welfare state construction and retrenchment in Mexico and Mauritius

The case study of Mexico by Viviane Brachet-Marquez and Orlandina de Oliveira analyses women's access to employment and social benefits under the two policy regimes that have marked the Mexican political economy over the past 60 years: a period of state-directed development accompanied by import substitution industrialization (ISI) and welfare state construction; this phase came to an abrupt end in 1982 as a result of the financial debacle and the debt-linked policy conditionalities which ushered in a harsh neo-liberal policy set-up (deflationary macro-economics, welfare state retrenchment, financial and trade liberalization), with severe economic and social consequences.

The history of social legislation in Mexico, as the authors underline, must be traced to the Mexican Revolution (1910–17) and the subsequent corporatist arrangement that was forged between the post-revolutionary (and authoritarian) state/party and its important social constituencies (peasants, labour). The basic conditions for industrial employment were legislated in 1932 – guaranteeing a minimum wage, paid vacations, severance pay, paid maternity leave and so on. In this way the state/party Partido Revolucionario Institucional (PRI) sought to legitimize its own rule, which perhaps more than any developmental imperative animated state policy in the social field.

The most important development in the 1940s was the creation of social insurance. However, rather than slowly consolidate different groups of beneficiaries into a unified system to facilitate pooling and cross-subsidization (as in Korea), the beneficiaries were segmented into a number of distinct schemes with vastly different and unequal entitlements. Social legislation for those outside the formal labour force (i.e. the rural population and the urban poor) was slow to emerge and meagre in benefits. Nevertheless, from the early 1970s serious efforts were made to sustain standards of living in the face of growing inflation by controlling the prices of basic items of consumption and exempting them from value-added taxation. As a result of these measures both the proportion and the absolute numbers of poor people diminished steadily until 1981 – a significant achievement by any standard.

While women benefited from some of the general subsidies that the state offered on items of urban consumption, their ability to access social benefits linked to employment prior to the 1980s was limited given their relatively low rates of labour force participation (although some women clearly benefited from these social provisions mediated by their relations to male 'breadwinners'). Women's presence in the industrial labour force remained below 5 per cent for much of the 1930s and 1940s, and went up only slowly during the period of ISI (from around 13 per cent in 1950 to 16 per cent in 1970). Moreover, women industrial workers remained concentrated in labour-intensive industries where they received low wages and were even used as non-wage home workers with no rights to social benefits.

Much of this was to change as a result of the financial debacle in 1982, which provided an opening for the international financial institutions to impose a harsh stabilization and adjustment package on Mexico through debt-related 'policy conditionalities'. As the authors indicate, during the 1980s and 1990s, the period when women's employment in industry, and particularly in export industry accelerated, social provisioning – whether in the form of employment-related benefits or universal subsidies on items of basic consumption – was massively curtailed. At the same time deflationary macro-economic policies choked employment and cut real wages. Whereas prior to 1982, in the so-called ISI era, the state's pro-business industrial policies (low wages, high tariffs) were somewhat tempered by measures aimed at maintaining minimum living standards, in the subsequent period these implicit subsidies were increasingly eroded and/or targeted to a dwindling proportion of the 'deserving' poor. Thus with extensive income contraction, declining real wages and the rising monetary cost of subsistence, family survival has increasingly relied on the intensification of women's *paid* work as a *distress* response,[11] as well as of their unpaid care work in both individualized and collective forms (Gonzalez de la Rocha, 1994).

At the same time women industrial workers seem to confront a number of adverse labour market conditions. First, the proportion of women in the industrial labour force, and particularly in the *maquiladoras* or industrial assembly plants, has fallen in recent years as men have been hired in more technologically advanced industries and occupations. Second, the demand for women's labour has been extended, with employment growth shifting from the higher-paying, better-protected factories on the Northern border to a range of small establishments and sweatshops in the interior provinces which provide work that is lower-paid, less visible and has poorer access to protection and regulation. Finally, while there is some evidence that women workers in *maquiladora* cities, particularly in the North, are better protected and better paid than those in non-*maquiladora* cities in the interior, two provisos are in order. First, women employees in the *maquiladora* sectors (now not jut confined to the Northern border states) only have entitlements to a limited and declining range of non-wage benefits, and have little or no access to gender-specific support such as childcare provision or maternity leave, 'both major necessities for women workers and *de jure* mandatory entitlements for all women employed in the formal sector' (Brachet-Márquez and de Oliveira, this volume). Second, the incorporation of women workers in the export sectors has spurred neither the design of women-friendly social policies, nor the extension of existing employment-related benefits to this new category of industrial workers. On the contrary they chronicle a steady decline in the mandatory protection of formal sector workers in Mexico as state enterprises were privatized, large scale retrenchments were implemented and domestic enterprises were squeezed by trade liberalization which exposed them to competition from cheaper imports.

Another country where women are being displaced from export-oriented production processes is Mauritius – not because male workers are being recruited into skill-intensive production processes, but rather because industrialists are hiring migrant female labour in order to side-step the alleged shortcomings of the local labour force, such as its high levels of absenteeism and low productivity. However, unlike Mexico, Mauritius has managed remarkably well to fight off the erosion of its relatively generous welfare state, which continues to act as a bulwark against social dislocation and impoverishment, especially at a time when the export industry is shedding workers in large numbers.

Sheila Bunwaree provides a useful analysis of the efforts made to construct a welfare state along the lines of western democracies in Mauritius, largely as a response to the island's deep-seated ethnic tensions and conflicts, and demonstrates how this attempt to provide universal entitlements (to health, education, pensions and food and housing subsidies) intersected with an ethnically segmented labour force. The issue of migrant labour and ethnic identity has not been one that has been stressed in earlier analyses of women's employment in export production, although it has been an issue in countries like Malaysia.

In the early 1970s Mauritius embarked on a major industrial development strategy – with the export-oriented garment sector as its central pillar – in order to diversify its economy away from reliance on sugar exports and escape the limitations of its small domestic market. Crucially, in Mauritius export production was not located in an enclave-type of EPZ but was widely dispersed throughout the island. This particular feature of the EPZ facilitated the absorption of married women: more than 40 per cent of the female workforce was married and above 25 years old, leaving few untapped reserves of 'cheap' female labour. As far as the ethnic composition of the workforce is concerned, initially at least the Creole population tended to dominate in the EPZ.

Moreover, the universal social provisions that were available to all citizens in Mauritius – such as free healthcare, education, pensions – were also enjoyed by women workers in the export sectors, almost by default rather than design (importantly, Bunwaree notes that there are inadequate health services for woman-specific conditions, and similar biases are evident in the Occupational Health and Safety Act which tends to privilege health hazards that inflict male workers, rather than those affecting women workers, such as repetitive strain injury). It could even be argued, as the government's own rhetoric on social development suggests, that the welfare state provided the country's 'social scaffolding' which in turn underpinned its economic success. In other words, welfare provisions effectively subsidized the export-oriented production processes by providing a workforce that was educated, healthy and well-nourished and a society that was relatively cohesive. Much of the welfare state edifice was funded through the tax on sugar exports despite the controversies and vested interests that surrounded its imposition.

However with the rising demand for workers in the early 1990s the export-oriented sector came up against a shortage of 'appropriate' labour. In the 1990s entrepreneurs increasingly relied on expatriate workers from countries like China, Bangladesh, India, Sri Lanka and Madagascar to meet the demands for expanded and 'flexible' production, which was required to compete with cheaper labour sites in Asia and elsewhere. These workers were often accommodated in dormitories near the factories. Although the recruitment of foreign labour was acceptable in the early 1990s because of the apparent shortage of local labour, and the reluctance of Mauritian women to work anti-social shifts and overtime, the practice has continued unabated in more recent years despite the rising levels of unemployment (especially among women). This is generating considerable social tension and a certain degree of suspicion towards migrant women workers.

Managers interviewed in a recent study voiced a preference for expatriate workers because they 'willingly work long hours and do not ask for holidays and sick leave'; they also praised the skills and speed of foreign workers preferring them to local workers who 'with their social and family obligations seem demanding, lazy and overall less productive' (Clean Clothes Campaign, 2002). Moreover, whilst Mauritian women industrial workers often had curtailed social and economic benefits due to the dispersed nature of the production facilities, the evasion of social security contributions by small-scale enterprises, and the low level of organization and unionization, expatriate workers have little access to any such benefits. Since their work permits specify that their right to remain in Mauritius is limited (usually to three years) and applies only to a specific employer, they are not in a position to utilize state provided education services and their access to health care is also restricted. The nature of their contractual relations also precludes their access to unemployment benefits or old age pensions (since their right to residence is terminated in the event of redundancy). When the downturn in demand for exports occurred in the late 1990s as the result of the East Asian crisis and the prospect of phasing out the Multifibre Agreement (MFA) (which has facilitated preferential prices and access to EU and US markets for Mauritian exports), these workers had no protection from summary dismissal and deportation.

Mauritius is an interesting case. In terms of social policy it is among the handful of developing countries that has aspired to construct a social democratic welfare state, inclusive of all its citizens. Moreover, despite the pressures from international financial institutions urging welfare retrenchment in recent years, the public provision of health and education remains free of 'user charges' (even though there is evidence of growing private sector provision). In the initial years at least the export-oriented firms seem to have benefited from the social provisioning that was available to the work force through the welfare state. However, since the mid-1990s the Mauritian EPZ – which continues to specialize in labour-intensive and low-skill products and has not been able to upgrade itself to more skill- and capital-intensive production processes – has come under severe pressure. Accelerated liberalization and globalization seem to have created the conditions for what some economists refer to as 'immiserising growth', with constant downward pressure on manufacturing wages determined by global labour cost competitiveness (Jomo, 2003). Under these pressures the Mauritian EPZ no longer seems able to hire a workforce with social and family obligations (even if these are somewhat tempered by the availability of welfare provisioning). As the above-mentioned report concludes, what managers seem to be saying is that to survive and compete in the global market they need a workforce that can make itself available 24 hours a day, prepared to do shift work and unencumbered by any social obligation.

Late liberalization: the case of employment in India's export sector

The trajectory of liberalization and opening up of the economy in India has followed a different trajectory from the countries in East and South East Asia. Jayati Ghosh argues that by the time Indian industry had been extensively de-protected – that is by the 1990s, the feminization of labour in export processing had peaked in the rest of Asia; and a trend towards an increasing male share of export employment was manifest. However she suggests that, unlike in other countries much of the export production in India took place not in large formal sector factories, but in the unorganized sector. Although accurate statistics on informal employment is difficult to obtain, she presents data from the Census of Manufacturing Establishments which indicate that in the urban unorganized manufacturing sector the share of women also declined in India from 14.2 per cent to 11.1 per cent. However she suggests that a large proportion of manufacturing production has been shifted to home-based subcontracting activities in small units that are below the scale used for the manufacturing census, where employment is on the basis of very low paid piece-rate work with virtually no non-wage benefits. This is the result of the nature of industrial regulation which has favoured subcontracting rather than growth and agglomeration in Indian industry, as entrepreneurs seek to avoid the labour protection and regulation which has been a characteristic of Indian industrial policy over many decades. Given, as she demonstrates, the fact that women are the overwhelming majority of the labour force working in the unorganized and unrecorded sectors of the economy women's role in these sectors has not brought with it concomitant improvements in social protection.

Moreover even in the apparently 'organised' formal sector factories in the EPZs, women's employment has been precarious and unprotected. In spite of generally extensive non-wage benefits for women in India, including maternity leave and benefits, the right to organize and collective bargaining and specified minimum wages, these benefits are rarely if ever actually afforded to women workers in export factories. Research evidence suggests that wages are below the government minimum wage rate, often being paid on piece rates rather than according to regular wage contracts. Working hours frequently exceed those laid down in the regulations, with no overtime payments for excessive hours. Basic health and safety precautions are rarely observed and women commonly face dismissal if they become pregnant. Given these kinds of working conditions which prevail because the EPZs are constituted to lie outside the regulations for the protection of workers in the formal sector, the fact that women continue to form the majority of the workforce in these export sectors has not led to the improvements in social protection and working conditions of women workers. And whilst export production in India has continued to involve many thousands of women, the fact that much of this has taken place in informal and unorganized workplaces, including home-based work, has exerted downward pressure on pay, working conditions and consequently has not provided the political or economic basis for the development of social policies which support women workers.

Export-oriented employment in South Africa: Neo-liberal contradictions

At the beginning of this chapter we referred to the European debates about the connections between open economies and social policy, and the argument that the welfare state was essentially a response to the challenges of economic integration. In her contribution to this cluster Gillian Hart tackles a rather similar set of issues but from the vantage point of developing countries and seen through a 'gender lens' (which explores the connections between production and the conditions of reproduction of labour). In doing so she poses some fundamental questions about the viability of the neo-liberal project on its own terms, particularly in the context of profound social inequalities.

Of the six case studies that are included in this cluster, in the recent decade South Africa seems to have followed most closely the conventional neo-liberal package (even without the policy conditionalities imposed on indebted countries such as Mexico) – of tight fiscal austerity, monetary discipline, wage restraint, trade liberalization and so on – in the hope that this would lure private investment (both domestic and foreign), unleash rapid export-led growth (as in the East Asian scenario), tighten the labour market and drive up wages. However, as Hart goes on to argue, to date the flows of foreign direct investment have been negligible while domestic capital has continued to flow out of the country, and all indications are that employment has continued its precipitous decline. To explain why industrial production in small-scale, decentralized, Taiwanese-owned firms (destined for export markets) have operated so problematically in South Africa, Hart draws on her extensive historical and anthropological research in two contrasting localities of the KwaZulu Natal province.

The Taiwanese-owned export-oriented industrial operations in this province have been the site of intense labour tensions and conflicts, to the point where their viability has been seriously undermined. Given the way in which racial and gendered differences were being constructed against each other, Hart suggests, the Taiwanese industrialists have been largely incapable of creating a negotiated labour regime with their predominantly female workforce. In other words the industrialists' understandings of racial difference have undermined their capacity to engage with workers on anything but openly coercive and hostile terms. This had led to anger and resentment on the part of women workers who feel that they are treated in inhumane ways. Hart argues that 'gendered constructions of localism and familialism, using the idioms of kinship and paternalism, that are central to the way managers and workers negotiate with one another in different parts of Asia ... are simply unavailable' to the majority of Taiwanese industrialists operating in South Africa (Hart, 2002: 192).

Second, and again in contrast to the situation prevailing in Taiwan and southern China, the conditions of labour reproduction in South Africa have been extremely unfavourable, given the way in which the workforce has been historically dispossessed and thrust into a radically commoditized form of livelihood. Ironically, these tensions have been amplified in recent years as the ANC government has embraced the neo-liberal policy package. Fiscal restraint at the national and provincial level has led to the massive shedding of basic welfare functions by the state (evident in the rise in service charges in the townships). Hart argues that the intensity of labour conflict in the industrial firms in KwaZulu Natal derives not only from the inability of the majority of Taiwanese industrialists to deploy gendered forms of negotiation on the factory floor, but also from the *absence* of the sort of social wage subsidy that characterized Taiwanese and Chinese industrial trajectories. One rough indication of this 'subsidy' is the gap between nominal and real wages in the two settings: while wages in the Taiwanese knitwear factories in KwaZulu Natal were nearly double those in southern China in terms of the prevailing exchange rates, the real wages were almost 30–40 per cent lower. It is the absence of this sort of social wage subsidy that can in part at least explain the intensity of labour conflicts that have been unleashed on the factory floor.[12] In other words the absence of 'social policy' in a harshly commoditized and unequal social context – driven historically by racialized processes of land dispossession and livelihood commodification, and reinforced in the dominant neo-liberal climate through processes of fiscal restraint and welfare retrenchment – that has effectively undermined the ability of export-oriented production processes from taking root in South African conditions.

Conclusions

To capture the diversity of gendered constructions of labour markets and social policy arrangements and how these are in turn shaped by both government policy and global forces operating in radically different ways (in different contexts and at different times), we have looked at the female employment/social policy nexus across diverse regional contexts. In this concluding section we attempt to draw some useful pointers from our case studies.

Globalization is a highly uneven process. Because state capacities differ, the ability to exploit the opportunities of international economic change – rather than simply succumb to its pressures – will be much more marked in some countries than others (Weiss, 1997: 26). The two East Asian countries in our cluster – Korea and China – have been, *relatively* speaking, in a better position to exploit the opportunities offered by global economic integration. Korea, along with a handful of other countries, was a pioneer in nurturing labour-intensive, export-oriented manufacturing in the 1960s and 1970s, and today China seems to be following in its footsteps. In this process they have provided employment for a predominantly female work force. While there are serious questions about the terms on which women were included in the labour force (to which we shall return further below), it is nevertheless true that in terms of sheer numbers of jobs provided these two countries have been in a much stronger position, than say Mexico, Mauritius and South Africa where export-oriented production processes remain weak and fragile.

And yet neither in the globally 'successful' countries, nor elsewhere, have labour markets been a site of gender equality. The ways in which labour markets are socially constructed – the sectoral distribution of women's employment, the nature/size of the firms in which they are employed, the occupations in which they are clustered, the nature of their contracts, the definitions of 'skill' and so on – reproduce gender inequality and embed those inequalities in access to both direct and indirect benefits of employment, including welfare entitlements. And yet despite persistent gender inequalities, it is important to ask whether women have been able to register some gains through the labour route.

In the case of Korea, as we have seen, while labour markets and welfare entitlement remain unequal, it is nevertheless noteworthy that by the mid-1990s about 40 per cent of female workers had obtained regular full-time jobs (even though more than 60 per cent had temporary or daily work). While this record is far from ideal, the gains that women workers have registered are not negligible, especially in comparison to conditions prevailing in other countries. The serious challenge confronting Korean women workers is how to hold onto these gains in the face of increasing pressures for labour market flexibility. Ominously, the 1997 crisis represented a serious regression in gender equality: the ease with which enterprises rid themselves of regular workers during the crisis interrupted the slow progress that women in particular had made in accessing the more secure jobs so that by the end of 1999 women had a *lower share* of such jobs than in 1990.

The other encouraging development in Korea – again in relative terms – is that rather than retrench the different social insurance programmes that are in place, serious efforts are being made to consolidate different groups of beneficiaries into a unified system to facilitate pooling and cross-subsidization. Again, the extent to which women stand to gain in this process is an open question and much will depend on how strictly benefits are linked to labour market contributions. But the general direction in which social policy is moving seems to be far more enabling here than in countries like Mexico where there has been large-scale employment related welfare retrenchment, in favour of narrowly targeted poverty alleviation programmes.

The situation of Chinese women workers in the current era also looks less encouraging than their Korean counterparts. In addition to the fact that large numbers of female employees from the state owned enterprises have lost their jobs and their work-related welfare entitlements, the largely migrant female work force that is now being recruited into the export-oriented industries has little or no entitlement to social protection or welfare benefits in its place of work. This marks a serious regression as far as gender equality is concerned.

Developments in Mexico have been highly contradictory. During the period of welfare state expansion women were largely excluded from labour-based welfare entitlements given their low levels of labour force participation. However, the period of economic crisis and welfare state retrenchment has coincided with women's large-scale entry into the labour force in both export and non-export sectors with little or no welfare entitlements. It seems to us that much of the 'global' debate about export-oriented employment for women has been implicitly premised on this kind of scenario. Needless to say, in a period of economic stagnation and welfare retrenchment, labour force entry has neither facilitated accumulation nor acted as a conduit for welfare entitlements. As such it has tended to be of a 'survivalist' nature.

A very different scenario emerges from Mauritius. Welfare entitlements in Mauritius were won through a non-labour route, and the welfare state was largely a response to divisive ethnic politics. This citizenship-based model facilitated women's access to welfare entitlements. While wages in the EPZs where women are employed remain low, women workers are nevertheless able to enjoy certain social provisions thanks to the inclusive way in which the welfare state was constructed. While Mauritius seems to have maintained its welfare state relatively intact, it has been far less successful in coping with global competition. In recent years levels of unemployment in the export-oriented manufacturing sector have soared as local women workers are displaced by more "flexible" migrant workers.

In South Africa too the export-oriented manufacturing plants remain highly fragile under the dual pressure of global cost competitiveness on the one hand, and the locally and historically constructed system of labour reproduction marked by brutal processes of dispossession and commodification, on the other. This set of powerful constraints fuels intense labour unrest and conflict that threatens the viability of these export-oriented production processes. It is in such contexts of profound social inequalities that the contradictions of the neo-liberal project emerge most sharply.

So to answer the question we posed in the opening paragraphs of this article – whether paid work can be the route to welfare entitlement for women in developing countries – we can say that in the five countries included in our cluster only Korea comes close to answering this question positively, and even so the answer must be qualified with the important proviso that while a section of the female work force has managed to attain welfare entitlements through the labour route, a larger proportion has not and many more women remain outside the formal labour force, as informal sector workers as well as wives and mothers. In the other five countries a combination of factors – the powerful ways in which gender inequality is constantly embedded in labour markets as well as the global and local pressures for welfare retrenchment – have denied women industrial workers the opportunity to obtain welfare entitlements through the labour route. In places like Mauritius where inclusive welfare states have been constructed, women have been able to access certain welfare entitlements, almost by default rather than design. Elsewhere the pressures for labour market 'flexibility' and fiscal restraint combine to deny vast numbers of women – regardless of their employment status – any meaningful access to welfare.

Notes

1. This chapter draws on the findings of the UNRISD research project on Globalization, Export-Oriented Employment for Women, and Social Policy. Financial support for this project was provided by the Rockefeller Foundation and UNRISD's core funders, the governments of Denmark, Finland, Mexico, the Netherlands, Norway, Sweden, Switzerland and the United Kingdom.
2. Women argued that the capacity to bear children was equally important and should entitle them to citizenship. The 'maternalist' demands for social protection and provisioning have been extensively analysed in the US context by Theda Skocpol (1992) in her classic study, *Protecting Soldiers and Mothers: The Political Origins of Social Policy in the United States*.
3. There are of course economic arguments which suggest that in open economies wages have to remain low. As Seguino and Grown (2002), put it,

higher wages – once a benefit in the form of a demand-side stimulus in more closed economies – in more open economies have a potentially negative demand-side effect on exports and investment demand, assuming, of course, that wage increases do not affect labour productivity.

4. Katzenstein's work focused on 'corporatism' as the central institutional mechanism that allows the small open and vulnerable economies of Europe to respond effectively to changes in the global economy by compensating for those changes politically and economically. A parallel argument, but without the political economy analysis, was reiterated more than a decade later by economists critical of the dominant neo-liberal thinking. Based on a cross-country quantitative analysis, Rodrik documents a positive and robust association between an economy's exposure to foreign trade and the size of its government (Rodrik, 1999); the most plausible explanation for this association, he argues, is that government expenditures are used to provide social insurance against external risk. In other words, social protection may be the only alternative to trade protection, if social disintegration is to be avoided.

5. Huber and Stephens (forthcoming) accept that there has been significant retrenchment in welfare states in recent years, but in their view the retrenchment was generally moderate, and driven by domestic forces (such as budgetary pressures due to the rise in unemployment as well as demographic factors such as population ageing) rather than external ones.

6. This shift in attitude on the part of the Bretton Woods institutions was manifest in the IMF programmes in Korea, Thailand and Indonesia following the 1997–98 financial crisis, where according to Chang (2001) both the IMF and the World Bank put unprecedented emphasis on building 'social safety network' devices.

7. One could of course argue that 'full employment' was not a gender-neutral social objective. This is an important issue that is discussed further below.

8. Also at the international level, labour unions and others concerned with global social justice have demanded that international trade regulation takes responsibility for its social effects. Although the demands for a 'social clause' have been largely rebutted (for being a disguised form of Northern protectionism and so on), it is important to recognize that the logic behind this approach is again one that rejects the artificial separation of the 'economic' from the 'social' in the context of international policy frameworks.

9. Corporate welfare originated in the 1920s during the Japanese colonial period and was largely the product of an arrangement between the state and the corporate sector whereby the former pressured the latter to provide non-wage benefits in return for financial rewards such as tax reductions and special loans.

10. The fact China maintains a non-convertible currency, state control over its banking system and a broadly 'gradualist' strategy is taken by some to suggest that it violates some of the key elements of IMF/World Bank prescription for 'successful integration' (Jomo, 2003).

11. As the authors show, women's labour force participation rates jumped up from 21 per cent in 1979 to nearly 36 per cent in 1999.

12. These pressures have been amplified in recent years by the influx of cheap imported knitwear items from China – the other side of trade liberalization.

References

Bhattacharya, D. and M. Rahman (2002) 'Female Employment under Export-Propelled Industrialization: Prospect for Internalizing Global Opportunities in the Apparel Sector in Bangladesh', in C. Miller and J. Vivian (eds) *Women's Employment in the Textile Manufacturing Sectors of Bangladesh and Morocco*, Geneva: UNRISD.

Chang, H. J. (2001) *The Role of Social Policy in Economic Development – Some Theoretical Reflections and Lessons from East Asia*, background paper prepared for the project 'Social Policy in a Development Context', Geneva: United Nations Research Institute for Social Development (UNRISD).

Charmes, J. (1998) *Informal Sector, Poverty and Gender: A Review of Empirical Evidence*, Washington, DC: World Bank.

Clean Clothes Campaign (2002) *Made in Southern Africa*, Amsterdam: Clean Clothes Campaign.

Cook, S. and S. Jolly (2000) *Unemployment, Poverty and Gender in Urban China: Perceptions and Experiences of Laid Off Workers in Three Chinese Cities*, Research Report 50, Sussex: Institute for Development Studies.

Cornia, G. A. (2000) *Preliminary Comments on the Paper 'Social Policy in a Development Context'*, presented at the 'UNRISD Conference on Social Policy in a Development Context', Stockholm, 23–24 September.

Croll, E. (1999) 'Social Welfare Reform: Trends and Tensions', *The China Quarterly*, 159: 684–99.

Edgren, G. (1982) *Spearheads of Industrialisation or Sweatshops in the Sun?: A Critical Appraisal of Labour Conditions in Asian Export-Processing Zones*, Bangkok: ILO-ARTEP.

Elson, D. (2000) *'Comments to the Session on Social Policy and Macroeconomic Performance: Integrating "the Economic" and "the Social"'*, presented at UNRISD Conference on Social Policy in a Development Context, Stockholm, 23–24 September.

Elson, D. (2002) 'Gender Justice, Human Rights and Neo-Liberal Economic Policies', in M. Molyneux and S. Razavi (eds) *Gender Justice, Development and Rights*, Oxford: Oxford University Press.

Elson, D. and N. Cagatay (2000) 'The Social Content of Macroeconomic Policies', *World Development*, 28(7): 1347–64.

Esping-Andersen, G. (ed.) (1996) *Welfare States in Transition: National Adaptations in Global Economies*, London and Geneva: Sage/UNRISD.

Ghosh, J. (1999) *Trends in Economic Participation and Poverty among Women in the Asia-Pacific Region*, Internet version available at <www.macroscan.com/Gender/Gender%20Issues.htm>

Gonzalez de la Rocha, M. (1994) *The Resources of Poverty*, Oxford: Blackwell.

Gough, I. (2000) *Welfare Regimes in East Asia and Europe: Comparisons and Lessons*, presented at 'Towards the New Social Policy Agenda in East Asia', Parallel Session to the Annual World Bank Conference on Development Economics Europe 2000, Paris, 27 June.

Greenhalgh, S. and J. Li (1995) 'Engendering Reproductive Policy and Practice in Peasant China: For a Feminist Demography of Reproduction', *Signs*, 20(31).

Hart, G. (1995) 'Clothes for Next to Nothing: Rethinking Global Competition', *South African Labour Bulletin*, 9(6): 41–7.

Hart, G. (2002) *Disabling Globalization: Places of Power in Post-Apartheid South Africa*, Berkeley, CA: University of California Press.

Heyzer, N. and T. B. Kean (1988) 'Work, Skills, and Consciousness of Women Workers in Asia', in N. Heyzer (ed.) *Daughters in Industry: Work Skills and Consciousness of Women Workers in Asia*, Kuala Lumpur: Asian and Pacific Development Centre, 3–30.

Holliday, I. (2000) 'Productivist Welfare Capitalism: Social Policy in East Asia', *Political Studies*, 48: 706–23.

Hsiung, P-C. (1996) *Living Rooms as Factories: Class, Gender and the Satellite Factory System in Taiwan*, Philadelphia: Temple University Press.

Jomo, K. S. (2003) *Globalization, Export-Oriented Industrialization, Female Employment and Equity in East Asia*, Geneva: UNRISD mimeo.

Kabeer, N. (1995) Necessary, Sufficient or Irrelevant? Women, Wages and Intra-household Power Relations in Urban Bangladesh, *IDS Working Paper No. 25*, Brighton: Institute of Development Studies.

Katzenstein, P. (1985) *Small States in World Markets: Industrial Policy in Europe*, Ithaca and London: Cornell University Press.

Kwon, H-J. (2001) 'Globalization, Unemployment and Policy Responses in Korea', *Global Social Policy*, 1(2): 213–24.

Mkandawire, T. (2001) *Social Policy in a Development Context*. PP-SPD 7, Geneva: UNRISD.

Molyneux, M. (1996) *State, Gender and Institutional Change in Cuba's 'Special Period': The Federación De Mujeres Cubanas*, research paper 43, London: Institute of Latin American Studies.

Orloff, A. (2002) *Women's Employment and Welfare Regimes: Globalization, Export Orientation and Social Policy in Europe and North America*, PP-SPD 12, Geneva UNRISD.

Park, C. B. and N. Cho (1995) 'Consequences of Son Preference in a Low-Fertility Society: Imbalance of the Sex Ratio at Birth in Korea', *Population and Development Review*, 21(1).

Pearson, R. (1998) 'Nimble Fingers Revisited: Reflections on Women and Third World Industrialisation in the Late Twentieth Century', in C. Jackson and R. Pearson (eds) *Feminist Visions of Development: Research, Analysis and Policy*, London: Routledge.

Pearson, R. (1999) *Gender and Economic Rights*, background paper prepared for the project 'UNRISD Report: Visible Hands', Geneva, unpublished mimeo.

Polanyi, K. (1957) *The Great Transformation: The Political and Economic Origins of Our Time*, Boston: Beacon Press.

Razavi, S. (1999) 'Labour-Intensive Growth, Poverty and Gender: Contested Accounts', *Development and Change*, 30(3).

Rodrik, D. (1999) *The New Global Economy and Developing Countries: Making Openness Work*, Washington, DC: Overseas Development Council.

Seguino, S. (1997) 'Gender Wage, Inequality and Export-Led Growth in South Korea', *Journal of Development Studies*, 34(2): 102–32.

Seguino, S. and C. Grown (2002) *Feminist-Kaleckian Macroeconomic Policy for Developing Countries*, University of Vermont, mimeo.

Skocpol, T. (1992) *Protecting Soldiers and Mothers: The Political Origins of Social Policy in the United States*, Cambridge, MA: Harvard University Press.

Standing, G. (1999) *Global Labour Flexibility: Seeking Distributive Justice*, Houndmills: Macmillan Press Ltd.

Tzannatos, Z. (1995) '*Growth, Adjustment and the Labour Market: Effects on Women Workers*', presented at 'the Fourth Conference of the International Association for Feminist Economics', Tours, France, 5–7 July.

UNDESA (1999) *1999 World Survey on the Role of Women in Development: Globalization, Gender and Work*, New York: United Nations.

UNIFEM (2000) *Progress of the World's Women 2000*, New York: UNIFEM.

UNRISD (2000) *UNRISD 2000+: A Vision for the Future of the Institute*, Geneva: UNRISD.

Weiss, L. (1997) 'Globalization and the Myth of the Powerless State', *New Left Review*, 225 (Sept./Oct.): 3–27.

Wolf, D. L. (1992) *Factory Daughters: Gender, Household Dynamics and Rural Industrialization in Java*, Berkeley, CA: University of California Press.

World Bank (2000) *Entering the 21st Century: World Development Report 1999/2000*, New York: Oxford University Press.

2
Korea's Miracle and Crisis: What Was in It for Women?

Hyoung Cho, Ann Zammit, Jinjoo Chung, Insoon Kang

Introduction

The 1948 Constitution of the newly established independent Korean state institutionalized the concepts of civil rights and modern social welfare. The democratic principles included that of equality between men and women, the right of labour to form trade unions, to negotiate with employers and to participate in organized activities. Moreover, the Constitution mandated the state to provide social assistance for citizens unable to earn a livelihood due to physical disability, old age or other reasons (OECD, 2000: 127).

Soon Korea was to embark on an unprecedented process of rapid and far-reaching industrialization:

> ... in 1955 the Republic of Korea was unequivocally an industrially backward agrarian economy. It was acknowledged to have such little scope for development that in the 1950s the US Congress denied it funds for developmental purposes (Krueger, 1995). The country's net value per capita in manufacturing output was US$ 8 per year, compared to $7 in India and $60 in Mexico. Since then the Republic of Korea has transformed itself into an industrial giant. It is arguably the most advanced country in the world in electronic memory chip technology. Before the Asian crisis, the Republic of Korea expected to become the fourth largest car producer in the world by the year 2000. (Singh, 2000: 5)

The central issue for this chapter is how women fitted into this picture; what was their role in this burgeoning economy and how did economic growth and structural change affect their position? In other words how far were the principles and gender aims of the 1948 Constitution and future legislation embodying these and related ideals realized in practice?

As Orloff (2002) rightly emphasizes a complex interplay of different forces affects women's economic and social advancement. Employment, and the policies that facilitate or constrain it, social policy, equal opportunity legislation, women's activism, the corpus of law, as well as cultural and religious traditions that assert prohibitions and predispose employers and policy makers to perceive labour in gender specific ways, all play a part. This chapter focuses on two of these factors – *employment* (an objective of macroeconomic policy with considerable social consequences) and *social protection* policies (a subset of social policies) that in turn have implications for employment.[1]

The nature of the broad policy regime within which employment and social welfare policies took shape in Korea is a matter of some contention: some argue that throughout the period under study – 1950s to 2001 – the approach was developmentalist, though with a gradual shift away from interventionism from the late 1980s onwards, as elements of 'liberal' economic policy were introduced. For others, the measures introduced under the aegis of the IMF to deal with the severe economic crisis beginning in 1997 ushered in a distinctly different regime.

We start by summarizing the main policy characteristics of the 'developmentalist' regime and the factors that influenced the incorporation of growing numbers of women into the labour force over the 40-year period until the economic crisis. This is followed by an overview of the changes in women's labour market position during the early developmental period and subsequent period of economic crisis. We then outline briefly the evolution of social protection and assess it from a gender perspective.

Developmentalism

With the rise to power of the post-1961 Park military regime, the stipulations and the labour-related laws passed in the 1950s were put in abeyance for several decades, while Korea pursued a process of 'compressed' capitalist industrialization, with security, growth and economic development as the priority goals under a 'developmentalist' policy regime (Deyo, 1987; Kim, E-M, 1997; Chibber, 1999).[2] Government intervention to force the pace of industrialization was achieved through strong state intervention in investment decisions that was facilitated by the development of structural ties between the state, the banking sector and the *chaebol* (large diversified business groups that accounted for a large proportion of domestic production and exports (Amsden, 1989; Wade, 1990; Lindström, 1993; Kim, E-M, 1997; Seguino, 2000a)). The specific policies to achieve industrialization and growth through import substitution and export promotion growth varied from one economic plan to another, while the central strategy involved reliance on domestic financing rather than foreign direct investment and foreign aid. Until the mid-1970s, following the first 'oil shock', industrial policy aimed to promote light industry, the output of which was increasingly destined for export markets. Thereafter, and until the late 1980s, the focus turned to promoting more capital- and technology-intensive 'heavy' industries and petrochemicals (Seguino, 2000a).

Until the late 1980s, this *dirigiste* approach was facilitated by the authoritarian nature of the political regime, under which political and trade union activism were prohibited.[3] Despite periodic strikes, protests and riots that were often forcefully repressed, the state enjoyed a certain degree of legitimacy, due partly to a residual anti-communist sentiment among the public and perhaps also to the benefits delivered by the burgeoning economy.

The new democratic regime elected at the end of 1987 continued the essentially *dirigiste* approach to economic policy of its authoritarian predecessor. However, faced with weakening international competitiveness, partly due to a tight labour market and rising wages as well as low cost competition, the government introduced a modest degree of liberalization of trade and financial markets in order to achieve financial and industrial restructuring (Seguino, 2000a). Industries in relative decline were given less government support, tight government control over the investment decisions of the *chaebols* was relinquished and in 1991 short-term capital flows were liberalized and domestic financial markets were subject to less regulation.

In 1992, the Labour Ministry, intent on raising productivity, introduced measures to achieve the 'rational management of labour' whereby wages and working conditions could be settled through more autonomous negotiations between employers and employees (Oh, 1993; Kim, Chang-gon, 1997). Other measures to increase labour market flexibility included changes that made it easier to end labour contracts and to substitute permanent full-time workers by casual workers or workers on short-term contracts. These new capital–labour relations served to weaken the trade unions which had become increasingly powerful since 1987 and hence facilitated government efforts to achieve industrial restructuring.[4] The government's 'human resource policy' aimed to draw 'underutilized' labour such as housewives into the labour market. In practice, they were brought into the more deregulated labour market as low-waged workers. The increased flexibility in labour markets enhanced the power of employers over trade unions.

Whatever the general policy trend, the financial crisis that erupted towards the end of 1997 led to a severe economic crisis.[5] With the country on the verge of default, the new government of Kim Dae-Jung that was inaugurated in the midst of the 1997 crisis introduced deflationary measures demanded by the IMF, as part of the conditionalities attached to its standby credit of US\$58 billion.[6] On IMF insistence, a further restructuring of the financial and business sectors was embarked upon, with a view to dismantling the *chaebol* and breaking the close relations between these and the government. In the IMF's view, the 'Asian way of doing business' ('crony capitalism' or close government–business relationships) was the fundamental cause of the crisis as it fettered market forces and prevented the efficient allocation of capital. To rid Korea of chronic 'crony capitalism', Korea was put under pressure by the IMF to restructure the financial institutions and the *chaebol* and to adopt Anglo-Saxon methods of corporate governance, which were partly achieved through mergers and acquisitions (Feldstein, 1998; Hwang, 1999; Singh, 1999).[7]

For some, these policies heralded the end of the developmental state, but for others 'the dismantling of the developmental state was effectively finished by ... 1995' (Chang and Evans, 1999). A shift in the direction of liberalization and deregulation, if not wholesale adoption of 'Washington consensus' policies, was in any case necessary if Korea was to conform with its multilateral commitments under the Uruguay Round Agreements requiring it to implement changes in a wide range of trade and trade-related matters so as to promote economic liberalization and deregulation. Moreover, Korea's entry into membership of the OECD in 1996, symbolizing its success in effecting the transition from extreme poverty to powerful industrial status in the course of just four decades, made it more susceptible to the liberalizing influence of co-members.[8]

Nevertheless, in dealing with financial and corporate sector problems, the government adopted a strongly interventionist approach. Rather than leaving the market to achieve restructuring of the financial sector, the banks were forced by the government to wipe out bad loans and sell underlying assets to government agencies for restructuring or scrapping.[9] While government public discourse conveys an espousal of neoliberal policies, actual practice suggests that 'developmentalism' still underpins Korean policy in various ways, and indeed the re-invigoration of the state's interventionist role ensured a rapid recovery and fast renewed growth. Whatever the case, the key concern here is to assess the gender implications regarding employment and social welfare of the accumulation process and the economic crisis. In this context, an appropriate starting point is World Bank President Wolfensohn's (1999: 12) perspective on this issue:

> While macroeconomic management is never perfect – there will always be some fluctuations in output and employment – the most effective safety net is a policy which maintains full employment. ... Formal safety nets are but an imperfect stop-gap measure in addressing the failures of effective macro policies to maintain the economy at full employment.

The validity of this statement depends, of course, on how far it embraces a concern for gender equality both with regard to the terms and outcomes of work, and on the nature of the safety net.

From a gender perspective, the key issues to analyse concerning women's access to paid labour are the relative terms on which female and male workers are employed, particularly regarding their contractual status, their remuneration and possible side benefits, and their access to social protection. Labour markets are highly gendered constructs, whose characteristics are determined by factors such as the division of family responsibilities between male and female household members and the extent to which social protection and provision arrangements are gender neutral, allowing equal access to the world of paid work for men and women. In turn the pattern or female/male insertion in the labour market is also a strong determinant of male/female wage differentials and also access to social welfare arrangements that are rooted in paid employment. Only by analysing these interrelated issues it is possible to arrive at any conclusion regarding how well women were served by full employment and safety nets. Below we focus first on women's employment status and subsequently their access to social welfare.

Economic growth, crisis and women's employment

For the purposes of our analysis the data has been organized in a manner that allows one to identify trends and experience pre- and post-crisis, with 1997 the crisis year as the separating point. This is not only because the crisis was a turning point with respect to policy but also because there are well-founded reasons for supposing that women were more likely to be disadvantaged than men by economic crisis (Singh and Zammit, 2000).[10]

Growth and employment pre-crisis

It is important to appreciate that, from the beginning of the 1960s until the 1997 economic crisis, Korea maintained an annual rate of growth of real GDP of about 8 per cent a year. Capital accumulation and growth throughout the four decades generated what was tantamount to full employment for men and increasing levels of employment for women, and an overall growth in real wages averaging about 7 per cent a year.[11]

In the early years, the demand for labour for light industries was met by drawing on young female labour from rural areas, following an agrarian reform aimed at raising productivity (Kay, 2001).[12] Continuing industrial expansion drew increasing numbers of unskilled married women into a wide range of light industries and services (Chung, 1996). Increasing educational opportunities for women and rising skill levels enabled women to gain employment in a wider, though still limited range of occupations.

The number of economically active women (aged 15 or more) grew continuously since the period when Korea was a Japanese colony until 1997, the year of economic crisis. The percentage rose from 35.9 per cent in 1970 to peak at 49.5 per cent in 1997, after which it declined to 47.0 per cent in 1998 (Korea National Statistical Office, 1970–99).[13]

Over the period 1970 to 1997 the numbers of women in paid employment rose almost two and a half times, and the proportion of the labour force comprising women rose from 36.5 to 41.2 per cent. The sectoral distribution of women's employment changed significantly over this period. The absolute numbers in agriculture, forestry and fishing increased in the 1970s but declined thereafter; in mining there were large swings in the numbers of women employed, but over the long term there was a considerable decline. Manufacturing and then services absorbed the greatest numbers from the growing female labour force.

The numbers of women in services, including public services, increased about five and a half times between 1970 and 1997, and the sector's share of women's jobs rose from nearly 31 per cent in 1970 to just over 68 per cent in 1997 (Table 2.1). The ratio of female to male workers in this sector increased from 31.6 per cent to 41.8 per cent over the period (Table 2.2). The manufacturing sector accounted for about 12 per cent of women's jobs in 1970 and 28 per cent in 1990, after which both the absolute numbers and the share declined (Table 2.1). The female

Table 2.1   Sectoral composition of the female labour force, 1970–97

Sector	1970	1990	1997
Agriculture, Forestry and Fishing	57.3	20.3	13.2
Mining	0.3	0.1	2.3
Manufacturing	11.8	28.1	18.3
Services*	30.6	51.5	68.2
Total	100	100	100

* Indirect social capital and other services.

Source: Korean National Statistical Office, Data base; <http://www.nso.go.kr/cgi-bin/ sws_999.cgi>

Table 2.2   Women's share of employment by sector, 1970–98 (%)

	1970	1980	1985	1990	1995	1996	1997	1998
All sectors	36.5	38.2	39.0	40.8	40.4	40.7	41.2	40.4
Agriculture, Forestry and Fishing	41.5	43.7	42.9	46.2	47.4	47.6	48.2	47.6
Mining	11.0	8.9	3.2	10.1	7.4	8.7	7.7	0
Manufacturing	32.8	39.1	38.6	41.5	41.0	36.6	35.6	34.5
Services	31.6	34	37.7	38.5	40.4	40.9	41.8	40.9

Source: Korean National Statistical Office, Data Base; <http://www.nso.go.kr/cgi_bin/ sws_999.cgi>

share of total manufacturing employment was 32.8 per cent in 1970, 41.5 per cent in 1990 and 35.6 per cent in 1997 (Table 2.2). Nevertheless, in 1997 this sector still employed almost four times the number of women it had in 1970.[14] The post-1990 decline in absolute numbers of women workers in manufacturing together with the lower share of manufacturing in total women's employment point to a 'defeminization' of manufacturing employment in Korea as in other export-oriented economies in Asia (United Nations, 1999; Seguino, 2000a; Jomo, 2001).[15]

Despite a changing industrial structure resulting from the government's promotion of heavy industry and petrochemicals, women were mainly employed in light industry. Moreover, even in 1997 there was still a high (if declining) ratio of female to male workers in some light industries that, in terms of their share of total employment, were in decline (textiles, wearing apparel, leather goods, footwear, pottery, china and earthenware). At the same time one notes a considerable decline in the proportion of women's jobs in electrical machinery and professional and scientific equipment over the period 1970–97.

Table 2.3 shows the distribution of the female and the male labour force according to types of contract in the 1990s. Even after three decades of industrial development and high growth, only about 40 per cent of female workers had regular full-time jobs, while just over 60 per cent had temporary or daily work.[16] The bulk of employed women therefore faced considerable insecurity and instability regarding employment and income (Han, 1998). However, contrary to the common belief that all Korean males had life-long jobs, only about two-thirds of male workers had regular contracts.[17]

The relative proportions of females and males within each category of waged and salaried workers are more revealing on this matter (Table 2.4).

Table 2.3 Composition of the female and male employed labour force by type of contract, 1990–99 (%)

	1990		1997		1999	
	Female	Male	Female	Male	Female	Male
Regular	37.5	64.5	38	64.5	30.4	60
Temporary	39.6	22.4	45.2	22.8	45.6	25.4
Daily	22.8	13.1	16.8	12.7	23.9	14.6
Total	100	100	100	100	100	100

Source: Table constructed from data from the Korean National Statistical Office Data Base; <http://www.nso.go.kr/cgi-bin/sws_999.cgi?ID=DT_1BA9502&IDTYPE=3>

Definitions: *Regular workers* are those on permanent contracts. *Temporary workers* are fixed term workers (both full-time and part-time) with contracts of at least one month and up to one year. *Daily workers* have a contract of less than one month and receive daily-based wages.

Table 2.4 Female and male proportions of each category of waged and salaried workers, 1990, 1997 and 1999 (%)

	Regular		Temporary		Daily		All waged/ Salaried	
	Female	Male	Female	Male	Female	Male	Female	Male
1990	26.6	73.4	52.3	47.7	51.8	48.2	38.3	61.7
1997	27.6	72.4	56.2	43.8	46.2	53.8	39.3	60.7
1999	24.9	75.1	54	46.0	51.8	48.2	39.6	60.4

Source: Table constructed from data from Korean National Statistical Office Data Base; <http://www.nso.go.kr/cgi-bin/sws_999.cgi?ID=DT_IBA9502&IDTYPE=3>

Men had the lion's share of regular jobs, while women constituted a higher proportion of employees on temporary contracts and daily contracts. Tables 2.3 and 2.4 also provide an initial indication of the differential impact of the 1997 economic crisis on female and male workers, an issue discussed below.

Wage differentials

During the period 1980 to 1992, wage growth in the Korean manufacturing sector was rapid – women's earnings rose 13.8 per cent a year and men's 12.4 per cent (Seguino, 2000a: 444). Nevertheless, despite gradual improvement in women's wages, the gender wage gap was far from closed (Seguino, 2000a; Jomo, 2001). The average all industry (excluding agriculture) ratio of women's to men's wages was 42.9 per cent in 1980, rising to 53.4 per cent in 1990. (In all industries, in firms with 10 or more employees, the average monthly payment for women was less than one half of the average for men until 1990.) Data for 1997 and 1998 based on a slightly different industrial classification indicates that by 1997 the ratio was 61.0 per cent. Notwithstanding the improvement, the gender wage inequality in Korea was one of the largest among OECD countries for which data is available (OECD, 2000).

Variations between industries were considerable. In 1980, the ratios ranged between 41.9 per cent (electricity, gas and water) to 58.3 (transportation, storage and communication). In 1990, again the spread ranged between the same industries: 47.1 (electricity gas and water), 79.2 (transport storage and communication). In 1997/98: ratios fell in a range between 50.4 per cent and 83 per cent.[18]

Given the heavy concentration of women in particular sectors and industries (thus widely known as 'women's jobs'), and the preponderance of temporary and daily work among women, it is hardly surprising to find wage differentials tilting decidedly in favour of male workers. In 1980, in manufacturing (when manufacturing employed about 45 per cent of women workers), the ratio was 43.8 per cent, marginally higher than the average all-industry ratio of women's to men's wages. In 1990 (when manufacturing absorbed 39 per cent of female workers) it was 51.1 per cent. Since 1990, it has not exceeded the all-industry average, and the ratio of 54.8 per cent in 1997 was among the industries with the lowest ratios (see note 18).

Seguino (2000a) suggests that the implementation of the 1986 minimum wage legislation may have contributed to the narrowing of the gender wage differential in Korea. However, as she points out, 'the

1988 implementation covered only 4.2 per cent of firms employing 10 or more workers and was based on a two-tiered system, with minimum wages for a number of female-dominated industries set lower than in other industries. In 1990, the original law was amended to cover all firms with 10 or more employees' (Seguino, 2000a: 445). The relocation abroad of some light industry enterprises giving rise to the dismissal of female labour, together with greater competition for irregular jobs from male workers due to the greater flexibility of the labour market, may also have contributed to the persistence of female–male wage differentials.

Push and pull factors regarding women's employment

Contrary to those who see a tight labour market situation as sufficient to effect a reduction in gender gaps, the continuing demand for female labour over almost four decades did not bring about equality for women in the field of work. A sizeable proportion of women did not enter the labour force and of those that did there was a proportion in continual flux owing to the numbers who were temporary or daily workers. And though the wage gap narrowed, wage equality was still far off. Other important factors determining the amount and type of work undertaken by women and the terms of their engagement were clearly significant.

In the early years of industrialization employers preferred to hire young unmarried women rather than men or married women as employees who, in addition to their alleged dexterity, were socialized to accept their situation and gender inequality as an acceptable outcome. Women's passivity could thus be counted on to minimize conflict in the workplace and to keep wage and related costs low. Moreover, needing less time off to deal with family responsibilities, unmarried women would be given preference over married ones, being regarded as more reliable and more productive workers. Nevertheless, the fast pace of industrial development kept up the demand for labour and the ranks of female labour were gradually swelled by married women, being partly facilitated by crèche facilities in many factories. Nevertheless, the male breadwinner/female carer dichotomy persisted as the accepted norm, and women's paid work outside the home was perceived as an addition to their basic household functions.

Cultural norms and traditions, and practices such as the continuing *hoju-je* family registry system that defines the status of each family member in relation to the *hoju*, or male householder, have perpetuated paternalism and institutionalized discrimination, by predisposing employers and policy-makers to perceive labour in gender specific ways.[19] Employment practices reflected patriarchal norms, and 'preferred' jobs were reserved for men (the heads of family and rightful bread-winners), and a 'glass ceiling' has limited the number of women occupying positions that involve the exercise of authority, such as senior managerial and administrative jobs. Seguino (2000a) points to some improvement in the gender distribution of managerial and administrative jobs and of professional and technical jobs during the period 1980 to 1992, both economy wide and in the manufacturing sector. Improvement was, however, greater in the latter than in the former, where, by definition, employees are part of a pecking order of positions of authority. Evidence of these subtle pressures affecting women's participation in the labour market became more manifest during the economic crisis.

Women in the labour movement

The above data on women's position in the labour market, prevailing gendered assumptions on the part of employers, and continuing paternalistic attitudes might suggest that Korean women passively accepted their lesser status. However, their participation in the labour movement demonstrates otherwise.[20]

During the 1970s and early 1980s, workers in light industries such as textiles and electronics strove actively to improve the terms and conditions of work, characterized by low wages, long working hours and limited labour rights, despite the fact that strikes and mobilizations were illegal. Until the late 1970s, women, the bulk of workers in these industries, were often at the forefront of these struggles that were frequently met with police violence or that of male employees or thugs hired by employers (Kang, 2001). Women workers led the famed wildcat strikes in Tongil Textile Company incident and the YH Trading Company.[21] In addition to being prompted by their own grievances, the prominence of women workers in sit-ins and demonstrations is attributed by some to the fact that young female workers would expect to leave the workforce on marriage or pregnancy and hence were less concerned than male workers about being blacklisted.

During the 1970s, 1980s and 1990s the proportion of women employees who belonged to trade unions was higher than the proportion for males.[22] However, women constituted a lower percentage of total trade union membership than men, due to three main factors. First, the absolute numbers of women registered in trade unions was lower than the number of males, second, less than 40 per cent of women workers were full-time regular employees who are those most likely to join a union and third, trade union membership tends to be higher in large-scale work places, whereas most women work in SMEs where union organization is always more difficult. In 1995, the rate of unionization in firms with more than 300 workers was over 80 per cent and only 5 per cent in firms with less than 100 employees. In firms with less than five employees it was considered to be negligible (Martin and Torres, 2000).

Women's influence in union matters has been limited by their generally lower numbers and the fact that they gained high-ranking positions in unions less frequently than men. Male-dominated labour organizations contributed little if anything over the years to improving women's status or to raising women-specific issues (Chung *et al.*, 2000). Women workers themselves were of the view that while their trade union has played a considerable role in improving workers' rights, they had not shown interest in dealing with specific women's rights, even in instances where women outnumbered men among the membership (Chung *et al.*, 2000; Kang, 2001). This situation can be attributed to two principle factors: the male-centred culture and hierarchical structure of trade unions. The perception that women's employment is supplementary to that of the male breadwinner is still widely shared among trade union leaders as well as among government bureaucrats. It is only relatively recently recognized as a problem and the Korean Confederation of Trade Unions (KCTU), the largest union federation, now aims to recruit women to at least 20 per cent of the executive positions in the Confederation (Chung *et al.*, 2000).

The gender bias of the 1997 economic crisis

Gender biases in the labour market were clearly demonstrated at the time of the 1997 economic crisis, which exacerbated women's already inferior position (Cho, 1998; Kim and Mun, 1999). The combination of policies implemented under the aegis of the IMF in response to the financial crisis led to a precipitate fall in consumption (9.6 per cent) and investment (21 per cent in 1997–98 and 20 per cent in 1998–99 GDP (Shin, 2000)). In the year 1997 to 1998 GDP fell by 5.8 per cent, and in the period 1998 to 2000, GDP was 12 per cent lower than what it otherwise would have been (Crotty and Lee, 2001). This sharp contraction in economic activity had a severe impact on employment: unemployment rose from half a million in 1997 to 1.85 million in 1998, representing an increase from an annual rate of 2.6 per cent in 1997 (while the monthly rise in December 1997 was 3.1 per cent) to 7.8 per cent in 1999. If the underemployed are also included the rate was over 10 per cent (the highest level for 40 years). Moreover according to the KCTU, if the considerable numbers who withdrew from the labour force between 1997 and 1999 are also counted in, the unemployment rate was six times higher.

In his 1997 election campaign Kim Dae Yung had emphasized the need to pay attention to equity and welfare measures, promising measures to avert mass dismissals of labour, but once in power these did not feature on his immediate agenda. Laws were, however, introduced to bring about greater flexibility in the labour market, allowing firms to dismiss workers for 'urgent managerial reasons', thus responding to the chaebol's interest in reducing the power of the unions and being able to dismiss labour (Chang, J., 2001; Crotty and Lee, 2001).[23] Such changes were argued to be necessary in order to attract foreign investment which would subject the *chaebol* to competitive pressure and render the overall economy more efficient and competitive.

Between 1997 and 1998 unemployment grew fastest among those with relatively poor education, the middle-aged, heads of household and the precariously employed. A gender analysis (Table 2.5) reveals the following:

- the decline in total women's employment was almost three percentage points greater than that of men (−6.9 per cent compared with −4.1 per cent), though taking the period 1997–99 there was less of a difference;

Table 2.5 Changes in female and male employment, 1997–99 (%)

	1997–98		1998–99		1997–99	
	Female	Male	Female	Male	Female	Male
Total labour force	−6.9	−4.1	2.7	0.6	−4.4	−3.6
Self-employed	−11.5	−0.4	5.7	−0.6	−6.4	−0.7
Unpaid family labour	6.2	13.4	−7.2	10.1	−1.5	23.6
Waged and salaried workers	−9.7	−6.7	5.5	1	−2.8	−5.7
Regular	−18.8	−6.2	−5.8	−6.5	−23.5	−12.3
Irregular	−4.1	−7.4	11.4	14.7	6.6	6.2
Temporary	−4.5	−4.3	0.6	9.8	−3.9	5
Daily	−3	−12.7	40	24.4	35.7	8.4

Source: Table constructed from data from the Korean National Statistical Office Data Base; <http://www.nso.go.kr.cgi-bin/sws_999.cgi>

- there was an increase in *unpaid family workers*, though the increase was much higher for men than women and even in 1999 the ranks of male unpaid family workers increased;
- among the *self-employed* there was a far greater percentage fall in the numbers of self-employed women than men, though they increased between 1998 and 1999;
- with respect to *employed workers* (i.e. all waged and salaried workers), women's employment declined far more than men's. This was particularly the case among regular workers: the numbers of female regular workers fell by 18.8 per cent, while the number of male regular workers fell by 6.6 per cent.[24] Between 1998 and 1999, the fall in the numbers of female and male regular workers was 5.8 per cent and 6.5 per cent respectively;
- among *temporary* workers, the numbers of women workers declined by 4.5 per cent between 1997 and 1998 and rose by less than 1 per cent in 1999, (For males, the decline was 4.3 per cent followed by an increase of 9.7 per cent.);
- *daily-based workers* experienced some of the biggest changes: the numbers for women declined by 3 per cent between 1997 and 1998 and rose by 40 per cent the following year. (For males, the figures were a decrease of 12.7 per cent followed by a rise the next year of 24.4 per cent.)

Statistics on the contractual status of female and male workers (Tables 2.3 and 2.4) indicate that, even before the crisis and more recent changes in labour laws intended to increase labour market flexibility, a high percentage of workers were non-regular workers, whose situation is characterized by insecurity, and poorer terms and conditions of employment. Data on the composition of the female and of the male labour respectively force respectively by type of contract (Table 2.3) and the female and male proportion of each of the three categories of contract (Table 2.4) indicate the labour market changes occurring due to the combined effect of crisis and greater labour market flexibility.

From Table 2.3 one observes that:

- the events of 1997–99 seem to have put the clock back as far as women are concerned: a lower proportion of them have regular jobs than they had in 1990 (30.4 per cent compared with 37.5 per cent);
- the gains registered with respect to the proportion of women workers in temporary work between 1990 and 1997 were maintained in the crisis years; whereas the improvement indicated by the fall in daily work between 1990 and 1997 was reversed during the crisis;

Table 2.4 indicates that:

- the crisis more than wiped out the gains made by women relative to men in their *share* of regular jobs;
- as a result of the crisis, the gains in women's share of temporary jobs between 1990 and 1997 were partly reversed;
- the improvement registered in women's relative labour market position between 1990 and 1997 in terms of the declining proportion of women relative to men in temporary work was all lost as a result of the crisis.

The above data provides strong evidence that the crisis was disastrous from the point of view of labour market equality for women. The earlier introduction of labour market flexibility made it legal for employers to rid themselves of regular workers during the crisis, thus putting more male workers in competition with female workers for temporary jobs. The crisis interrupted the slow progress made in women's access to more secure and better paid jobs such that, by the end of 1999, women had a lower share of such jobs than in 1990.[25]

The extent and pattern of job loss by women during the crisis (and the temporary decline in women's labour force participation rate) can be partly explained both by discriminatory practices on the part of employers and internalized social norms and related pressures that prompted women to relinquish their jobs 'voluntarily'. Indeed, government and press comments at the time demonstrated forcefully that women were expected to provide a caring supportive role with respect to their newly unemployed husbands whose loss of job was considered to be 'social death' and cause for depression and suicide.

To sum up on the employment front, government efforts to foster rapid capital accumulation and full employment served to some extent as a surrogate social policy. Indeed, the employment policies until the late 1980s provided lifetime job security for a considerable proportion of males, affording a certain protection for male workers and their families. Increasing paid employment in urban areas gave many women the opportunity to escape the confines of rural family life. Moreover the continuing and significant rise in real wages over a long period also contributed significantly to general welfare. But, the gender distribution of the benefits was highly skewed. Women's participation in the paid labour force was clearly limited by familialism (leaving service provision to families) and the gendered division of tasks related to household care, based on the norm that women's primary role was that of unpaid wife/mother, in the absence of the kinds of state support that would facilitate this. Temporary and/or part-time work may have provided the flexibility needed by some women to fulfill family responsibilities. But the sectoral distribution of their employment, the size of the firms in which they were employed, the occupations in which they were clustered and the nature of their contracts combined to ensure that both the direct benefits (stability of employment, remuneration and non-wage benefits), and indirect outcomes (access to social welfare insurance, and security in old age) were less beneficial than those for males.[26] Indeed, until the crisis, the cushioning of unemployment, ill health and poverty by means of direct social welfare policies were almost non-existent, especially for those in temporary jobs or small firms.

The partial and uneven work trajectory of many women perpetuated their financial dependence on a male 'breadwinner' and made it difficult for women and perhaps their family to sustain an independent and sufficient material base. Employment on this basis also hindered career enhancement, lowered the likelihood of a rising income over the years and reduced the possibility of accumulating savings.

The developmentalist welfare state and beyond

The above discussion focused on employment which clearly constituted part of social policy if this is understood as 'state policies, practices and institutions that directly influence the welfare and security of various groups within a particular society' (UNRISD, 2000: 9). However, social security or social welfare, a subset of social policies that consist of particular forms of direct social assistance or insurance in relation to a variety of social needs or conditions, evolved only slowly.[27]

This was very much by design: in the words of President Park (whose military coup put him in power from 1961 to 1979), 'Korea cannot afford to ape blindly the income or welfare policy of other advanced countries. Should we expand welfare in disregard of reality, it would only dampen the enthusiasm of some hard-working people. Should welfare policy, in opposition to its goal, encourage indolence and a psychology of dependence among some people, it would have harmed not only development, but also welfare' (a quote from President Park's biography (1979: 102) cited by Shin, 2000: 86).

The resulting regime is characterized by Holliday, (2000) – referred to in Gough (2000: 6) as 'productivist welfare capitalism', whereby corporate provision and state-promoted social insurance were used to reinforce the position of the productive elements in society. For social support during the developmentalist period, the population relied on a variety of sources: the extended family, civil society organizations, corporate welfare schemes, social insurance and public assistance – the relative importance of each changing over time.[28] Social protection programmes (see below) developed in a limited and piecemeal fashion, within what one author terms 'peripatetic adaptive learning and development strategies with the prime goals of nation-building' (Goodman and Ito, 1996).

These social welfare arrangements (see further below) are taken by some to suggest that until the crisis of the mid-1990s, the South Korean developmentalist state completely subordinated the welfare needs of labour and the population at large to that of economic growth and development, its strategic priority (Shin, 2000). The complex sharing of responsibilities that went beyond the state, the 'market' and the household hardly lived up to 1948 Korean Constitution's mandate that the state provide social assistance for citizens unable to earn a livelihood due to physical disability, old age or other reasons (OECD, 2000: 127).[29] Nevertheless, the developmentalist regime's heavy emphasis on social policies made a considerable contribution to improving welfare while also bolstering the regime's developmental efforts; considerable investment went into education, housing and health that, in addition to generating a healthy, increasingly skilled and productive population needed by a growth-oriented development strategy had a redistributional effect and made for a 'contented' labour force. Together with indirect measures to protect SMEs, and hence employment, these policies performed both direct and indirect welfare functions. Apart from raising standards of living, all these contributed to broad social cohesion and industrial peace (Chang, H-J, 2001).

Korea's approach to social welfare was not unique. In a comparative study of welfare regimes in East Asia and Europe, Gough (2000: 4) suggests that in East Asia, '[T]he welfare mix in the region is one of relatively low public responsibility (in terms of expenditure, provision and regulation), extensive family provision and redistribution, and growing private markets and community-based organizations. ... Within the public sector priority is given to social investment in health and education, notably basic health care and primary education with very little attention to social protection. In all countries state personnel are supported most generously' (Esping-Andersen, 1996). This approach to social protection in Korea continued until growing labour market problems associated with declining competitiveness in the 1980s and the economic crisis of the 1990s called it into question.

The social protection afforded through state provided social welfare schemes and through social insurance initiatives (see later) was greatly limited until the later 1980s (Kwon, 1997; White and Goodman, 1998; Shin, 2000), leaving corporate welfare, 'market' provision and household provision to plug the gap.

Corporate welfare

Corporate welfare in fact made an important contribution throughout the period, particularly for workers in the *chaebol* (Song, 1995).[30] During the early period of industrialization in the 1960s, Japanese style corporate welfare was adopted by the labour-intensive, export-led light industries that employed young women with a rural background.[31] Corporate welfare was also provided in the heavy and chemical industries that were developed: during the 1980s large companies supplemented wages with retirement allowances, bonuses, housing loans, partial support for private insurance and organizing credit unions and special savings schemes for low-income workers, offering wedding loans and scholarships for education (Kim Y-M, 2000). Large corporations in Korea also provided vocational training for workers.

Far from being an expression of corporate charity, its expansion was the product of an arrangement between the state and the corporate sector. In part it corresponded to the need for healthy, contented and productive workers. But in the 1980s, unwilling to yield to labour movement pressures for public welfare provision, the government used its close relationship with business to press employers to extend their non-wage financial benefits in return for finance from the government, including tax reductions and special loans.[32] (The financial benefits were part of the government's industrial development strategy.) Corporate assumption of responsibility for workers' welfare went even further in that, together with workers, companies bore the bulk of the costs of social insurance schemes. Thus apart from wages, workers' welfare was largely dependent upon corporate policies regarding non-wage benefits and contributions (Park, 1996; Rou, 1997).[33] However, the economic crisis and the post-crisis pressures for corporate restructuring have posed a critical challenge to corporate-based welfarism (Kim Jeong-Han, 2000; Ministry of Labour, 2000).

The capacity of larger firms to provide more extensive benefits and the probability that regular workers in firms of whatever size were the main beneficiaries suggests that male workers were more likely to derive advantage than women. Nevertheless, child-care facilities would have been of particular importance for women in view of their prime responsibility for family matters.

There is evidence that the gap in welfare (corporate welfare and social insurance provision) between large and small- and medium-sized firms may have been attenuated if not narrowed in recent years. The new more competitive environment and the post-crisis corporate governance reforms are causing large firms in particular to scale back fringe benefits. However, only detailed research will reveal the extent to which the non-wage benefits available to women in small and medium firms have declined, and whether the widening scope of the social insurance and assistance schemes can compensate working women for those non-wage benefits that eased their double burden and provided a measure of greater immediate economic security.

Social protection

The state's role regarding social protection was mainly that of regulator, rule-maker and fund manager rather than that of provider and its share of the cost of various welfare benefits was negligible. This continued to be largely the case even when, from the 1980s onwards, in parallel with the change in political regime and shifts in economic policy under changing economic conditions, the coverage of state-promoted insurance schemes was extended. The continued supplementing of industrial workers' wages with non-wage corporate welfare benefits and the gradual widening coverage of social insurance schemes are deemed by some to have helped prolong the life of the developmentalist regime.

Over the last four decades, four social insurance schemes – Workers Compensation or Industrial Accident Insurance, Pensions Schemes, Employment Insurance and Health Insurance – have formed the core of non-corporate social welfare provision, together with a very minimal public safety net. From a very narrow base, their scope extended only slowly. However, in the new political climate following the 1987 democratic elections, there was growing pressure from trade unions and others for improved welfare provision. Debate hinged on whether Korea should proceed towards a full-fledged welfare state embodying citizen rights as advocated by the 'idealists' or whether it should continue to follow a 'pragmatist' route of social insurances largely tied to employment or on 'partnership' between the public and private sector (Chang, H-J, 2001; Chung, Y-t, 2001; Kwon, 2001, 2003).[34]

The issue partly revolved around whether the increasing integration of Korea into the global economy, its shift towards neo-liberal policies and its concern to maintain competitiveness and fiscal balance would impede further expansion of state-promoted social insurance and social assistance (Shin, 2000: 84). In the event the political contest between 'pragmatists' and 'idealists' was settled for the time being at least by the eruption of the 1997 economic crisis and the ensuing election of a new president Kim Dae-jung.[35] A tripartite (government, employers and employees) commission was established that managed to reach agreement on labour market reform, unemployment protection measures and labour retraining schemes, rooted in what was termed a 'productive welfare' philosophy.[36] The issue of social safety nets was high on the policy agenda, but with IMF blessing. As President Kim Dae Jung announced '… we have no option but (to pledge) to install a US-style safety net in the form of unemployment insurance and training programmes' (New York Times, 18 January 1998, quoted in Crotty and Lee, 2001).[37] There ensued a substantial widening of the protections afforded under the four social insurance schemes and revamping of the government's social assistance programme, as outlined briefly below.

The evolution of social insurance

Workers', compensation   for job-related injuries was the first insurance scheme to be enacted for working people (1962) being deemed essential in a country embarking on an ambitious development programme (Kwon, H-J.,2001). Financed solely by employers' contributions, the scheme initially covered only workers in companies with more than 500 employees, whatever the economic sector. In 1992 it was extended to all workplaces with more than five employees and from July 2000 onwards to all wage and salary earners, both regular and irregular. However, in the case of temporary and daily workers, observance of the rules tends to be lax except for those employed in the construction sector. There is therefore an element of gender discrimination, in that women tend to be clustered in small firms and, as elsewhere in the world, such firms do not comply fully with government regulations.

Pension provision   was first introduced under the 1961 Public Employees Pension Programme that provided compulsory occupational schemes for military personnel, civil servants and teachers in private schools. In 1988 a national pension insurance scheme was introduced for those employed in firms hiring ten or more employees. The scheme was extended in 1993 to those with five or more employees and again in 1999 to workers in firms of less than five workers. At that point it became compulsory for all regular workers and for certain irregular workers depending on the length of work contract.[38]

Shin (2000) estimates that in 1999 the national pension scheme covered around 41 per cent of the total labour force. Of total pension holders, around 26 per cent were women. According to the OECD

(2000), about 62 per cent of the population aged 18 to 60 paid pension contributions in 2000. As elsewhere, the level of pension benefits varies according to the number of years and level of contributions. (The current requirement is 20 years.) At the turn of the century, only one quarter of those in the retirement age bracket received a retirement pension and the average sum received was very low in relation to Korean living standards (OECD, 2000: 124). It will be only in 2008 that full old-age public pensions will be provided for those workers who were eligible to begin contributing in 1988 once membership was widened and made less exclusive (OECD, 2000: 124).

Once again, the fact that a greater proportion of women were irregular workers and often in small firms prejudiced their being able to benefit from pension insurance plans. Even with the recent reforms, it is clear that a greater proportion of female as compared with male workers are likely to lose out.

Health insurance   was initially introduced in a very limited way in 1963. It was extended to enterprises with more than 500 employees in 1977, and in 1988 became obligatory for the whole population, either as direct contributors or dependents, while the government paid contributions for those with no employer. In 2000, the multiplicity of insurance schemes was integrated into a unified National Health insurance system.[39] Irregular workers with very short-term contracts and temporary workers are generally covered as residents ('regional members') under the national health insurance.

Employment insurance   introduced in 1995, applied only to workplaces with 30 or more employees, thus excluding small-scale workplaces and people in the informal sector.[40] Eligibility for unemployment benefits required at least one year's contributions.[41] In view of the very inadequate coverage of the scheme and the rising unemployment associated with the economic crisis, the Employment Insurance Programme was extended first to all workplaces with ten or more employees, and then later that year to all workplaces.[42]

Nevertheless, the social protection afforded is far from comprehensive. In July 1999, only 66 per cent of paid workers were eligible to be insured under the employment insurance, and, of those eligible, only 71 per cent were actually covered. Thus only 47 per cent of paid workers were insured. This meant that only one in eight of the unemployed received unemployment benefits.[43]

The Ministry of Labour's annual statistics on employment insurance show a slight improvement in the numbers of women contributing both in absolute terms and as a percentage of the total number contributing, but even in the year 2000 women comprised only 31.33 of contributors. The OECD (2000) data indicating the numbers and proportions of workers eligible for employment insurance and those actually covered does not provide a gender break-down. However, Martin and Torres (2000: table 5) indicate that, in 1999, only 11.7 per cent of female unemployed workers acquired the right to receive unemployment benefits, though the figure for males was only 11.8 per cent.

Social assistance

In 1969 a Livelihood Protection Programme was introduced ostensibly to guarantee a decent living for those officially classified as poor outside the age group 18–65. Provision of relief (in cash or kind) was means-tested and took into account both the claimant's assets and also the earning capacity of members of the extended family (OECD, 2000).[44] Persons over 65 years of age who did not receive a pension, had no means and no family support qualified. The level of benefits was not sufficient to keep people above the poverty line (Kwon, 2003: 76). By the end of 1997, only 2.3 per cent of the total population received public assistance benefits. Some were only allowed access to medical and educational assistance. Those also receiving a living allowance amounted to only 0.8 per cent of the total population (Shin, 2000). The Ministry of Health and Welfare put the number of recipients a little higher at 3.1 per cent (Kwon, 2003: 76).

In 1997 the economic crisis prompted the introduction of a scheme targeted largely at the unemployed. Taking both programmes together, only about 4.4 per cent of the population were beneficiaries in 2000, and only 55 per cent of the population in poverty in 1999 received benefits under these programmes (OECD, 2000: 127). Due, among other things, to the strict eligibility criteria and administrative problems, the programmes proved inadequate.

With regard to livelihood protection benefits, women comprised 58.5 per cent of total beneficiaries in 1998, though the proportion of women rose in the age groups from 50 years and above, reaching almost three times that of men after 60 years of age (OECD, 2000: table B.1). However, to assess whether the welfare needs of women as a group were being met one would need data on the gender incidence of poverty in the different age groups and the terms and nature of the assistance provided.

A Minimum Living Standard Guarantee (MLSG) programme was introduced in October 2000 to replace the Public Assistance programme and aimed to guarantee a decent living for the poor, defining the poverty line in relative terms, unlike the absolute poverty approach in the earlier Public Assistance scheme. It is a citizen-based scheme, providing protection irrespective of employment status, in contrast with the health, pensions and employment insurances that depend on insertion in the labour market. In principle, the MLSG underwrites the entitlement of *all* citizens to a minimum standard of living. How adequate this is and how far in practice it delivers to all in need is something that requires detailed research.

An important qualification to the above is that family support is still taken into account in means testing. Elderly women are more likely than males to live with adult children (helping with household tasks and childcare) and hence possible social assistance will be reduced by the assessed level of need and family support.

Pragmatists and idealists: feminist's dreams?

Based on an analysis of the situation prior to the economic crisis, Gough (2000: 5) concluded '... on the Richter scale of social development East Asia achieves something akin to the liberal alchemist's dream: good welfare outcomes at very low cost in terms of public social expenditure'. Moreover, his analysis showed Korea to have been at the top of the league in most respects, compared with Malaysia, Thailand, Philippines and Indonesia.[45] But how far can Korea's experience be said to conform to a feminist's dream, both prior to and after the social welfare reforms? It is open to serious question whether the wider scope of social insurances and the MSLG scheme can be considered a step towards a more women-friendly system or whether in the words of Siim (1993) it is a 'modernized gender system'. From a feminist perspective the recent reforms seem to have little 'idealist' content.

Table 2.6, combined with the earlier data regarding the employment status of women (Tables 2.3 and 2.4), tells the story. The data in Table 2.6 indicates that regular workers, mainly concentrated in large enterprises, are on the whole well covered. Though larger numbers of workers in small- and medium-sized firms have now become eligible for membership of social insurance schemes, Table 2.6 suggests that full implementation of the social insurance programmes has not yet been achieved in such enterprises (Kwon, 2003). This, and the fact that women predominate in the temporary and daily work categories (Tables 2.3 and 2.4) and that

Table 2.6 Social insurance coverage by employment status in 2001 (%)

	National Pension Programme	National Health Insurance	Employment Insurance Programme
Wage and salary earners	51.8	54.3	46.9
Regular employees	92.7	94.8	80.0
Temporary employees	19.3	22.2	20.7

Note: Both regular and temporary employees are included in the category 'wage and salary earners'.

Source: Kim, W. (2001).

these categories of workers are mostly employed in medium- and small-scale firms, indicates that women continue to fare worse.

Essentially the new system extends the previous welfare rights attached to full-time (male) workers to wider sectors of the labour market, namely smaller firms and temporary and part-time labour. It seems to assume that the standard worker is akin to the proverbial regular male employee who, even if with no life-time job, can still achieve a full work record for pension purposes. The post-crisis welfare system, like its predecessor, is predicated on the assumption that 'men "specialize" in paid work while doing little unpaid, mainly care-giving work and women do the bulk of unpaid work, increasingly in combination with paid work. ... Women do a second shift at home' Orloff (2002: 4).

While the new expanded system may in principle have introduced some improvement, it does little to remove the basic shortcomings of such a system when one considers the characteristics of women's labour market participation that are themselves often partly determined by the household (read wife/mother) provision of (unpaid) welfare and care services, in the absence of state support for the same.

Furthermore, employment-related social insurance approaches tend to discriminate against women who undertake unpaid 'care work' in the home rather than become full-time 'workers' in the formal labour market. Generally such work is not counted as employment and hence the 'carers' (mainly women) do not qualify for social insurances in their own right. For women providing unpaid family care, the only safety net is that provided via dependence on a male breadwinner, something that neither guarantees security nor facilitates women's autonomy. The lack of adequate state assistance with child-care prevents and perpetuates the partial employment of women that risks prejudicing their social protection especially in old age.

While the MSLG in Korea may provide some sort of safety net on a citizenship entitlement basis, there is need for detailed analysis of the extent to which it provides gender justice. To the extent that the tradition of family care for the elderly still affords a degree of protection against poverty, the burden of providing such care tends to fall on the shoulders of other women and can hence affect the level of their own eventual social welfare benefits.

There is therefore a *prima facie* case for concluding that the choice of a welfare system rooted in work-related insurances (and corporate welfare benefits, clearly tied to employment) in preference to a citizenship-based welfare system is likely to prejudice many if not most women, whether as paid workers or carers. The extent of the prejudice will only emerge from detailed research, including on how the health and pension contributions and benefits of the unemployed and especially women in irregular and or part-time work, are dealt with.

Conclusions

A growing raft of legislation in Korea has accorded women equal rights with men both in the workplace and more broadly. The 1948 Constitution affirmed the principle of equality between men and women and mandated the state to provide social assistance for citizens unable to earn a livelihood due to physical disability, old age or other reasons. The 1954 Labour Standards Law included measures to protect women workers and 'motherhood'.[46] The 1987 Equal Employment Law legislated for gender equality in employment practices, prohibited direct and indirect discrimination on the basis of sex, and established equal payment for work of equal value.[47] It affirmed that maternity protection did not constitute discrimination against male workers and it extended the duration of maternity leave provided under previous legislation to 60 days.[48] This legislation was subsequently supplemented by the ratification of the United Nations Agreement for Elimination of All Forms of Discrimination against Women, the amendment of the Family Law, the Basic Law for the Advancement of Women and the introduction of special laws on daycare, sexual violence, family violence, maternity benefits and the prohibition of gender discrimination (Kim, E., 1999). Nevertheless, the expectations regarding gender equality that might be harboured on the basis of these 'first tier' legal instruments are not yet matched by objective reality.

Though for several decades Korea's chosen strategy has provided the sort of growth, stability and social development that countries under neo-liberal rules of the game in a globalized economy can hardly dream of, looked at through a gender prism it has not proved particularly 'women-friendly'.[49]

While, there have been undoubted improvements in the economic and social position of women, the gender assumptions and household relation that underwrite women's employment status and social welfare arrangements, between which there is a complex interplay, have resulted in a skewed distribution of the benefits in favour of males.

Specifically, women in the labour force have been prejudiced on two accounts. First, better corporate non-wage benefits were provided by large firms, whereas the bulk of the female labour force was concentrated in small and medium enterprises that could ill afford the same level of benefits. Second, the key employment-related social insurances providing economic security during and beyond working life were only extended to medium and small firms with considerable delay. They in any case directly benefit only a limited number of working women owing to the high proportion in temporary and daily work.[50] Thus, corporate welfare and social insurances resulted in inequities between industries, firms and workers and prejudiced the chances of many women benefiting from some of the social insurance schemes especially in relation to qualifying for a pension (Choi, 1992).

The increased openness of the Korean economy now limits both the possibility of guaranteeing full employment as a surrogate social policy and of extending corporate welfare. In principle, therefore, the state-sponsored social insurance and assistance system has an even more important role to play. But, apart from the fact that it lacks full implementation in precisely the employment situations where women are heavily concentrated, the expanded system still appears to have an inherent gender bias (with women's interests continuing to be largely ignored).

Women will continue to be vulnerable to low income and poverty in old age, owing to the current nature of female employment patterns and their responsibility for unpaid care provision. Resort to social assistance as a safety net, when earned income and pensions are inadequate, is notorious for its defects and stigmatization; and women are likely to be disproportionately affected. Moreover the fact that elderly women continue as helpers/carers while living with the family reduces their claims for social assistance and independent income. These problems will persist unless work–welfare policies are extended to encompass unpaid care-giving, voluntary work and other socially valued but unremunerated activities, or unless society recognizes the value of such work by attaching to it a financial reward, or some combination of these two.

Experience and research indicate that there is no single way to reduce unemployment, raise employment and labour market participation. Different economic strategies that are equally effective in achieving these goals have quite different implications for social justice and gender equality. Some may further commodify the labour market and supplement it with a residual welfare state, others may promote a more distributive system based on social solidarity and citizen rights. This is a research field rich in potential for those with gender equality as an objective. Nevertheless, greater progress in the direction of greater gender equality in Korea will also depend on whether and how the 'ideological' bases of direct and indirect gender discrimination in these areas are addressed. That, however, is a social and political process that depends as much as anything on women themselves working to diminish the influence of attitudes that determine these matters. But detailed research on the gender distribution of contributors and beneficiaries and the levels of benefits associated with the formal welfare system in Korea could also make an important contribution to improving women's status.

Notes

1. For an overview of research on the ways in which both employment and social policies interrelate in effecting changes in women's economic status and gender equality under different policy regimes in the advanced developing countries have been the subject of considerable research, see Orloff, 2002.
2. This developmentalist strategy was introduced following the toppling of a conservative anti-communist regime that had received strong backing, including financial aid, from the United States in the 1950s and early 1960s. Developmentalism has been adopted by various latecomers in the industrialization process, particularly in Latin America and East Asia, though the specific pattern of economic development and the style of state intervention have reflected idiosyncratic characteristics and differing historical experiences.
3. Freedom of association, collective bargaining and collective action were guaranteed under the labour laws that had been introduced in 1953. However, the post-1961 regime exercised firm control over the labour movement in view of its association with the overthrown leftist regime and because the unions' economic objectives conflicted with the regime's concern to keep labour costs low in the interests of achieving rapid capital accumulation. (The 1953 Labour Union Laws were amended in 1963, 1973/74, 1980/81 and 1987. For a review of these and other laws regulating workers rights and so on see Lindström, 1993: 96–102.)
   In the 1960s and the 1970s the relationship between the state and the Federation of Korean Trade Unions (FKTU) was essentially of a corporatist nature (Lindström, 1993). In return for recognizing the FKTU as the sole trade union confederation and for labour legislation that would shield the union leadership from being challenged from below, the state demanded industrial

peace. Moreover, bargaining at enterprise level in industries such metal working and textiles meant that many unions were company dominated (Choi, 1983). The 1980 Labour-Management Council Law (amended in 1987) specified that all bargaining should take place at enterprise level within Labour-Management Councils, a law that circumscribed even further the bargaining power of unions.

The growth of heavy and more technologically advanced industries reinforced male leadership of the growing labour movement. Organized labour protests against the repressive government and oppressive labour conditions were frequent, and confrontation between labour and the police became more violent. In response to rising labour unrest, in the early 1980s the government relaxed many of its anti-labour measures and legalized trade union activities and revised its labour laws. The 'Workers' Great Struggle' following in the wake of the civil movement's campaign for democratization in June 1987 forced the government to give greater attention to workers' demands for improved working conditions and for more humane treatment. The dip in membership figures for a few years following 1980 reflects the change to enterprise-based unions and the law that restricted unions to workers in plants with more than 30 employees. For an overview of the history of unionism in Korea and its political dimensions, see Lindström, 1993: 118–40.

4. Legislation was introduced to legalize temporary workers hired out by 'dispatch agencies' – so-called because they employed workers dispatched from their previous jobs. They became common in the 1990s. Agency workers could be hired out to firms for up to two years in a wide range of occupations and could be used as temporary replacements for absent employees. They attracted the hostility of trade unions keen to protect full-time permanent jobs (OECD, 2000; Crotty and Lee, 2001).

5. In a nutshell, the immediate cause of the financial crisis was a balance of payments crisis. A growing balance of payments deficit, associated with the high level of private foreign borrowing and shrinking trade surplus, and the crisis in other South East Asian economies, caused foreign creditors to call in their loans to local banks. The increased short-term foreign credits (from US$12 billion to US$67 billion between 1993 to 1996) due to earlier financial liberalization had been largely deployed for long-term investment (Crotty and Lee, 2001). Indebted firms therefore had difficulty in complying, thus prejudicing the position of local banks *vis a vis* their foreign creditor banks. Interest rates rose rapidly and growing capital flight led to a run on the currency and a greatly devalued exchange rate (around 30 per cent). IMF insistence on deflationary policies aggravated the economic crisis (Stiglitz, 2002).

6. Criticism of 'crony capitalism' now rings hollow in view of recent revelations pointing to the extent of corporate misgovernance and malfeasance under the Anglo-Saxon corporate governance system, particularly in the United States.

7. These policies and the IMF interpretation of the crisis are regarded by a number of economists as excessively one-sided, ignoring the role played by financial liberalization (Kim and Cho, 1999; Singh, 1999; Stiglitz, 2002, among others).

8. There has been a flourishing controversy over the causes of South Korea's economic success. Orthodox economists (e.g. Balassa, 1991; Krueger, 1995), have argued that free markets, free trade and export-orientation were recipes for rapid economic growth. World Bank (1991) concluded that 'Economic theory

and practical experience suggest that (government) interventions are likely to help provided they are "market friendly"'. The Bank's definition of 'market friendly' was one that clearly circumscribed the extent and intensity of state intervention. A number of non-orthodox scholars argue that, to the contrary, in the successful economies like Japan and South Korea, the government had played a leading role with heavily interventionist policies and regulated trade and capital flows (Singh, 1997; Amsden, 1989; Wade, 1990). In its study of the 'miracle' economies of East Asia, the World Bank (1993) acknowledged that there was very considerable government intervention in these economies, but argued that such interventions, particularly those in the field of industrial policy, had a limited effect. For the Bank, success was basically due to 'fundamentally sound, market-oriented policies' (p. 35). The debate continues over whether it is 'market-friendly' or 'industrial' policies that are the key to rapid development and over whether 'close' or 'strategic' integration into the world economy is the most appropriate approach.

9. One quarter of the financial institutions closed, and banks were merged, nationalized or closed (and about half the staff dismissed). Credit was redirected from 'inefficient' chaebol to small- and medium-sized enterprises (SMEs) and half of the biggest chaebol were closed or broken up. Others cut their debt and raised profitability (Pilling, 2002).

10. These authors have argued this case in the context of unfettered international capital flows, where the rhythm, particularly of private flows, exhibits considerable volatility, creating problems for macroeconomic management and frequently generates financial and economic crisis.

11. Women already formed a growing part of the industrial labour force in Japanese factories in Korea in the 1920s and 1930s during Japanese colonial rule (1910–45) (Cho and Kang, 1995).

12. As Yoo (2000: 2) notes, 'Perhaps nothing was more striking than the arrival of women of various social backgrounds to the city' ready to fill the new positions in textile, shoe and garment factories or service jobs. Many of the female migrant workers were the saviours of their families: many provided financial support for their families left behind in rural homes. Notably, a significant part of their incomes went towards paying for the education of their brothers. To some extent they continued to be victims of a long-standing patriarchal familialism, while now becoming victim to the segregation of labour markets on a gender basis as well (Lee, 1996). The preference for young unmarried female workers reduced the employment opportunities in this sector for married women, who had little alternative but to take part-time jobs or to do subcontract work under poorer working conditions in this or other sectors.

13. This ratio is considerably lower than international standards, and the overall employment–population ratio in Korea has been somewhat lower than the average for OECD countries (Martin and Torres, 2000).

14. The figures presented here for absolute numbers of female workers are drawn from the authors' working paper on this subject.

15. In Korea, conscious government policy led over time to a shift in the inter-sectoral distribution of employment. The *share* of total employment in textiles, wearing apparel and rubber products experienced a considerable decline (other light industries undergoing a lesser decline), while there were

substantial increases in the percentage shares of non-electrical machinery, electrical machinery and transport equipment, and lesser increases in other heavy industries and chemicals. These newer industries principally employed male workers, either due to the physically demanding nature of the work, to the fact that males had the appropriate skills, or to 'gender-typing' of jobs.

16. Regular employees are those employed on a full-time basis under a contract of one year or more, or under an open-ended contract of at least one year. Temporary employees are those employed either full-time or part-time on short-term contracts of at least one month and less than one year. Daily employees have a contract for less than one month and receive daily-based wages.

17. Less secure jobs also brought poorer wages: a temporary worker would receive two-thirds of a regular worker's wage (Kim, J-S, 1999).

18. Data from authors' working paper.

19. *Hoju-je* is founded on the principle that males are superior to females and treats a married woman as an instrument for the paternal lineage of her husband's family. A daughter must remain first in her father's registry and keep his surname until she marries and is transferred to the name of her husband's family registry. There is a ranked order for who may be considered a householder. If the household has no living father, his son, no matter how young, succeeds to the position. Then follow in order, his grandson, unmarried daughter, wife and his mother. This pecking order defines legal rights over a daughter. A child born of an extramarital relationship can be registered as a lawful family member even in the face of objection by the wife. Current family law contains around 70 principles relating to *hoju-je*, and some lawyers argue that it is a central element of the entire civil law. Others legal specialists argue *that hoju-je* is a symbolic remnant of the traditional family system and its abolition of *hoju-je* will not enhance humanitarian standards or establish equality between the sexes, and should therefore be retained (Park Soon-mee, 2002).

20. The women's movement has been another active force campaigning for women's rights.

21. The struggle of young women employees – the majority of the 4000 employees – of the YH wig-producing company occupies an important place in South Korea's labour history. They had managed to gain an autonomous and democratic union in the factory in the 1970s. In 1979, in the face of economic troubles, the company announced its imminent closure, causing some women workers to meet to discuss the matter. Riot police broke up the meeting, so other forms of protest were organized and the management announced a reversal of its decision. Within one month it reversed this decision, prompting women workers to hold a sit-in. Following intervention by the riot police, the women took refuge in the opposition New Democratic Party (NDP) headquarters, which riot police stormed. This ended in the death of one striking worker, injury to other workers, party members and journalists and the arrest of the leading women trade unionists and several party members. But to no avail: the factory was closed down, and the chairman of the NDP was forced to resign.

22. The proportion of employed persons enrolled as trade union members reached its peak level of 17.2 per cent in 1990 (table 10).

23. In this text, the terms workers and employees are generally used interchangeably.
24. The high percentage of 18.8 per cent results from the combined effect of two factors: women constituted a smaller percentage of the regular labour force and their rate of job loss was higher.
25. There is some evidence that the women departing from temporary and daily jobs were partly replaced by new female entrants to the labour market such as the wives of males who had become unemployed (Korean Women's Development Institute (KWDI, 1999)).
26. Even if family care substitutes for a pension for the elderly, and keeps them out of poverty, the burden of this welfare provision generally falls on other female members of the family, who may prejudice their own future security or suffer a heavy double burden by providing such care. Such family care systems are not guaranteed to persist, as past experience regarding the role of the extended family shows.
27. Gough (2000) warns that care is needed in using the term 'welfare regime' in the Asian context, as it is frequently used to denote 'state hand-outs or charity'. It is contrasted to 'development', as in human resource development or social development, concerned with investing in people and productivity-enhancing institutions.
28. Changes in Korean society consequent on industrialization, urbanization and changes in the composition of the labour force have tended to reduce the effective role of the extended family. Nevertheless, the resources of kin are taken into account in determining levels of social assistance. For a detailed discussion of the nature and role of NGOs in the field of social assistance, see OECD (2000).
29. Since the constitution also affirmed the principle of equality between men and women there are grounds for assuming that the word citizens embraced both female as well as male nationals. Moreover, seen above, the full-employment policy (deemed to contribute to economic security), did not result in full employment for women.
30. Corporate-based welfare originated in the 1920s during the Japanese colonial period. In the absence of statutory standards on the terms and conditions of work, 'patrimonial gifts' served both as a means of disciplining labour and as an incentive system, which also encouraged lifetime commitment to the company, Park (1999).
31. Corporate welfare in this period reflected the need to secure the labour of young, mainly female migrant workers. In addition to mandatory paid maternity and monthly menstrual leave funded by employers, the latter provided dormitory or other housing facilities, free meals and transportation to and from workers' homes during holidays.
32. This puts in question the Park (J-S) (1996) suggestion that 'by default more than design, the vacuum of social protection has spurred the rise of company sponsored occupational welfare, especially in Japan'.
33. Apart from severance pay and paid maternity and menstrual leave, there was no formal legal requirement that companies provide welfare measures, corporate welfare therefore responded to changes in the internal and external economic, social and political environment (Rou, 1997).
34. The total cost of corporate welfare increased by 30 per cent a year over the decade from 1988. As a proportion of total labour costs, welfare costs

increased from 4.8 per cent in 1988 to 8.5 per cent in 1992 and stabilized at 7 per cent around 1995 (Kim, Y-M, 2000).

35. For an account of the advocacy coalitions relating to social policy in Korea, see Kwon, 2003.
36. Retraining programmes introduced to get the unemployed back to work were deemed to be insufficiently targeted at disadvantaged labour groups (Martin and Torres, 2000: 9). Our earlier analysis would suggest that women were among those who missed out.
37. Social safety nets grudgingly or otherwise became accepted by the World Bank, in the context of the Asian crisis, being seen as a legitimate means of attenuating poverty, averting major social unrest and the possible rejection of the policies perceived by many to have precipitated the crisis.
38. Voluntary contributors by such as the self-employed, unemployed and housewives are assessed on the amount of their property and non-wage income. Those unable to afford contributions have to rely on extremely meagre public assistance programmes. Married women who never entered the labour force receive a derived pension on the death of the husband related to his contributions.
39. In 1996, the level of public and private expenditure on health in Korea as a percentage of GDP was the lowest (4 per cent) in the OECD, comparing with, for example, Sweden (8.6), the United Kingdom (6.9), Japan (7.2) and Germany (10.5). The public share of total health expenditures was considerably lower than in these other countries, some of which were based on a social insurance model and others financed by general taxation (Kim, Y-M, 2000).
40. Social protection for the unemployed was not high on the government agenda prior to this date, owing to the fact that there was full employment (Kwon, 2000).
41. Due to the size of establishment covered, in 1995 the scheme covered only 35.3 per cent of waged and salaried workers (Kwon, 2000). In June 1998, only 7.8 per cent of the unemployed were eligible for benefits (Kwon, 2000).
42. The Employment Insurance Programme also provided training and job security grants (Kwon, 2000).
43. For those unemployed who took up the payment incentives for job seekers, the daily 'job-seeking allowance' amounted to only 50 per cent of the so-called 'basic daily wage' at the time of separation, and was for a period of three to eight months, depending on the age at the time of job loss and the length of time over which insurance contributions had been made (OECD, 2000).
44. The criteria of capacity (to earn) of extended family members, rather than actual income, is a comparatively strict interpretation of family support criteria compared with other OECD countries (OECD, 2000: 129).
45. See Kwon (1998) for a comparative analysis of welfare systems in East Asia.
46. 'Women-specific' measures including the protection of 'motherhood', maternity leave and daycare services have often operated to discriminate against women. See Chung (2001) for research on the extension of maternity protection.
47. Grievances regarding gender discrimination can be brought to the Ministry of Labour or the Ministry of Gender Equality.
48. Women's organizations subsequently campaigned with success to have paid maternity leave extended to 90 days and the government has agreed to share

the cost of the extra 30 days. The cost of the other 60 days are borne by the employer. On the extension of maternity protection, see Chung (2001).

49. While there is clear evidence of a gender bias in the distribution of the benefits from Korea's process of compressed capital accumulation, it can be also argued that women made a significant contribution to the success of the government's development strategy, by providing relatively cheap labour in export-oriented light industries that helped to keep export goods more competitive than what they otherwise would have been. Seguino (2000b: 1223) shows a positive link between gender wage inequality and growth, operating through capital accumulation, industrial restructuring, technological change and productivity growth. It is significant that, in 1990, despite industrial restructuring to more technology intensive industries, the industries in which women's employment share was significant produced about 44 per cent of the country's foreign exchange earnings (Seguino, 2000a: 442).

50. Voluntary membership of the schemes was possible and therefore employers could, if they chose, facilitate membership for non-regular female workers. However, this would seem unlikely to occur with any great frequency as smaller firms would be less able to afford the contributions and it is less likely that there were enterprise unions to press the case in smaller enterprises.

References

Amsden, Alice H. (1989) *Asia's Next Giant: South Korea and Late Industrialization*, New York: Oxford University Press.

Balassa, Bela (1991) *Economic Policies in the Pacific Area Developing Countries*, New York: New York University Press.

Chang, Ha-Joon (2001) *'The Role of Social Policy in Economic Development – Some Theoretical Reflections and Lessons from East Asia'*, paper prepared for the United Nations Research Institute for Social Development Project on Social Policy in a Development Context, Geneva: UNRISD.

Chang, Jiyeon (2001) *Kyoungjeweewoa yeosongweo nodong (Economic Crisis and Women's Labour)*, Seoul: Korea Labour Institute.

Chang, Ha-joon and Peter Evans (1999) *The Role of Institutions in Economic Change*, mimeo, Cambridge University, Cambridge and University of California at Berkeley, Berkeley.

Chibber, Vivek (1999) 'Building a Developmental State: The Korean Case Reconsidered', *Politics and Society*, 27(3): 307–46.

Cho, Hyoung and Ee-Soo Kang (1995) 'Historical Formation of Industrial Division of Labor under the Japanese Rule', Korea Research Foundation, *Collection of Works Commemorating the 50th Anniversary of Korean Independence: Women.*

Cho, Soon-Kyung (1998) 'Economic Crisis and the Politics of Female Employment', *Journal of Korean Women's Studies Association*, 14(2): 5–33.

Choi, Jang-jip (1983) *Interest Conflict and Political Control in South Korea: A Study of the Labour Unions in Manufacturing Industries, 1961–1980*, unpublished doctoral dissertation, Department of Political Science, Chicago: University of Chicago.

Choi, Sook-Hee (1992) 'Women's Employment Structure and National Pension Plan', *Yeosung Yeongu*, Spring.

Chung, Jinjoo (1996) *Development, Work and the Family in the Making of Korean Working Women*, unpublished PhD thesis, Toronto: University of Toronto.

Chung, Jinjoo (2001) *Research on Extension of Maternity Protection*, report submitted to the Department of Gender Equality, Government of Korea, Seoul.

Chung, Jinjoo, Hyun-baek Chung and Mi-kyung Kim (2000) *Integrating Women Executives into Decision-Making Rank in the Trade Union*, report to the Korean Federation of Trade Unions, Seoul.

Chung, Yeon-taek (2001) 'Reality of Korean Social Welfare and an Alternative Welfare Model', *Economy and Society*, 50: 72–105.

Crotty, James and Kang-Kook Lee (2001) *Economic Performance in Post-Crisis Korea: A Critical Perspective on Neoliberal Restructuring*, working paper series No. 23, Political Economy Research Institute, Amherst: University of Massachusettes.

Deyo, Frederic C. (ed.) (1987) *The Political Economy of the New Asian Industrialism*. Cornell: Cornell University Press.

Esping-Andersen, Gøsta (1996) 'After the Golden Age? Welfare Sate Dilemmas in a Global Economy', in Gøsta Esping-Andersen (ed.) *Welfare States in Transition: National Adaptations in Global Economics*, London: Sage.

Feldstein, Martin (1998) 'Refocusing the IMF', *Foreign Affairs*, March–April.

Goodman, Roger and Peng Ito (1996) 'The East Asian Welfare States: Peripatetic Learning, Adaptive Change, and Nation-Building', in Gøsta Esping-Andersen (ed.) *Welfare States in Transition: National Adaptations in Global Economics*, London: Sage.

Gough, Ian (2000) *Welfare Regimes in East Asia and Europe: Comparisons and Lessons*, paper presented at parallel session to the Annual World Bank Conference on Development Economics Europe 2000, Paris, 27 June.

Han, Myung-Hee (1998) 'Reality of Women's Employment: Unstable Employment', *Jejeong*, 445: 43–5.

Holliday, Ian (2000) 'Productivist Welfare Capitalism: Social Policy in East Asia', *Political Studies*, 48: 706–23.

Hwang, Sangin (1999) *Korean Economy under IMF Guided System*, Korea Institute for International Economic Policy, Seoul.

Jomo, K. S. (2001) *Globalization, Export-oriented Industrialization, Female Employment and Equity in East Asia*, mimeo, Geneva: UNRISD.

Kang Insoon (2001) *History of Women's Labour Movement*, Seoul: Hanul.

Kay, Cristóbal (2001) *Asia's and Latin America's Development in Comparative Perspective: Landlords, Peasants, and Industrialization*. Working Paper Series No. 336, The Hague: Institute of Social Studies.

Kim, Chang-gon (1997) 'Shinkoungyoung Jeokryak Goyoung Bulan (New Management Strategy and Employment Insecurity)', Special issue: 761–88.

Kim, Elrim (1999) *Accomplishment and Remaining Problems after Enforcement of Equal Employment Law*, Seoul: Korea Women's Development Institute.

Kim, Eun Mee (1997) *Big Business, Strong State: Collusion and Conflict in South Korean Development, 1960–1990*, New York: SUNY Press.

Kim, Jeong-Han (2000) Eesipilsekirl Kiyeop Bonkjirl weehan Bangwhangkwh Daewan (*Directions and Alternatives of Corporate Welfare for the 21st Century*), Report to the Korean Labour Institute.

Kim, Jin-Soo (1999) 'Changes of Corporate Welfare in the Era of Economic Crisis', Kangnam Daehak *Hankook Sahoebokji (Kangnam University Korean Social Welfare)*, 4: 361–75.

Kim, W. (2001) 'The Institutional changes in the National Pension Programme'. Paper presented at Korean Social Security Conference, June (in Korean).

Kim, Yeon-Myung (2000) *Sahwoe bokjiwa Nodong Woondongee Bangwahng (Social Welfare and Direction of the Labour Movement)*, Report submitted to the Korean Confederation of Trade Unions.

Kim, Soohaeng and Bokhuyan Cho (1999) 'The Southern Korean Economic Crisis: Contrasting Interpretations and an Alternative for Economic Reform', *Studies in Political Economy 60*, Autumn.

Kim, Taehong and Youkyung Mun (1999) *Yeoseongwoe Silopgwa Dawanoel chawaseo (Women's Unemployment and Search of Alternatives)*, Report, Seoul: Korean Women's Development Institute.

Korea National Statistical Office, Statistics of various years, internet edition <http://www.nso.go.kr/cgi-bin/>

Korea Statistical Information Office Data Base, internet edition <http://www2.kwdi.re.kr:8090/ucgi-bin_/stat_fnd_n>

Korean Women's Development Institute (KWDI), *Yearbook of Women's Statistics*, Statistics Database, various years.

Korean Women's Development Institute (KWDI) (1999) *Changes of Women's Role and Family Life Affected by Unemployment*, Report, Seoul: *Women's Development Institute*.

Korean Women's Development Institute (KWDI), *Women's White Paper*, 1999.

Krueger, A. O. (1995) 'East Asian Experience and Endogenous Growth Theory', in T. Ito and A. Krueger (eds), *Growth Theories in Light of the East Asian Experience*, Chicago and London: University of Chicago Press.

Kwon Huck-ju (1997) 'Beyond European Welfare Regime: Comparative Perspectives on East Asian Welfare Systems', *Journal of Social Policy*, 26(4): 467–84.

Kwon, Huck-ju (1998) 'Democracy and the Politics of Social Welfare: A Comparative Analysis of Welfare Systems in East Asia', in Roger Goodman *et al.* (eds) *The East Asian Welfare Model: Welfare Orientalism and the State*, Routledge: New York.

Kwon, Huck-ju (2000) *East Asian Social Policy in the Global Context. The Korean Case*, paper presented at the UNRISD Conference on Social Policy in a Development Context, Sweden, 23–24 September.

Kwon, Huck-ju (2001) *The Economic Crisis and the Politics of Welfare Reform in Korea*, Department of Public Administration, South Korea: Sung Kyun Kwan University, Mimeo.

Kwon, Huck-ju (2003) 'Advocacy Coalitions and the Politics of Welfare in Korea After the Economic Crisis', *Policy and Politics*, 31(1): 69–83.

Lee, Heo-jea (1996) 'Korean Patriarchy and Women', *Women and Society*, 7: 160–76.

Lindström, Lars (1993) *Accumulation, Regulation, and Political Struggles. Manufacturing Workers in South Korea*, Stockholm Studies in Politics, 46, University of Stockholm.

Martin, John P. and Raymond Torres (2000) *Korean Labour Market and Social Safety-Net Reforms: Challenges and Policy Requirements*, Paris: OECD.

Ministry of Labour (2000) *Report on Labour Costs*, Ministry of Labour, Seoul.

OECD (2000) *Pushing Ahead with Reform in Korea. Labour Market and Social Safety-Net Policies*, Paris: OECD.

OECD, Social Expenditure Database, various years.

Oh, Gunho (1993) 'Labour Policy of the State and the Capital', in *Industrial Restructuring and Labour Class of the Korean Economy*, edited by Korean Association of Industrial Society Research, Seoul: Hanul.

Orloff, Ann Shola (2002) *Women's Employment and Welfare Regimes*. Globalization, Export Orientation and Social policy in Europe and North America. Social Policy and Development, paper no. 12, Geneva: UNRISD.

Park, Jun-Shik (1996) 'The Structure and Function of Korean Corporate Welfare', *internet edition*, <http://www.hallym.ac.kr/~jsp/data/36.html>

Park, Soon-mee (2002) 'What's in a Name? For South Korean Women, Everything', *International Herald Tribune*, 21 October.

Park, Soon-Won (1999) *Colonial Industrialization and Labor in Korea: The Onoda Cement Factory*, Cambridge MA: Harvard University Press.

Pilling, David (2002) 'The Korean Renaissance: Lessons for a Humbled Japan', *Financial Times*, 25 October.

Rou, Jinsuk (1997) 'Development and Determining Factor of Korean Corporate Welfare System', *Trends and Vision*, Summer.

Seguino, Stephanie (2000a) 'The Effects of Structural Change and Economic Liberalization on Gender Wage Differentials in South Korea and Taiwan', *Cambridge Journal of Economics*, 24(4): 437–59.

Seguino, Stephanie (2000b) 'Gender Inequality and Economic Growth: A Cross-Country Analysis', *World Development*, 28(7): 1211–30.

Shin, Don-myeon (2000) *Social and Economic Policies in Korea 1960 to the Present: The Dynamics of Ideas, Networks and Linkages*, unpublished PhD thesis, Bath: University of Bath.

Siim, Birte (1993) 'The Gendered Scandinavian Welfare States: The Interplay between Women's Roles as Mothers, Workers and Citizens in Denmark', in Jane Lewis (ed.) *Women and Social Policies in Europe*, Aldershot: Edward Elgar.

Singh, A. (1997) 'Catching up with the West: A Perspective on Asian Economic Development and Lessons for Latin America', in Louis Emmerij (ed.) *Economic and Social Development into the XX1 Century*, Inter-American Development Bank, Washington DC: The John Hopkins University Press, 222–65.

Singh, A. (1999) ' "Asian Capitalism" and the Financial Crisis', in J. Michie and J. Grieve-Smith (eds) *Global Instability*, New York and London: Routledge.

Singh, A. (2000) *Global Economic Trends and Social Development*. United Nations Research Institute for Social Development (UNRISD), occasional paper 9, Geneva.

Singh, Ajit and Ann Zammit (2000) 'International Capital Flows: Identifying the Gender Dimension', *World Development*, 28(7): 1249–68.

Song, Ho-geun (1995) 'History and Reality of Korean Corporate Welfare', *Studies of Korean Corporate Welfare*, Seoul: Korean Labour Institute.

Stiglitz, Joseph (2002) *Globalization and Its Discontents*, New York: Norton.

United Nations (1999) 'Employment and Displacement Effects of Globalization', chapter 2 in *World Survey on the Role of Women in Development: Globalization, Gender and Work, 1999*, Division for the Advancement of Women Department of Economic and Social Affairs, New York: United Nations.

UNRISD (2000) *UNRISD 2000 +: A Vision for the Future of the Institute*, Geneva: UNRISD.

Wade, R. (1990) *Governing the Market*, Princeton: Princeton University Press.

White, Gordon and Roger Goodman (1998) 'Welfare Orientalism and the Search for an East Asian Welfare Model', in Roger Goodman *et al.* (eds) *The East Asian Welfare Model: Welfare Orientalism and the State*, London and New York: Routledge.

Wolfensohn, James D. (1999) *A Proposal for a Comprehensive Development Framework, A Discussion Draft*, World Bank, 21 January.

World Bank (1991) *World Development Report 1991: The Challenge of Development*, New York: Oxford University Press.

World Bank (1993) *The East Asian Miracle*, New York: Oxford University Press.

Yoo, Theodore Jun (2000) *You Make Me Feel Like a Natural Woman: The Politics of Gender in Colonial Korea*, paper presented at the 2001 Association for Asian Studies Annual Meeting, Chicago, 22–25 March.

3
The Impact of Export-oriented Manufacturing on the Welfare Entitlements of Chinese Women Workers

Delia Davin

> *Although tending the field is very hard work, we have a lot of free time. When your work is done you can play with your village friends. Here you have to hold your urine until they give you the permit to go to the bathroom*
>
> (SEZ woman worker interviewed in Lee, 1995: 384).

Introduction

This chapter is concerned primarily with the impact of employment in the export-orientated industries of China on women workers and in particular on their access to social welfare. It discusses the way in which the economic reforms and the growth of non-state industry have affected non-wage benefits to workers. It shows that women workers in the new export-oriented industries receive high wages by the standards prevailing in the older state industries, but have little job security, work long hours in poor conditions and lack the health and welfare benefits formerly enjoyed in China's state-owned industries. However, it would be an over-simplification to argue that involvement in the global economy has reduced security and welfare provision for the whole workforce. Access to welfare in pre-reform or 'socialist China' was by no means as comprehensive or as generous as is sometimes believed. Entitlement depended on residence and occupation. Urban workers benefited from the system, but peasants, the majority of the population, had little access to public provision. In difficulties caused by bereavement, disability, sickness or old age they depended on the family.

The first section of this study offers an overview of the social welfare regimes of China before and after the economic reforms. The next section looks at the female workforce of the export-processing industry and describes their lives and the controls and pressures to which they are subject. The following section considers how migration and work affect women workers' life-chances, family relations and entitlements. The last section looks at state policy on social welfare. It discusses the state's unwillingness either to maintain the old costly system in state-owned industries or to extend entitlements to the migrant workforce. It also considers differences of interest between provincial and national officials.

Entitlements to social welfare in China before and after the economic reforms

Neither in contemporary China, nor indeed in China prior to the economic reforms, did the labour force enjoy universal or equal access to non-wage benefits. The labour force was, and is, highly stratified. The major cleavage is between the urban and the rural population (Cheng and Selden, 1994). Since the late 1950s, people registered as urban residents have had access to higher status employment and have enjoyed superior entitlements compared to the rural population.

For the urban population, entitlements also depend on occupational status. In pre-reform China social welfare was distributed through the enterprise. State employees in government offices, state owned-enterprises and schools enjoyed job security, pensions, paid sick leave and maternity leave, free healthcare and subsidized housing. The treatment of those who worked in enterprises operated by *local* government or by collectives depended on the profitability of their enterprise but was less generous (Davis, 1989, 1995).

Entitlement to welfare was not directly dependent on gender in this model. It was dependent on an individual's job and was equal in most ways for employees of the same grade. The dependants of a state employee were entitled to half price medical treatment. A female state employee could have family members recognized as her dependants. The important exception to the gender blindness of the model was housing which was 'by custom' provided to the couple by the man's work unit.[1] The female worker's access to accommodation was thus normally through a man, a situation that disadvantaged women in two ways. Unmarried and divorced or separated women had great difficulty in securing independent accommodation. Married women often had to commute considerable distances, whereas their husbands normally had only a few minutes walk from homes provided by the work unit to the work unit itself.

However, the major gender discrimination in entitlements was not in the model itself but in its application. Men greatly outnumbered women in the formal state sector and also predominated in the senior grades. As a result more men enjoyed the welfare benefits associated with this type of employment. They also tended to receive higher pensions because these were calculated as a proportion of final salary. In the smaller enterprises owned by *local* government or collectives where welfare provision was much less satisfactory the workforce was often predominantly female.

Since the economic reforms, there have been great changes in the social welfare regime in the cities. A labour market is developing (Wang, 1998). Although the State is still the employer for much of the urban population, employment in privately owned, foreign-invested and jointly owned Sino-foreign enterprises is growing rapidly. Prior to the economic reforms, the State allocated school and university graduates to jobs. Most then remained in the same enterprise for the rest of their working lives. Now, by contrast, young people can seek their own jobs and move on when they think they can better themselves. Some who had secure jobs in the state sector have chosen to give up the security of a job for life in exchange for the greater potential, but greater risk, of business or a job in the private sector. (The Chinese expression for this action, *xiahai*, – 'jump into the sea' – conveys the common feeling that it needs courage to break away from the protective environment of state employment.)

The development of large-scale private employment has made it necessary to rethink the distribution of welfare. The old system, in which state-owned enterprises distributed and even funded welfare for their employees, was difficult to extend to the growing private sector. Moreover, many state-owned enterprises were struggling to survive in the new economic climate and policy makers began to argue that they must be relieved of the burden of paying non-contributory benefits. Interest in the development of contribution-based insurance systems grew in the 1980s and these were introduced in many cities in the 1990s (Krieg and Schädler, 1994).

It is not easy to provide an overview of welfare provision in China today because regions and cities have been required to experiment with their own systems. China lacks uniform national provision. However certain generalizations can be made. Few villages enjoy any cover beyond minimal help for the completely destitute. In urban areas social welfare is increasingly separated from its enterprise base but is still connected to employment as contributions are taken from the wage. Decentralized provision makes local governments responsible for the accumulation and distribution of social welfare funds. Family responsibility for the sick, disabled or elderly is strongly emphasized. Both marriage law and inheritance law require family members to support each other. Inheritance is related to the fulfilment of this obligation.

The result of the reforms is that permanent workers in large enterprises are increasingly covered by a contribution-based social insurance system rather than by enterprise-based welfare. However, older workers in state-owned enterprises still often depend on enterprise-based welfare. Contract workers, workers in small, collective or private enterprises and migrant workers tend not to be covered at all. Employment in a state-owned enterprise no longer confers the security or the entitlements once associated with it. As China developed greater contact with the world economy, adopted an export-orientated growth policy and tried to attract foreign investment, the inefficiency and uncompetitive management of state industrial enterprises became more apparent. Under increasing pressure to make cuts, they lay off workers and trim budgets wherever possible. There have been reports of enterprises that reduce their deficits by ceasing to make pension payments for months at a time (Hussain, 2000: 11). The State has often had to give subsidies to enable its enterprises to discharge their welfare obligations. Welfare rights formerly enjoyed by state workers have gradually been eroded. Job security for life has come under particular attack. It was vilified as an iron rice-bowl that made workers complacent and gave them no incentive. Such allegations have been used to justify lay-offs and changes in contract conditions since the start of the economic reforms. In October 1986, state enterprises were instructed to give no new permanent posts. All work henceforth was supposed to be on fixed contract (Sargeson, 1999: 34). Contrary to official policy, some enterprises even deprived established workers of their existing tenured status. Throughout the 1990s, enterprises laid off workers, sometimes severing their contract completely, sometimes paying a percentage of their former salary. By 1997, there were 14.4 million laid-off workers, called in Chinese *xiagang gongren* – workers who have left their posts (Hussain, 2000: 10). Numbers might have been greater still but for the fear of a threat to social order.

The policy of phasing out enterprise-based responsibility for social welfare is being implemented only gradually. Pilot insurance systems were set up in many cities in the 1980s and in 1986 a contributory unemployment system was introduced to cover workers in formal employment in the urban areas (Hussain, 2000). Insurance also covers retirement, healthcare and work injuries. Premiums can be as much as 10 per cent of a worker's salary. The 1994 Labour Law of the People's Republic lays down 'The State shall develop social insurance, establish social insurance systems and funds so that workers can obtain help and compensation when they are old, ill injured at work, unemployed or giving birth' (Warner, 1995: 187). However, in practice, these systems are still thought to cover only limited numbers while enterprises, including even newly established ones in the private sector, are still the important providers of health, welfare, pensions and housing in the urban areas (Francis, 1996). Benefits vary greatly in accordance with the profitability of an enterprise and its ability to provide and the extent to which non-wage benefits are perceived as beneficial to the recruitment of labour.

Changes in social welfare have also come about through the major changes in the structure of employment that have accompanied the economic reforms. An increase of numbers in the types of employment not usually covered by social insurance has been produced by the following overlapping developments:

1. large increases in non-state employment and in self-employment;
2. increases in numbers employed on temporary contracts;
3. growth in the numbers of migrant workers laid off as soon as there is no need for their services.

In addition to the insurance entitlement associated with employment, urban people enjoy other welfare entitlements. Even if they are not employed in government enterprises or covered by contributory systems, they can receive shelter and sustenance under a welfare system administered by the municipal bureau for civil affairs. This system of entitlement is limited to the urban population with permanent residence and migrant workers are specifically excluded (Hussain, 2000: 11). Indigent migrants are expected to return to the villages to be supported by their families. If they do not leave willingly they may be forced to go, and there are frequent reports of the deportation of unemployed migrants from cities.

Social welfare in the rural areas before the economic reforms was provided either by the family or by the institutions of collective agriculture

(Davin, 1994). Some communes had a cooperative medical service and most had some minimal support entitlement for the least fortunate. This system guaranteed care, food, shelter, healthcare and burial for orphans or old people without relatives to help them. The use of this 'five guarantees system', however, entailed a loss of status for the peasants who therefore only resorted to it in desperate straits. After the economic reforms, township and village committees acquired responsibility for the modest provision that survived decollectivization. Many still guarantee a minimal subsistence level to the destitute but this is not universal. In any case, only those without any family qualify for such aid. Otherwise, in most rural areas, the economic reforms resulted in disappearance of the limited health and welfare systems that had been funded through the institutions of collective agriculture. When peasants fall on hard times, it is the family, including both co-resident members and more distant relatives, that is more than ever the major source of help. The increasing importance of networks of kin, friends and fellow villagers that can be called on in times of need is emphasized in many of village studies of post-reform China (Chan *et al.*, 1984; Potter and Potter, 1990; Yan Yunxiang, 1996).

These great inequities between the entitlements of the comparatively well off urban population and those of the poorer rural population are under-pinned by the still significant limitations on demographic mobility. It is harder for a rural person to settle permanently in a large city within China than it is for a European citizen to move across frontiers in Europe. Peasants are denied urban residential status, even if they migrate to the cities. The definition 'urban' or 'rural' is based on residential registration at the place of origin rather than facto residence. Prior to the economic reforms, restrictions were even more severe. People with rural registration (*hukou*) were not allowed to live in towns. An urban *hukou* was necessary not only to obtain jobs in the urban areas, but even to obtain grain rations or schooling for children there. Rural to urban migration was therefore difficult if not impossible except when sponsored by the State to recruit extra labour. The development of a private market in grain after the economic reforms made it harder to keep the peasants out of the cities and the rapid expansion of the demand for labour forced the State to relax these iron controls (Davin, 1999; Solinger, 1999). Rural people are now tolerated in the cities as 'guest workers' but are treated as second class citizens. They have to pay for the temporary work permits they are required to obtain and they are still excluded from the best jobs by the *hukou* system. Job requirements for high status employment specify an urban *hukou*. Some cities have issued regulations listing jobs that are to be reserved for those with an urban *hukou*. Inevitably, rural migrants predominate in employment that urban people shun: service jobs in restaurants and repair shops, building and construction, domestic work and petty commerce. In export-oriented industry the majority of assembly-line workers are migrants.

Migrant workers in the urban areas are largely excluded from social welfare because they lack the urban *hukou*. They cannot obtain permanent employment in state industry with better entitlements and the sorts of jobs they take are rarely covered by insurance schemes. They are specifically excluded from the welfare schemes run by the city bureaux of civil affairs to relieve urban poverty. I will look in detail at the particular position of migrant women assembly-line workers in the following sections.

Export-oriented manufacturing industry and new types of employment

Export-oriented manufacturing

Export-oriented manufacturing has produced a huge growth in industrialization in China since the reforms. Many new enterprises engage in manufacturing or processing for the export market although others only aspire to do so. The new industries tend to be assembly-line operations with a high volume output and rather basic needs in terms of work skills. The labour force in this sector therefore has its own characteristics and its welfare regime is minimal in comparison to that of state industry. The new enterprises are generally owned or part-owned by foreign, overseas Chinese, Taiwan or Hong Kong interests but may also be privately owned by Chinese, or belong to local governments or collectives. The situation is further complicated by the fact that ownership and management are not always the same. A foreign-owned enterprise may be locally managed. Moreover, in exchange for gifts or 'management fees', local officials will sometimes register a foreign or privately owned enterprise as a collective in order to shelter it from government health and safety requirements (Lee, 1998: 55–62). There are great concentrations of export-oriented industry in the special economic zones (SEZs) set up in the 1980s, but export processing zones (EPZs) have since been established in every part of China. Export processing is not therefore an activity confined to foreign invested-enterprises nor indeed to EPZs.

The size of the workforce in export-oriented industry

The difficulty in defining export-oriented manufacturing leads to problems in quantifying the labour force that it employs. The sector is

Table 3.1   Employment by ownership of enterprise in China (all urban except TVEs) in 1994 and 1998 (numbers employed)

	1994	1998
1. Urban state-owned units	112 140 000	90 580 000
2. Enterprises funded by Hong Kong, Macao and Taiwan capital	2 110 000	2 940 000
3. Foreign-funded enterprises	1 95 0000	2 930 000
4. Privately owned, shareholding, jointly owned and corporations	6 760 000	20 510 000
5. Collectively owned enterprises	32 850 000	19 630 000
6. Town and village enterprises	120 170 000	125 370 000

Source: From SSB, *China State Statistical Yearbook*, 1999, Section 5.

not an official employment category for China's State Statistical Bureau. The Bureau does, however, collect data on numbers employed in foreign-funded enterprises, enterprises funded with capital from Hong Kong, Macao and Taiwan, private enterprises and town and village enterprises (TVEs). The table above (Table 3.1) provides figures for 1994 and 1998 to give some idea of the rise of these enterprises and associated employment compared with the state and collective sectors, which although still important, are suffering some decline.

Although these data can give us some idea of the relative importance of employment in different sectors, they are highly imperfect as an indicator of the numbers in export-oriented industry. It is probably that the great majority of enterprises in categories two and three could be so defined although they will also include non-manufacturing enterprises. Conversely, there is also substantial export-processing in enterprises in categories four, five and six of ownership and no doubt some in category one.

Another perspective on numbers can be gained from the data for migrant workers in Guangdong (home province to the first SEZs and to an enormous amount of export processing). Surveys have come up with figures of around 10 million migrants from outside the province of whom the majority find employment in export processing (Lee, 1998: 68). Migrants are notoriously difficult to enumerate (Davin, 1999). As one local official said, 'They are too many and we are too few. They come and go so quickly that sometimes even their employers cannot keep track of their whereabouts. Counting these workers is almost impossible' (Lee, 1998: 70). It is also difficult to provide a breakdown of the labour force in export processing by sex. However it is clear that export-processing industries depend more heavily than the older state-owned industrial sector on female workers. Official figures show that 39.3 per cent of the workforce of state-owned enterprises was female in 1994, the figure was 50 per cent for urban collectives (SSB 1999: 148). The data from studies of export-processing enterprises show female workforces of the order of 80 per cent (Knox, 1997: 29; Scharping, 1997; Lee, 1998: 68–9; Tan Shen, 2000). The lives, conditions of work and access to welfare of this labour force, whatever its exact numbers, are obviously worthy of discussion.

The location of export-oriented manufacturing industry and labour recruitment

Processing enterprises in China are chiefly located in three types of industrial area. The first, and perhaps the most studied, are the SEZs. These areas in the south of China are modelled on free trade or EPZs elsewhere in the world. China's SEZs were opened in 1984 with tax breaks and other concessions to attract foreign investment in the hope of accelerating economic growth and bringing in modern, high tech production methods and know-how. Since the early 1980s, the SEZs have drawn in capital from the outside world and labour from all over China. Subsequently, first investment incentives were extended to the whole eastern seaboard and then trade and investment regulations were generally liberalized. Consequently, foreign-invested manufacturing enterprises have grown up in all the coastal provinces including in old established urban areas such as Guangzhou, Shanghai and Tianjin. They are also found in much smaller numbers in the inland provinces. Chinese-owned private industry has also flourished, especially in small-scale enterprises that undertake processing work for larger foreign-owned plants Finally many of China's rural industries, the so-called TVEs (town and village enterprises), also produce goods or components which are eventually traded on world markets.

From the start, enterprises in the SEZs recruited migrant labour because the local labour force could not meet their rapidly expanding needs. Even when export-processing industry was established in existing centres of population as was often the case in the 1990s, it has tended to employ high proportions of migrant labour. Local people shun assembly-line work if they can find higher-status or less tedious work. Employer preference is probably also a factor, there is abundant evidence that employers prefer to take on young rural women whom they regard as docile and easy to control (Chan, 1998). Young migrants can also be signed on and laid off easily in response to fluctuations in the market. Employers may deliberately exploit regional identities and difference among workers from different provinces to reduce the potential solidarity of the workforce (Pun Ngai, 1999). The labour force in most TVEs, by contrast, is local. Some TVEs may also attract migrants from distant rural areas, but most of their workers are peasants from nearby villages. Rural people compete fiercely for assembly-line jobs because they are more remunerative than agricultural work. In some industrializing areas, the local rural population has transferred almost completely into non-agricultural employment, and leases its land to migrant cultivators from other provinces.

To summarize, migrant labour is attracted to export-processing industry in all three types of industrializing areas. It dominates in the labour force of the SEZs, and indeed the population of these zones (Lee, 1998: 69). In the older industrial areas and in the villages, the proportion of migrant labour in the assembly-line workforce depends on the availability of other more desirable work locally. The household registration system provides the means by which the most desirable jobs can be reserved for local people by the simple expedient of requiring a local *hukou*.

New industries and urban life

The dominance of the migrant population in the SEZs and their extraordinarily rapid growth gives life in the zones a particular flavour. Growth has been based on inward investment. Direct foreign investment into China reached over US$3 billion in 1988, US$30 billion by 1994 and it was over US$40 billion in 1995 (SSB, 1996: 554). By 1994, the SEZs had absorbed a seventh of total foreign investment into China. The SEZs were particularly attractive to foreign investment not because of the concessions made to investors and their proximity to Hong Kong and Taiwan, two of the major sources of investment. However, foreign investment also went to other areas of China as restrictions were relaxed in search of cheaper labour and fresh opportunities.

In the original SEZs the process of urbanization is far advanced. Skyscrapers dominate city skylines. Villages whose economies only two decades ago were based on rice and fish have been absorbed by urban sprawl, their paddy fields built over with factories, roads and cheap dormitory housing. Industries set up on greenfield sites have produced the development of new urban settlements where almost everyone is a migrant. The 10 million migrant workers in the SEZs of Guangdong

Province come from all over China, but the largest numbers are from the interior provinces where the impact of the economic reforms has been less pronounced and the economy is expanding less rapidly. Most enterprises in these areas were created with foreign capital and management practices, wage rates and working conditions are quite different from those that prevail in state enterprises.

There is a clear hierarchy of work in the zones and new industrial areas. Many of the managers, engineers and technicians are expatriates, but some of these jobs also go to a new, prosperous Chinese middle class. The best jobs are monopolized either by local urban people or by urban people from elsewhere. White collar jobs in tourist and hotel services also go to local people or to the best qualified of the migrants. Most managerial, supervisory and technical posts are held by men, whereas the assembly line and service workers are predominantly female (Tan, 2000).

There are also differences of status dependent on resident registration in the SEZs. At the top of the hierarchy are local people who always had local registration or those who were given it as an inducement to move to the zones when they were first set up. Most of these permanent workers are older, better educated and much better paid. They tend to live in good accommodation and enjoy various fringe benefits (Ip, 1995: 272–80). By contrast the majority of the workers in the zones have temporary work contracts and temporary residential status. Most come from other areas and have rural *hukous*. Unless they can find another job they will return home when their work contract ends. Temporary workers have no right to remain in the zones once their employment is ended.

The manufacturing industries of these areas are mostly labour-intensive and require only moderate skills. They include electronics assembly-line work, garment-making, and shoe and toy manufacture. The Chinese State has made huge investments in the infrastructure of SEZs to attract foreign capital. China has to compete for investment with other Asian countries such as Sri Lanka, Malaysia and the Philippines where living conditions are more attractive to foreign managers. Much of China's success is owed to its linguistic, cultural and sentimental attraction for Hong Kong and overseas Chinese businessmen, but the availability of cheap labour with work discipline and basic education is also no doubt important.

Female workers in the export-oriented industries

In their classic 1980s study of female labour in EPZs in the Third World, Elson and Pearson observed that managers liked to recruit young rural women for assembly-line work (Elson and Pearson, 1981). Two decades later, managers in export-oriented industry in China, whether Chinese or foreign, come out with the same stereotypes and clichés to explain the same preferences. Young women are said to be dextrous, and to have small, delicate hands. This enables them to do fine work. Their patience allows them to spend long hours on repetitive tasks which men would not tolerate. Women are also regarded as easier to control and less likely to prove troublesome.

As we have seen, about 80 per cent of the workers in China's SEZs are female (Knox, 1997: 28). Most are recruited from rural areas of interior provinces where the less developed economy has little to offer them. Ordinary Chinese citizens cannot simply enter the SEZs at will; they need special permits. This provides an opportunity for various types of middlemen to profit. New workers may be recruited by state run labour bureaux or directly by the enterprises. Local governments in the sending areas also play a role. For example, some county governments in Sichuan sign contracts with labour bureaux in the coastal areas. They then establish recruitment offices and run long-distance buses to take young women on the long trip to the coast. County governments even run training schools in Sichuan to teach young people the skills they will need as migrants. Local governments explain these activities with reference to notions of welfare and protection. They point out that naïve young villagers are vulnerable, do not know how to find themselves jobs and are easily cheated or exploited when they migrate. All this is of course true, but local governments are probably also motivated by the recruitment fee, often paid by both the worker and the employer, that would otherwise go to a private labour contractor.

Factory managers in the SEZs can set their own wage rates and hire and fire at will. Most workers in the SEZs are between 16 and 25 years old. Employers want to maintain a young, docile labour force that can be worked hard with minimal health problems and actively discriminate against older workers who tend to be given the lowest paid jobs such as canteen work or gate-keeping (Lee, 1998: 81). The government of Shenzhen, the largest of the SEZs, does not permit permanent workers over 35 to take up jobs in the Zone (Summerfield, 1994: 729). Wages are far lower than in Hong Kong or Taiwan and hourly rates can be considerably below what is paid to urban workers in state industry in China. However, because the hours worked by factory workers in the SEZs are long, overtime increases the wages actually received. And despite all hardships, migrants continue to stream into the newly industrializing areas. Their attitude is pragmatic. Hardships can be endured and will be worthwhile if they can earn more, save and improve their prospects for the future.

Once they arrive in the economic zones, young workers are usually accommodated in dormitory blocks often belonging to the factory. It is worth considering the significance of this type of arrangement. Factory dormitories also appeared early in the Industrial Revolution in England in places where mills using water power created a demand for labour that could not be satisfied by the local population. Girls drawn in from elsewhere were accommodated in factory dormitories (Cruickshank, 1981: 15–17). Only when the arrival of steam power made it possible to locate industry in pre-existing centres of population, did the dormitories disappear.

The dormitory system has been common in labour-intensive industrialization in East Asia. Early Japanese industrialization housed a female labour force from faraway villages in dormitory accommodation (Tsurumi, 1990; Hunter, 1993) as did the factories of Shanghai in the 1920s and 1930s (Honig, 1986). Dormitories were also commonplace in industrializing Taiwan in recent decades (Kung, 1983). In all these societies, the dormitory system made it possible for factories to recruit cheap female labour from the rural hinterland. Accommodation is often part of the employment agreement where employers particularly wish to attract migrant women workers as in the case of assembly-line work, or indeed domestic service. Dormitories solve the new arrivals' problem of where to live and provide some supervision. Dormitory janitors exclude men. Sometimes an older woman is employed to keep an eye on the young women. Long working hours, dormitory curfews and communal sleeping and living arrangements restrict opportunities for young women to develop relationships with men. Parents are concerned about their daughters' welfare away from home and are acutely aware that the preservation of virginity is crucial to a young woman's marriage prospects in rural China. The dormitory system helps to assuage such concerns. The choice of occupations for young women reflects the same concerns. Parents are reported to prefer that their daughters should take up factory work where discipline and dormitory confinement provide proper conditions for young women. Service work in beauty parlours and restaurants is suspect because it involves contact with all sorts of people. Parents fear lest such employment should result in the loss of a daughter's reputation (Lee, 1998: 82–4).

Dormitory accommodation also gives employers additional control over the lives of their workers, even outside working hours and helps them in the struggle to retain labour, countering the inclination of many young women to move from one job to another seeking better conditions (Lee, 1998: 86–7). Although employers use dormitories for the retention of labour over the short to medium term, the system plays a part in the high turnover of labour in the SEZs. Many plants lose 50 per cent of their labour force every year. Dormitory life is incompatible with marriage and family formation, and the system therefore discourages the formation of a permanent labour force. Few workers wish to live and work in these conditions for more than a few years.

The lives of young female workers in the SEZs are hard and restricted. The Chinese Labour Law of 1994 stipulates normal working hours of 44 hours a week with one day off. Overtime is supposed to be arranged only after consultation with the workers and the unions and should not exceed 36 hours per month (Warner, 1995: 177–92). However, working hours in export-processing industry tend to be much longer. When orders are high, a 10–12-hour day is normal (Knox, 1997: 31; Zhang, 1999: 37; Tan, 2000: 302; author's fieldwork 1994 and 2000). A refusal to work overtime may be recorded as an absence and bring dismissal. Remuneration is calculated on piece rates but workers must also achieve set production quotas. There are fines for being late, for refusing to work overtime, for speaking at work or during meals and even for infringements of the rules on uniforms or for going to the lavatory without permission or too often (Lee, 1995: 383; Knox, 1997: 31). It is often said that assembly-line work is so stressful that no-one could do it for more than a few years. Working conditions can also be unhealthy or even dangerous. Health and safety rules are not properly observed, there are frequent accidents and there have been horrific fires with much loss of life.[2]

Living conditions in crowded dormitory blocks bring little respite. Workers complain that there is round the clock noise and one shift moves off to work and another comes home to eat and sleep (Zhang, 1999: 38). Workers enjoy very little personal space. Often they sleep, dress, make up their faces, do their hair and keep their meagre possessions on their bunk beds Leisure time is spent chatting, window shopping, doing laundry, writing letters, reading and watching television if one is provided. Dormitory doors are usually locked at night to enforce curfews. Locked doors have been the cause of loss of life in dormitory fires.

Investigators reported monthly earnings of RMB 500–600 in the SEZs in the mid-1990s, by 2000 they could go to RMB 1000 or even higher (Knox, 1997: 31; author's fieldwork notes, 1994 and 2000). These were good rates. A survey of migrant workers in Guangdong Province in 1993 found that 53.6 per cent reported monthly incomes of RMB 300–500 and one-third earned less than RMB 300 a month (Tan, 2000: 298). Even these levels of remuneration are only achieved with a lot of overtime, the hourly rate is very low. The money is nevertheless an attraction. Many of the young women workers previously worked on family farms where they never received an independent wage. In the SEZs they can earn in a month more cash than a man in their home villages would make in a year. Their ability to earn and the experience they obtain can have a long-run impact on their relationship with their families, on their sense of themselves and on their future prospects.

Women workers and economic change: hopes, prospects, entitlements and welfare

The young woman worker in export-oriented industries is a person 'between worlds'. She is an industrial worker and usually lives in an urban settlement of some sort but without an urban *hukou* she cannot enjoy the full range of social welfare benefits accorded to the older industrial work-force. The new enterprises are supposed to pay social security premiums for their workers, but according to one survey in the Pearl River Delta in Guangdong Province, more than half failed to do so. Workers who are injured or ill are likely to be sacked and have to return home. Migrant workers are themselves very conscious that their situation compares unfavourably to that of permanent workers (Zhang, 1999: 37).

Many young workers are ambitions for personal development and hope to acquire more education, training, skills or even an urban husband (Lee, 1998: 80–2; Zhang, 1999). The cards, however, are stacked against them. Their employers see them as cheap and replaceable. Their work does not encourage training and other investment in human capital. Their living conditions make a long-term stay impossible and the State reinforces their difficulties by allowing them only temporary residence certificates. Family ties inevitably exert a pull and most return home to be replaced by a younger cohort.

Some women settle despite the obstacles. It is estimated that between a fifth and a quarter of Sichuan migrants will not return to their home villages (interview at SASS, Summer 1994). For the majority who do return, migration may confer advantages. They may have savings, new competencies and more sense of choice in life.

Interestingly, female migrants sometimes admit that they see migration as a way of gaining some autonomy. Lee (1998: 80–2) found that many young SEZ workers at first gave poverty as the reason for their migration. However, it soon became apparent that this was the 'respectable' explanation. As they talked more, many admitted that their primary motive was to escape from family restrictions and to experience a new life. Poverty was not simply a cover, they did send money back to their families or save it for their futures. But they also wanted to earn to be able to buy things without having to account for everything they spent. Some women even sought more fundamental freedoms. Lee (1998: 79–80) found that some hoped to avoid unwelcome betrothals by distancing themselves from home. In my fieldwork I have twice encountered migrant workers who were saving to pay off husbands from whom they wished to be divorced (Davin, 1999: 127–9).

Of course, in entering factory employment women accept a new form of control. As Hoy (1996: 355) observes:

> with many young women literally locked into factories and dormitories, bound by contracts, their wages remitted to families sometimes hundreds of kilometres away and used for the promotion of the family and individual family members other than themselves, we should not assume that growing numbers of women in the migrant labour force are always associated with a growing sense of autonomy and independence.

Yet we cannot either dismiss the voices of the many young women who affirm a sense of achievement and pride in the lives they make for themselves as factory workers (Lee, 1998: 80–4; 1999: 39). Hardship may be a price worth paying if the cash that they earn allows them to change something that they disliked in their past or that they wish to avoid in their future.

By taking such control over their lives and prospects they are challenging their traditionally prescribed gender roles within the family. But like other migrant workers they endeavour to maintain and reinforce family ties. Their remittances may go to pay for a brother's education or his marriage or enable parents to build a new house. Such contributions ensure young women their place in the web of obligation and responsibility that links Chinese families. Remitting is therefore a good strategy for the future when they may no longer wish or be able to stay in the destination areas. Family is an important source of long-term security and mutual assistance for everyone in China, and especially for rural people who have mnimal state entitlements.

The Chinese *hukou* system interacts with Chinese marriage practice to provide another obstacle to migrant settlement and ensures that most rural to urban migration is, for the moment at least, circulatory. Marriage between migrants and urban people is unusual. Partly this is a matter of status, – urban people tend to regard migrants as inferior. In addition marriage to an urban person does not give a migrant the right to an urban *hukou*. If an urban man marries a rural woman, they can only live together in an urban area for as long as she is employed and retains a temporary permit. Moreover a child inherits the mother's *hukou* not the father's. In the past, married couples with different *hukous* sometimes had to live apart for years (Ma *et al.*, 1996). The knowledge of the difficulties brought by these 'mixed marriages' is a strong disincentive. Nor is it easy for migrants to marry and settle together in the urban areas. Accommodation for migrants is usually for single people. Migrants have to pay for healthcare and if their children are not excluded from urban schools they have to pay high fees. Such discrimination ensures that most return to the rural areas to marry and bring up their children. Married men may continue to migrate on a seasonal basis even after they have children, leaving their wives or relatives to cultivate the land but once women return and have children they are less likely to leave again.[3]

The duration of migration for young women may be decided by all sorts of factors, the amount they are earning, whether they are needed at home or whether their remittances are more useful, whether they are homesick or are positive about their migratory experience. For all of them, however, marriage prospects must be a factor taken into account. Marriage is almost universal for women in China. The minimum legal age for women is 20. Most rural women get married in their early twenties.[4] There is evidence that women who have been migrant workers may delay marriage until their late twenties, perhaps they or their families wish to maximize their earnings. However, there is also a fear of leaving marriage too late when the pool of eligible young men will inevitably be smaller.

A sojourn as a migrant worker can increase a woman's value as a bride in various ways. First, she may have returned with some of her earnings as personal savings. Second, even if her remittances have gone to finance projects of her natal family such as house building or a brother's marriage, they can contribute to her family's economic status. The higher this status becomes, the better a woman's marriage prospects. Her family may also decide to recognize the contribution her remittances have made by giving her a large dowry. Finally, returned migrants sometimes come back with sufficient skills or capital to improve their income generating potential at home. A young woman with her own small business will be seen as a more desirable spouse. Potentially a period as a migrant worker can increase the young peasant woman's own economic standing in her home community and thus her chances of economic security through a good marriage.

We have already seen that another group of young women are involved in the export-processing industries work in TVEs while continuing to live in their own homes. In some ways they benefit just as the young female migrants do. They also have money of their own and are able to make recognized contributions to the family income. Judd (1994) has shown how this tends to affect gender relations within the family. With money of their own, these women may also seem more desirable marriage partners. Of course, they enjoy less freedom from family control than migrant workers do, and have less chance to broaden their horizons. None the less, with money of their own, they may negotiate more control, for example, in such matters as the selection of their marriage partners. On the positive side, they do not suffer the homesickness or vulnerability of the young women who find work far from home.

Workers in the established industrial labour force are the third group of women affected by the China's economic reforms and their associated entry into the world economy. They are usually state employees. China's economic reforms have involved the exposure of her industries to world markets. In this process many enterprises have been found to be uncompetitive. At the same time, an ageing workforce burdens them with higher pension and welfare bills. When state enterprises had to make economies the wages bill was an obvious target. Millions of workers have been laid off, transferred to lower-paid jobs or sent home on a fraction of normal pay. These measures involve at least a partial loss of welfare entitlements. It has been widely reported that a disproportionate number of the workers selected for this treatment are women. It is felt that they are less likely to make trouble and can be supported by their men. Laid-off women have become a much-discussed social category (Benyon, 2000). They usually look for new employment but their age and lack of qualifications tends to tell against them. If they find a new job it is likely to be poorly paid work such as cleaning.

The cohort of women most affected by cutbacks in China's state industry belong to a generation brought up to believe that women should be in the labour force and to draw their self-esteem from the contribution their work made to their society. They were told that the welfare benefits they enjoyed were an achievement of the revolution and something of which to be proud. The impact (for these women) of

China's incorporation into the global economy has been negative in terms of self-image, status and remuneration and has enforced dependence on husbands or other relatives.

Even younger women suffer discrimination in the new labour market. Many employers, whether state or private, prefer to hire men who they claim are more able, less costly in social security and do not have to take time off for family responsibilities.

The role of the State

It is a high priority for government in China to ensure economic growth and to attract foreign investment. De-emphasizing the difficult terrain of ideology, the post-reform government has based its claim to legitimacy above all on the extraordinary growth rates achieved by China in the 1980s and 1990s. Any serious setback to growth could threaten this legitimacy. To maintain high growth rates China must continue to attract foreign investment and for this China must continue to offer a cheap labour force. Chinese leaders are all too well aware that the labour-intensive industries are very cost sensitive. After all, much of the industry China has attracted was relocated from places such as Hong Kong, Taiwan and South Korea as a response to rising labour costs. At the same time, the Chinese government has an ideological commitment to workers' welfare and a constituency to please that may react badly to the perceived ill-treatment of workers, especially when that ill-treatment is at the hands of foreigners. The government wishes China to be seen as a modern state giving appropriate attention to the health and welfare of its citizens.

The ambivalence of the government in the area of social policy reflects these different pressures. Aware of the fiscal problems associated with the universalist welfare state model of western Europe, Chinese reformers have shown a clear preference for contribution-based social insurance linked to employment (White, 1998). As rural residents cannot easily be included in this model they are left to their own devices. Labour and trade union legalization of the 1990s laid down obligations on both the State and the enterprise to provide a wide range of social insurance and welfare benefits (Warner, 1995). Very significantly, the large and rapidly growing migrant labour force was specifically exempted from these national laws. In the SEZs, and in foreign-invested industry in general there is a clear reluctance to create a full and compulsory programme of social security and welfare rights for the labour force or even to enforce the rules that do exist. There has been insufficient effort to implement legislation or to create enforcement machinery. The same reluctance can be observed in the failure of the Chinese government bodies to enforce their own health and safety and anti-pollution legislation. One is left with the impression that these laws, like much Chinese legislation, set out what is considered desirable rather than what is actually expected to happen.

However any discussion of the Chinese State must acknowledge that it is not a monolithic unified body in relation to the labour force. There is a need to distinguish between the state at national level and at local levels. There is some communality of interest and overlap of agenda between the various levels but there are also important differences. There are also differences of interest between, for example, different provincial governments.

The provincial governments of the sending areas tend to be particularly concerned with migrants' rights. The government of the densely populated province of Sichuan, a major sending area, has attempted to defend migrant rights. It has argued that migrants should be allowed to acquire rights of residence in other provinces after a qualifying period of residence (fieldwork notes, 1994). It calculates and publicises the importance of migrant remittances in its provincial GNP. Its newspapers publicize bad conditions and factory accidents in export-oriented industries. Sichuan government officials even complain that it is unfair that Sichuan has to function as a nursery and a retirement home for the labour force while other provinces benefit from the productive years of its sons and daughters (fieldwork notes, 1994).

By contrast, the provincial government of Guangdong, the major destination area for migrants in China, has been resistant to the idea of giving residence rights to migrants. Its constituency is local people who, like people in other destination areas tend to lack sympathy for migrants (Davin, 2000). Guangdong is, of course, anxious to continue to attract foreign investment and to maintain its competitive edge over other investment destinations, including the poorer interior provinces of China. This may dispose its regulatory bodies to ignore the infringe-ments of health and safety and social security rules that are so obvious in its factories, and to side with management in the not infrequent labour disputes in the province (Knox, 1997).

Conclusion

It is difficult to draw a balance sheet for the effects of China's export-oriented industrial policy on the lives, security and welfare of her women workers. The majority of women who work in the export-oriented industries had no entitlement to social welfare in their village homes. The lack of non-wage benefits in their new employment does not represent a loss of anything they previously enjoyed. Their wages, although low by international standards, often allow them to acquire savings or to increase the resources of their natal families. Most migrants eventually return to their villages where the family-based system of security, mutual assistance and resource flow will in the end have greater relevance for them. A period as a migrant usually enables young workers to improve their position within their home society.

The position of women who joined the industrial workforce in earlier decades when there was a good level of job security and social welfare is different. The impact of China's economic reforms and of export-oriented policies has been negative for many of them. Millions have been laid off or had wages and other benefits reduced. Although as urban residents they may still enjoy a better standard of living and more entitlements than young migrants, they have suffered a net loss economically and in terms of security and self-esteem. It seems inevitable that when China's accession to the World Trade Organization reduces its ability to protect state-owned enterprises there will be an increase in these laid-off workers.

It is unlikely that these broad trends will see any dramatic changes in the short term. The government will try to attract high tech industry that requires a better educated workforce. Where it succeeds, a high labour turnover will no longer suit the needs of the employers, and in future they may perhaps seek to train and retain their young workers to a greater extent than they do today. In such cases they will presumably offer some non-wage benefits as part of the package. But most growth in employment will still be in the labour-intensive sector where China's main comparative advantage lies. Young rural people will continue to be willing to accept poor conditions and low wages on the assembly line because these jobs are more attractive than anything available to them in the villages. The willingness of these young rural workers to work for low wages makes China attractive to foreign capital. The state may try to control the worst excesses of managers in the export-oriented industries, but is bound to make China's competitiveness in the struggle for foreign investment its first priority. It cannot, therefore, force investors to fund an expensive system of social security, nor, with its weak fiscal base, does the Chinese State appear capable of taking this burden on itself. The Asian economic crisis and the recent downturn in the global economy must make the Chinese State more anxious to attract foreign capital and less willing to pay too much for welfare.

China's economic performance in the last two decades has been an enormous success. It enjoyed an extraordinary growth rate in excess of 10 per cent per annum in many years. It increased its share of world trade even during the years of international recession. Among the many factors contributing to this success has been the availability of plentiful female labour that is cheap because it accepts low wages and levels of social security. China therefore appears tied in to this mode of development for some time to come.

Notes

1. This custom was perhaps an unconscious reflection of the Chinese family system in which a woman joined a man's family on marriage. Exceptions to the system might occur if the woman's work unit had accommodation available and the man's did not. Interestingly, Beijing Municipality made a conscious decision to reverse the usual practice and give accommodation to its female employees in the 1980s (fieldwork notes, 1987).
2. Fires and industrial accidents in China's foreign invested industries have been widely reported. Details can be found in Knox, 1997 and in the Chinese Labour Bulletin published in Hong Kong.
3. There are of course exceptions. Zhang (1997) found that many young migrant women were determined to improve their qualifications in order to stay in the urban areas, some succeed in marrying urban people and some young women are able to leave their children with their mothers-in-law in order to return to factory work (fieldwork notes, Sichuan1994).
4. This cultural disposition to marry young is reflected in the official definition of 'late marriage'. Under the birth planning regulations there is a reward for marrying late. Males who marry at 25 and above and females who marry at 23 and above are eligible. (See, for example, the birth planning regulations of Liaoning Province in Scharping, 2000.)

References

Benyon, L. (2000) 'Changing Places, Changing Identities: Finding One's Place in Contemporary Chinese Urban Society', unpublished PhD thesis, SOAS, University of London.
Chan, Anita (1998) 'The Conditions of Chinese Workers in East Asian Funded Enterprises', *Chinese Sociology and Anthropology*, 30: 2–101.
Chan, A., R. Madsen and J. Unger (1984) *Chen Village, The Recent History of a Peasant Community in Mao's China*, Berkeley, CA: University of California Press.
Cheng Tiejun and Mark Selden (1994) 'The Origins and Social Consequences of China's Hukou System', *China Quarterly*, September, 139: 644–8.
Cruickshank, M. (1981) Children and industry: Child health and welfare in North-West textile towns during the nineteenth century. Manchester: Manchester University Press.

Davin, D. (1994) 'Family Care and Social Security in China before and after the Reforms', in Krieg, Renate and Monika Schädler (eds) *Social Security in the People's Republic of China*, Hamburg: Institut für Asienkunde, 103–13.

Davin, D. (1999) *Internal Migration in Contemporary China*, London: Macmillan.

Davin, D. (2000) 'Migrants and the Media' in L. West and Yaohui Zhao (eds) *Rural Labor Flows in China*, Institute of East Asian Studies, Berkeley, CA: University of California.

Davis, D. (1989) 'Chinese Social Welfare: Policies and Outcomes', *China Quarterly*, 119: 577–97.

Davis, D. (1995) 'Inequality and Stratification in the Nineties', in Lo Chin Kin *et al.* (eds) *China Review*, PP 19.1–25, Hong Kong: Chinese University Press.

Elson, Diane and Ruth Pearson (1981) 'The Subordination of Women and the Internationalisation of Factory Production', in Kate Young *et al.* (eds) *Of Marriage and the Market: Women's Subordination in International Perspective*, London: CSE Books, 144–66.

Francis, C. (1996) 'Reproduction of the *Danwei*: Institutional Features in the Context of China's Market Economy', *China Quarterly*, 147: 839–59.

Honig, E. (1986) *Sisters and Strangers: Women in the Shanghai Cotton Mills, 1919–1949*. Stanford: Stanford University Press.

Hoy, C. (1996) *'The Fertility and Migration Experiences of Migrant Women in Beijing, China', unpublished PhD thesis*, University of Leeds.

Huang, Xiyi (2001) 'Power, Entitlement and Social Practice: Resource Distribution North China Villages', Unpublished PhD Thesis, University of Leeds.

Hunter, J. (1993) 'Textile Factories, Tuberculosis and the Quality of Life in Industrializing Japan', in Janet Hunter (ed.) *Japanese Women Working*, London: Routledge.

Hussain, Athar (2000) 'Living in the City', *China Review*, 15(1): 8–11.

Ip, Olivia K. M. (1995) 'Changing Employment Systems in China: Some Evidence from the Shenzhen Special Economic Zone', *Work, Employment and Society*, 9(2): 269–85.

Judd, Ellen R. (1994) *Gender and Power in Rural North China*. Stanford: Stanford University Press.

Knox, A. (1997) *Southern China: Migrant Workers and Economic Transformation*, London: Catholic Institute for International Relations.

Krieg, R. and M. Schädler (eds) (1994) *Social Security in the People's Republic of China*, Hamburg: Institut für Asienkunde.

Kung, L. (1983) *Factory Women in Taiwan*, New York: Columbia University Press.

Labour Law of the People's Republic of China, 1994 in Malcolm Warner (1995) *The Management of Human Resources in Chinese Industry*, London: Macmillan.

Lee, Ching Kwan (1995) 'Engendering the Worlds of Labour: Women Workers, Labour Markets, and Production Policies in the South China Economic Miracle', *American Sociological Review*, 60(3): 378–97.

Lee, Ching Kwan (1998) *Gender and the South China Miracle: Two Worlds of Factory Women*, Berkeley, CA: University of California Press.

Ma Z., K. L. Liaw and Zeng Y. (1996) 'Spousal Separation Among Chinese Young Couples', *Environment and Planning*, 28: 877–90.

Potter, S. H. and J. M. Potter (1990) *China's Peasants: The Anthropology of a Revolution*. Cambridge: Cambridge University Press.

Pun Ngai (1999) 'Becoming *Dagongmei* (Working Girls): The Politics of Identity and Difference in Reform China', *The China Journal*, 42: 1–18.

Sargeson, S. (1999) *Reworking China's Proletariat*, London: Macmillan.

SASS (1994) Information collected by the author from briefing sessions at the Institute of Rural Development, Sichuan Academy of Social Sciences, September.

Scharping, T. (ed.) (1997) *Floating Population and Migration in China*, Hamburg: Institut für Asienkunde.

Scharping, T. translated (2000) 'Liaoning birth planning regulations' in 'The evolution of regional birth planning norms' special issue of *Chinese Sociology and Anthropology*, 32(3): 16.

Solinger, D. (1999) *Contesting Citizenship in Urban China*, Berkeley and Los Angeles, CA: University of California Press.

SSB (State Statistical Bureau) (1998 and 2000) *Zhongguo Tongji Nianjian* (China Statistical Handbooks for 1996 and 1999), Beijing: Statistical Publishing House.

Summerfield, G. (1994) 'Economic Reform and the Employment of Chinese Women', *Journal of Economic Issues*, 28(3): 715–32.

Tan Shen (2000) 'The Relationship between Foreign Enterprises, Local Governments, and Women Migrant Workers in the Pearl River Delta', in L. West and Yaohui Zhao (eds), *Rural Labor Flows in China*, Berkeley, CA: Institute of East Asian Studies, University of California: 292–309.

Tsurumi, Patricia (1990) *Factory Girls: Women in the Thread Mills of Meiji Japan*, Princeton: Princeton University Press.

Warner, M. (1995) *The Management of Human Resources in Chinese Industry*, London: Macmillan.

Wang Fei-ling (1998) *From Family to Market, Labor Allocation in Contemporary China*, Oxford: Rowman and Littlefield.

White, Gordon (1998) 'Social Security Reforms in China: Towards an East Asian Model?', in Goodman, Roger *et al.* (eds) *The East Asian Welfare Model*, Routledge: London, 175–97.

Yan Yunxiang (1996) *The Flow of Gifts: Reciprocity and Social Networks in a Chinese Village*, Stanford: Stanford University Press.

Zhang, Heather Xiaoquan (1999) 'Female Migration and Urban Labour Markets in Tianjin', *Development and Change*, 50: 21–41.

4
Globalization, Export-oriented Employment for Women and Social Policy: A Case Study of India

Jayati Ghosh[1]

This chapter seeks to examine the Indian experience with respect to women's employment in export-oriented manufacturing industry in the era of globalization. It also considers the role of social policy in providing work and survival security to women, by first evaluating the effects of state policy, and then considering other attempts to ensure minimum security to women workers. The first section sets out some of the issues with respect to the feminization of labour in export-oriented employment, and situates the discussion in the context of the experience of the high-exporting East Asian economies in the 1990s. The evidence pointing to a fall in the share of women in export-oriented manufacturing employment even *before* the onset of the East Asian crisis is considered, and the possible reasons for it are discussed. With this background, the next section briefly highlights the important trends with respect to aggregate female employment in the Indian manufacturing sector over the 1990s. It is argued that much of the use of female labour in export production in India has been in informal and unorganized workplaces, including home-based work, with associated implications for pay, working conditions and consequently also for social policy. The cases of Export Oriented Units (EOUs) and Export Processing Zones (EPZs) are then taken up in the third section, with specific attention to what such employment has meant for job, material and social security. Issues relating to social protection of female labour through the agency of the state and other examples of attempts to provide social security are considered in the final section. In this section there is also an argument for the need to have a macroeconomic perspective on the conditions for improving employment conditions for women workers, which would have wider applicability to other developing countries as well.

Women workers and export production in Asia: recent issues and trends

The link between export employment and the feminization of employment is now well known. (See Horton, 1995; Wee 1998 and Joekes, 1999 for discussions of some of this literature.) While feminization of employment can refer to either the absolute or the relative increase in numbers of women employed, or indeed the fact that growth in employment in the global economy has been insecure and badly paid jobs redolent not of the protected conditions of the male labour aristocracy but more akin to the secondary labour markets where most women have worked over the last hundred years (Standing, 1989, 1999). However most of the literature on this process in export-oriented employment has tended to look at the share of women to total workers in particular sectors. This is because the absolute increase in such employment (or even an increase in the share of women so employed to total female labour force) could be part of a fairly standard development pattern whereby more and more people are drawn into labour markets determined by changing patterns of labour demand, but need not tell us anything about any particular preference for women workers. By contrast, the relative increase in the share of women in total export employment, which was so marked for a period in parts of Asia, is a qualitatively different phenomenon. Of course, such feminization has obviously been reflected in more and more women being drawn into paid employment.

This process was most marked over the period 1980–95 in the high-exporting economies of East and Southeast Asia, where the share of female employment in total employment in the EPZs and export-oriented manufacturing industries typically exceeded 70 per cent. It was also observed in a number of other developing countries, for example, in Latin America in certain types of export manufacture.

Women workers were preferred by employers in export activities primarily because of the inferior conditions of work and pay that they were usually willing to accept. Thus, women workers had lower reservation wages than their male counterparts, were more willing to accept longer hours and unpleasant and often unhealthy or hazardous factory conditions, typically did not unionize or engage in other forms of collective bargaining to improve conditions and did not ask for permanent contracts. They were thus easier to hire and fire at will and according to external demand conditions, and also life cycle changes such as marriage and childbirth could be used as proximate causes to terminate employment.

Another important reason for feminization was the greater flexibility afforded by such labour for employers, in terms of less secure contracts. Further, in certain of the newer 'sunrise' industries of the period such as the computer hardware and consumer electronics sectors, the nature of the assembly line work – repetitive and detailed, with an emphasis on manual dexterity and fineness of elaboration – was felt to be especially suited to women. The high 'burnout' associated with some of these activities meant that employers preferred work forces that could be periodically replaced, which was easier when the employed group consisted of young women who could move on to other phases of their life cycle.

The feminization of such activities has had both positive and negative effects for the women concerned. On the one hand, it definitely meant greater recognition and remuneration of women's work, and typically improved the relative status and bargaining power of women within households, as well as their own self-worth, thereby leading to empowerment. (Such positive effects are documented in Heyzer (ed.) 1988, Joekes and Weston, 1994 and Kibria, 1995, inter alia.) On the other hand, it is also true that most women are rarely if ever 'unemployed' in their lives, in that they are almost continuously involved in various forms of productive or reproductive activities, even if they are not recognized as 'working' or paid for such activities. This means that the increase in paid employment may lead to an onerous double burden of work *unless* other social policies and institutions emerge to deal with the work traditionally assigned to (unpaid) women. For example, without adequate socially provided crèche and child care facilities, or adequate and accessible medical care and hospitalization, the job of looking after the young, the sick and the old, which is typically unpaid labour performed by women in a household, can devolve on girl children if the adult women are employed outside the home. Similarly the burden of regular housework typically continues even for women employed outside the home, except to the extent that these can be devolved to other household members or shifted to paid services.

Given these features, it has been fairly clear for some time now that the feminization of work is not necessarily a cause for unqualified celebration on the part of those interested in improving women's material status. On the other hand, it is also well known that the very process of feminization can also set in place social and political changes which improve the bargaining position of women not only within their own households, but also within the society and economy in general.

The exposure to paid employment has also played a major role in encouraging greater social recognition of women's unpaid work and led to greater social pressure for improving the conditions of all work performed by women in a number of countries. As more and more women get drawn into the paid work force, there is greater public and social pressure generally for improvement in their conditions of work and security of contract, for greater health and safety regulation in the workplace and for improvement in relative wages. Thus there are several reasons why, despite the acknowledged inferior conditions of such work, such a process of feminization in labour markets was generally welcomed by the women who were involved in it.

However, it is now becoming evident that the process of feminization of labour in export-oriented industries may have been even more dependent upon the relative inferiority of remuneration and working conditions, than was generally supposed. This becomes very clear from a consideration of the pattern of female involvement in paid labour markets in East and Southeast Asia, and more specifically in the export industries, over the entire 1990s.

It is well known that the expansion in export production which fuelled the economic boom in the East Asian region in the decade 1985–95 was largely based on the growing use of women as wage workers. Indeed, the Asian export boom was driven by the productive contributions of Asian women in many different ways: in the form of paid labour in export-related activities and in services, through the remittances made by migrant women workers, and through the vast amounts of unpaid labour of women as liberalization and government fiscal contraction transferred many areas to public provision of goods and services to households (and thereby to women within households).

Most countries of the region (barring a few important exceptions notably India) the period between 1985–97 witnessed a massive increase in the labour force participation of women. This process was most marked in the Southeast Asian region which was also the most dynamic in terms of exporting. Throughout Asia, as a consequence, the gap between male and female labour force participation rates narrowed, suggesting that this period was one in which – at least in terms of quantitative involvement – the gender gap narrowed. Indeed, this narrowing of the gender gap was not confined to overall employment – it also extended into wage differentials and even working conditions as the proportion of women involved in such activities grew.

In the exporting economies of Southeast Asia, these pressures were quite apparent, even if not always effective, from the early 1990s onwards, and to some limited extent they did contribute to a slight narrowing of the wage gap. But it is now evident that, as this more positive process occurred, there was in fact *a decline in the share of women employed in the export manufacturing sectors.* Thus, as the relative effective remuneration of women improved (in terms of the total package of wage and work and contract conditions), their attractiveness to employers decreased. This is discussed in a little more detail below, and is based on a more extended discussion of the issue in Ghosh (1999).

Most observers would not be surprised to find that the share of women in employment in the East Asian region has fallen in the very recent past, since this is after all a pattern well noted in economic downturns. It is obvious that the crash of mid-1997 dramatically altered both the potential for continued economic activity at the pre-crisis rate, as well the conditions of employment in the East and Southeast Asian region. When the export industries started to slow down from the middle of 1995, it became evident that continued growth of employment in these export-oriented industries could not be the same engine of expansion that they had served as over the previous decade. Obviously, therefore, there could be some setback to the feminization of employment that had been occurring, since the export industries had become the most important employers of women at the margin, especially in the large employment sectors such as textiles. Indeed, the very features which had made women workers more attractive to employers – the flexibility of hiring and firing and the more casual, non-unionized nature of labour contracts – are precisely those which are likely to render them to be the first to lose their jobs in any recessionary phase.

But in fact the reduced role for women workers (at the margin) was something that was coming into play even before the effects of the economic crisis worked themselves through. It is now apparent that even the earlier common assessment of the feminization of work in East Asia had been based on what was perhaps an overoptimistic expectation of expansion in female employment. Trends in aggregate manufacturing employment and female employment in the export manufacturing sector over the 1990s in some of the more important Southeast Asian countries, as described in Table 4.1, reveal at least two points of some significance. The first is that there is no clear picture of continuous employment in manufacturing industry over the decade even before the period of crisis. In several of these economies – South Korea, Singapore, Hong Kong China – aggregate manufacturing employment over the 1990s actually declined. Only in Malaysia, Indonesia and Thailand was there a definite upward trend to such employment.

Table 4.1   Trends in manufacturing employment and share of women workers

Country and year	Total manufacturing employment (000s)	Women employed in manufacturing (000s)	Share of women workers (%)
South Korea, 1992	4 828	1 931	40
South Korea, 1997	4 474	1 594	35
Malaysia, 1992	1 637	767	47
Malaysia, 1997	2 003	807	40
Indonesia, 1990	7 693	3 483	45
Indonesia, 1996	10 773	4 895	45
Thailand, 1990	3 133	1 564	50
Thailand, 1996	4 334	2 065	48
Singapore, 1991	423	189	44
Singapore, 1997	414	166	40
Hong Kong SAR, 1990	751	314	42
Hong Kong SAR, 1997	444	160	36

Source: ILO Yearbook of Labour Statistics, various issues.

Some may see the trend of reduction of manufacturing employment as a typical indication of a 'mature' economy, that is one in which the service sectors are achieving greater dominance and therefore there is a shift of labour away from secondary activities and towards a range of services. But remember that these are economies whose economic dynamism was fundamentally based on the ability to push out ever increasing quantities of manufacturing exports. And this reliance on exports was such that it fed into expectations in the rest of the economy, most particularly in the financial sector, thus creating conditions which made the crash possible. More significantly, it is precisely the ability of the manufacturing sector to respond (either to renewed export demand or to increased domestic demand resulting from a positive fiscal stimulus) which has determined the ability of the Southeast Asian economies to recover from crisis (Ghosh and Chandrasekhar, 2001). Thus, South Korea and Malaysia experienced partial recoveries which allowed both the volume of economic activity and employment to rebound led by the recovery in manufacturing activity. However Thailand has still not recovered even to pre-crisis activity levels, essentially because manufacturing growth has not picked up sufficiently. The renewed fears of stagnation, recession and possibly another financial shock that became widespread in the region in mid-2001 were again based on the slow-down in manufacturing activity. All this clearly points to economies which are still very much dependent upon increased manufacturing output as the basic reflection of economic expansion, which is quite far from the 'mature economy' situation.

The second point to emerge from the data over the 1990s is that, while they do show that female employment in manufacturing was important, the trend over the 1990s, even *before* the crash, was not necessarily upward. In most of the countries mentioned, there is a definite tendency towards a decline in the share of women workers in total manufacturing employment over the latter part of the 1990s. In Hong Kong and South Korea, the decline in female employment in manufacturing was even sharper than that in aggregate employment. Similarly, even in the countries in which aggregate manufacturing employment increases over the period 1990–97, the female share has a tendency to stabilize or even fall. Thus, in Indonesia the share of women workers in all manufacturing sector workers increases from an admittedly high 45 per cent to as much as 47 per cent by 1993, and then falls to 44 per cent by 1997. In Malaysia the decline in female share is even sharper than in South Korea: from 47 per cent in 1992 to only 40 per cent in 1997. A slight decline is evident even in Thailand.

This fall in women's share of employment is evident not just for total manufacturing but even for export-oriented manufacturing, and is corroborated by evidence from other sources. Thus Joekes (1999) shows that the share of women employed in EPZs declined even between 1980 and 1990 in Malaysia, South Korea and the Philippines, with the decline being as sharp as more than 20 percentage points (from 75 per cent to only 54 per cent) in the case of Malaysia.

In other words, what the evidence suggests is that the process of feminization of export employment really peaked somewhere in the early 1990s (if not earlier in some countries) and that thereafter the process was not only less marked, but may even have begun to peter out. This is significant because it refers very clearly to the period *before* the effects of the financial crisis began to make themselves felt on real economic activity, and even before the slowdown in the growth rate of export production. So, while the crisis may have hastened the process whereby women workers are disproportionately prone to job loss because of the very nature of their employment contracts, in fact the marginal reliance on women workers in export manufacturing activity (or rather in the manufacturing sector in general) had already begun to reduce *before* the crisis.

This is an important issue that clearly requires further investigation. The reversal of the process of feminization of employment in manufacturing has already been observed in other parts of the developing world, notably in Latin America (ILO, 1998). Thus Ghiara (1999) points out that in Mexico, as the share of exports in the machinery sector increased between 1987 and 1993, the proportion of women employed fell from 38 per cent to 29 per cent. Quite often, such declines in female share of employment have been found to be associated with either one of two conditions: an overall decline in employment opportunities because of recession or structural adjustment measures, or a shift in the nature of the new employment generation towards more skilled or lucrative activities requiring skills and training from which women have traditionally been excluded.

In the East Asian case, until 1996 at least the first factor would not have been important, and while the second factor is certainly likely to have played a role, it would not have explained the entire shift that can be witnessed. Also, the shift towards more skilled activities was more marked in certain countries such as South Korea, Singapore and Malaysia, and less evident in others such as Thailand and the Philippines. But there may be another process which is associated with widespread feminization of work, which creates conditions for its own unravelling over time. This relates to the relative cost of hiring women workers, and the relation to the perceived other advantages.

As mentioned above, one of the important reasons for preferring women workers in many export-related activities in particular, has been the lower reservation and offer wages of women. Throughout the East Asian region, women workers' wages have been consistently and significantly lower than male wages in the aggregate. The differentials have been particularly sharp in the case of South Korea, Malaysia and Singapore, where the average female wages were typically just above half those paid to male workers, as Table 4.2 indicates.

To some extent this reflects differences in the types of jobs for which women are used, which are typically at the lower skill and lower wage end of the employment spectrum. But it also reflects the general tendency for gender discrimination in pay, whereby women are paid less even for similar or identical jobs. This feature, which was quite marked in East Asia, is precisely the feature which tends to be rendered less potent as more and more women are drawn into employment. As women become an established part of the paid work force, and even the dominant part in certain sectors (as indeed they have become in the textiles, ready-made garments and consumer electronics sectors of East

Table 4.2 Female wages as per cent of male wages in manufacturing work

Average	Per cent
Bangladesh	71.7
Hongkong	65.9
South Korea	52.3
Malaysia	57.9
Philippines	84.0
Singapore	57.1
Sri Lanka	87.8
Thailand	63.8

Note: The data refer to an average of years for which data were available in the 1990s.

Source: ILO Yearbook of Labour Statistics, 1998.

Asia) it becomes more difficult to exercise the traditional type of gender discrimination at work. Not only is there an upward pressure on their wages, but there are other pressures for legislation which would improve their overall conditions of work.

It is worth noting that the female wage as a proportion of the male wage has been rising in most parts of East Asia in the 1990s up to 1997. Thus, in South Korea, the ratio of average female wages to male wages increased from 50 per cent in 1990 to 56 per cent in 1997, while in Malaysia it moved from 49 per cent to 57 per cent between 1990 and 1995. In Thailand it improved from 63 per cent in 1991 to 68 per cent in 1995. In Singapore it went up from 54 per cent in 1990 to 60 per cent in 1997. Hong Kong is the only economy in the region for which there is evidence of a decline in this ratio over this period, from 69 per cent in 1990 to 61 per cent in 1997 (ILO, 1999).

What this narrowing of the wages gap has meant is that women became less cheap as labour in exporting industry. To add to this, over this period there have been several moves towards protecting the interests of women workers, for example, in terms of slightly better maternity benefits and some improvement in the nature of contracts. In South Korea, a law which allowed women to be fired once they got married was repealed in the early part of this decade. Other legislation in other countries in the region has allowed for a modicum of benefits which were previously denied to women workers, to be provided. Thus, it has been observed that in several of these countries there were moves to ensure longer maternity leave of upto three months, provide better housing conditions and health care to young women workers and also (after the bad publicity offered by a series of industrial accidents) to work towards better compliance with minimal safety norms (Lim, 1994, 1996).

While this is fundamentally necessary and desirable, such social action reduces the relative attractiveness of women workers for those employers who had earlier been relying on the inferior conditions of women's work to enhance their export profitability. The rise in wages also tends to have the same effect. If this is in fact one of the explanations for the tendency towards reduced employment of women in export activities in the region, then it raises certain crucial questions which will become increasingly important. How is it possible to ensure a minimum provision of basic rights and privileges to women workers, and to improve the conditions of their work, without simultaneously eroding their attractiveness to employers and reducing the extent of female wage employment? How can such rights and basic labour standards be assured in the coming phase, in which heightened export competition is likely to be combined with a phase of aggregate employment contraction, as the full force of the current adjustment measures and the slowdown of the world economy are felt in the region?

These are already pressing concerns, as is evident from the growth of unemployment in the region, which is bound to accelerate in the coming period. Already, over the 1990s, female open unemployment rates in the East Asian region were much higher than those of men even in the expansionary phase. This is clear from Table 4.3 which describes open

Table 4.3   Unemployment rates (%)

	Total	Male	Female
Indonesia, 1996	4	3.3	5.1
Hongkong, 1996	2.8	3.1	2.3
Pakistan, 1995	5.4	4.1	13.7
Philippines, 1996	7.4	7	8.2
Philippines, 1997	7.9	7.5	8.5
Singapore, 1996	3	2.9	3.1
Sri Lanka, 1996	11.3	8	17.6
Thailand, 1996	1.1	1	1.1

Source: ILO Yearbook of Labour Statistics, 1998.

unemployment rates before the onset of the crisis of 1997. But now, as the exporting industries are hit and as the general economic decline is worsened by adjustment measures which are moving towards a downward harmonization of labour standards for all workers (men as well as women) the problem is likely to become more acute. Thus, in South Korea as a consequence of economic crisis, the fall in regular employment was much more severe for women than for men. Between 1997 and 1998, regular employment for men workers fell by 7 per cent, but that for women workers fell by 20 per cent (Korean Working Women's Network, 1998). Out of the 47 per cent of Korean workers employed in temporary capacity in 1998, 55 per cent were women. In addition, the proportion of women who were defined as 'economically inactive' increased by 6.4 per cent, indicating a strong 'discouraged worker' effect (Lee, 2001).

Also, as male workers were effectively forced to accept worse employment conditions, the working conditions for all workers deteriorated even as less women found employment at the margin. This process naturally gained momentum as the rate of growth of exports decelerated across the region from mid-1995 onwards, but the important point is that the process had started well before that, in fact during the height of the economic boom in these countries.

Indeed, with the onset of crisis and the recession of 1997–99, there appears to have been a shift to more insecure very small unit-based or home-based employment of women workers, in production chains based on a substantial dependence on outsourcing by large final distributors. Already this was a prevalent tendency in the region. For example, labour flexibility surveys in the Philippines have shown that the greater the degree of labour casualization, the higher the proportion of total employment consisting of women and the more vulnerable these women are to exploitative conditions (ILO, 1995). This became even more marked in the post-crisis adjustment phase (Pabico, 1999).

In Southeast Asia, women have made up a significant proportion of the informal manufacturing industry workforce, in garment workshops, shoe factories and craft industries. Many women also carry out informal activities as temporary workers in farming or in the building industry. In Malaysia, over one-third of all electronics, textile and garments firms were found to use subcontracting. In Thailand, it has been estimated that as many as 38 per cent of clothing workers are homeworkers and the figure is said to be 25–40 per cent in the Philippines (Sethuraman, 1998). Home-based workers, working for their own account or on a subcontracting basis, have been found to make products ranging from clothing and footwear to artificial flowers, carpets, electronics and teleservices (Carr and Chen, 1999; Lund and Srinivas, 2000).

This is of course part of a wider international tendency of somewhat longer duration: the emergence of international suppliers of goods who rely less and less on direct production within a specific location and more on subcontracting a greater part of their production activities. Thus, the recent period has seen the emergence and market domination of 'manufacturers without factories', as multinational firms such as Nike and Adidas effectively rely on a complex system of outsourced and sub-contracted production based on centrally determined design and quality control. It is true that the increasing use of outsourcing is not confined to export firms; however, because of the flexibility offered by subcontracting, it is clearly of even greater advantage in the intensely competitive exporting sectors and therefore tends to be even more widely used there. Much of this outsourcing activity is based in Asia, although Latin America is also emerging as an important location once again (Bonacich *et al.*, 1994). Such subcontracted producers in turn vary in size and manufacturing capacity, from medium-sized factories to pure middlemen collecting the output of home-based workers. The crucial role of women workers in such international production activity is now increasingly recognized, whether as wage labour in small factories and workshops run by subcontracting firms, or as piece-rate payment based homeworkers who deal with middlemen in a complex production chain (Beneria and Roldan, 1987; Mejia, 1997).

It has been suggested that a larger proportion of such subcontracting in fact extends down to home-based work. Thus, in the garments industry alone, the percentage of homeworkers to total workers has been estimated at 38 per cent in Thailand, between 25 and 29 per cent in the Philippines, 30 per cent in one region of Mexico, between 30 and 60 per cent in Chile and 45 per cent in Venezuela (Chen *et al.*, 1998).

All this may have special significance in India, where the process of open feminization of work is evident only in a very limited way in certain specific sectors and regions of export manufacturing. Despite the hype that is heard about the dynamic role of export employment, including in improving the conditions of women, there are few indications thus far that there has been any major shift in either the structure of production or female employment patterns. But there are important changes at the margin, which suggest that there is indeed a growing significance of female participation in export-oriented production in India, even if in ways rather different from the experience of the East Asian economies.

Women's employment in the Indian manufacturing sector, including in export employment

It is useful to begin by considering the overall evidence of the trends in female employment in urban India, and then focus on export-oriented activities, especially in manufacturing. In terms of aggregate urban employment, we have data from the small samples of the National Sample Survey (a major survey carried out periodically by the Indian government's Central Statistical Organisation, dealing with employment and unemployment as well as with consumer expenditure in separate surveys – hereafter NSS) covering the period up to 1999–2000.

It should be noted that the definition of economic activity used by the NSS is quite restrictive, and does not include the full spectrum of economic activities defined in the UN System of National Accounts, even though it now tries to take account of involvement in some household enterprises such as farm activities or small-scale artisan production or transacted service provision. It therefore excludes a significant amount of unpaid or non-marketed labour within the household, especially by women, including the processing of primary produce for own consumption, basic domestic handicraft production, services such as cleaning, child care and so on, which are undertaken within the household and not marketed. This means there is a likely underestimation of economic activity within the household, as well as of the work participation rates especially of women.

A word about the nature of definitions of work activity is also in order. The NSS data on employment is based on the distinction between 'principal' and 'subsidiary' status of activity as well whether the person is 'usually' engaged in the activity. Thus, a person is classified as 'usual principal status' according to the status of the activity (or non-activity) on which the person spent a relatively longer time of the preceding year. The activities pursued by a person are grouped into three broad categories: (a) working or employed (b) seeking or available for work (i.e. unemployed) and (c) not in the labour force.

A 'non-worker' (on the basis of the usual principal status) is someone whose major part of time in the preceding year was spent as either unemployed or not in the labour force. However, he or she could still be involved in some economic activity in a subsidiary capacity – when this is usually the case the person is referred to as a 'subsidiary status worker'. The two categories together – usual workers by both principal and subsidiary status – constitute 'all usual workers'.

Table 4.4 Work participation of urban Indian women, and per cent in manufacturing

	Work participation rate	Per cent in manufacturing	
		Usual status only	Usual + subsidiary status
1977–78	15.6	29.4	29.6
1983	15.1	26	26.7
1987–88	15.2	26.9	27
1993–94	15.5	23.6	24.1
1999–2000	13.9	23.2	24

Source: NSS, various rounds.

This detail can make quite a difference in the case of women workers – not only because much of their activity goes unrecognized, but because it is possible that they are classified as 'usually working' when in fact it may reflect underemployment or engagement in a subsidiary activity only. Indeed we shall find that there can be substantial variation in the type of employment contract depending upon whether the activity is a 'principal' one or a 'subsidiary' one.

Given this caveat, Table 4.4 provides an estimate of the overall work participation rate of urban women over the 1990s. This was more or less stagnant until the late 1990s, and then declined. This is extremely interesting, for it suggests that the picture that was being painted in the early 1990s, of a process of 'feminisation' of employment, especially export-oriented manufacturing at the margin, has not been substantial enough to counteract other forces which have made for downward pressure on work participation rates.

Since urban female unemployment rates have been approximately the same at around 7 per cent of the urban female labour force (according to usual status) or more than 9 per cent (according to the daily status definition) the decline in work force participation must reflect some other forces. One partial explanation is the increased involvement in education in the 6–15 age group, which has occurred and is certainly a positive feature. But this explains only about one-third of the fall in labour force participation. It is possible that even in urban soceities like that of India, with no effective social security or unemployment benefit system, there can be a discouraged worker effect due to the absence of available employment opportunities. Such a possibility tends to be confirmed by the significant percentage of those women who are described as

Table 4.5 Urban women workers by type of employment

	Principal status only			Principal + Subsidiary status		
	Self-employed	Regular	Casual	Self-employed	Regular	Casual
1983	37.3	31.8	30.9	45.8	25.8	28.4
1987–88	39.3	34.2	26.5	47.1	27.5	25.4
1993–94	37.2	35.5	27.3	45.8	28.4	25.8
1999–2000	38.4	38.5	23.1	45.3	33.3	21.4

Source: NSS, various rounds.

unemployed by the usual status by principal activity but are employed in some form of subsidiary activity, which amounts to 1.4 per cent of the urban female labour force, or nearly 20 per cent of the usually unemployed women.

Table 4.4 also shows that the share of urban women workers employed in manufacturing appears to have come down over this period. But there is an interesting, albeit small, variation depending upon whether usual activity alone is considered or usual plus subsidiary activities together. Those involved in manufacturing as a *subsidiary activity only* appear to have increased relative to all women working in manufacturing, and were just under 5 per cent of such workers.

The data on type of contract, described in Table 4.5, suggest that there has been a gradual shift away from casual employment towards regular employment, with self-employment broadly stable. In itself, this is a positive sign, since usually in urban India, except for a few cases at the very high income levels, regular employment suggests higher wages and better conditions than either self-employment or casual work. Notice, however, that this is much more marked for principal activity than it is for subsidiary activities, such that when both are considered together, self-employment remains much more dominant and accounts for nearly half of urban women workers; also that the discrepancy between the self-employed and regular workers becomes much sharper when sub-sidiary activities are included.

What could explain this very substantial difference once subsidiary activities are included? It can be argued that this has really taken two forms: the first is the increase in certain types of service activity, includ-ing domestic service; the second – and the important one for current purposes – is the increase in putting out home-based or other work as part of a subcontracting system for export and domestic manufacturing. Such work does not get fully incorporated in the employment statistics which are based on employers' records, and this may explain the paradox that even while women's share of employment in manufacturing has not increased, the dependence of the sector – and especially of export-oriented manufacturing – on the productive contribution of women may well have increased.

The data on women's employment in manufacturing in terms of category of enterprise confirms the picture that direct and formally recognized involvement of women has if anything come down in the period of the relative higher growth of exports in the early 1990s. This is shown in Table 4.6, which reveals that there has been a substantial decline in women's share of employment in Own Account Manufacturing Enterprises (OAMEs) in the period between 1989–90 and 1994–95. Employment in Non-Directory Manufacturing Establishments (NDMEs) (less than six workers) and in Directory Manufacturing Establishments (DMEs) (six or more workers) has remained broadly stagnant, which is itself significant considering that manufacturing output more than doubled over this period. Indeed, the overall stagnation of total employment in this area means that the absolute number of women employed in these enterprises declined.

However, while overall women's employment in manufacturing has decreased over this period, there are important variations across

Table 4.6 Female workers in unorganized manufacturing in India

	1989–90	1994–95
	In thousands of workers	
Own Account Manufacturing Enterprises	185	144
Non-Directory Manufacturing Enterprises	16	16
Directory Manufacturing Enterprises	33	32
	Per cent of total workers	
Own Account Manufacturing Enterprises	37.5	29.9
Non-Directory Manufacturing Enterprises	5.4	5.4
Directory Manufacturing Enterprises	10.6	10.1

Source: Census of Manufacturing Establishments (1996).

Table 4.7 Female workers to total workers by sector of urban unorganized manufacturing

	1989–90 (%)	1994–95 (%)
Food	20.4	17.2
Beverages	64	65.1
Cotton	41.9	36.1
Jute	80.4	67.4
Textiles	30.5	22.9
Wood	16.7	19
Paper	16.1	16.1
Leather	12.9	6.9
Chemicals	47.8	57.6
Rubber	13.5	12.9
Non-metals	25.9	28.5
Basic metals	2.9	6.3
Metal products	3.9	3
Non-electricals	5.5	1.7
Electricals	6.8	11.8
Transport	3.8	6.6
Other manufacturing	14.2	11.1
All industries	21.3	17.5

Source: Census of Manufacturing Establishments (1996).

particular industries. These can be gleaned from Table 4.7, which shows that the share of women employed and the trend over this period have varied quite remarkably across sub-sectors. In jute and beverages industries, the proportion of women was very high (as much as 80 per cent in jute) at the end of the 1980s, while in some others such as cotton and chemicals it was also quite high at nearly half the work force.

But the basic point remains that in most of these sectors the share of women declined over the first half of the 1990s, in some cases quite substantially. Only in the chemicals and non-metal manufacturing sectors was there any increase in the proportion of women employed. It is worth noting that these two sectors are also among the more hazardous industries. The involvement of women in own account small-scale activity in the chemicals industry in particular may become problematic because of the numerous health hazards associated with such production especially (but obviously not exclusively) on a small scale.

It is being argued in this chapter that home-based subcontracting activities, or work in very small units that do not even constitute small workshops often on piece-rate basis and usually very poorly paid and without any known non-wage benefits, may to some extent have substituted for both self-employment and more regular employment on a regular wage or salary basis. This is supported by some micro evidence relating to certain manufacturing sectors in particular towns and cities (Shah and Gandhi, 1992; Mukhopadhyay, 1999; Neetha, 2001). Deshpande (2001) found an increase in putting out tailoring activities in three Mumbai slums. Das (2001) reports an increase in the involvement of women in unregistered piece-rate payment based manufacturing in the ceramicware industry in Gujarat. Anand (2001) has documented the pattern of integration of home-based work with wider marketing channels in handicrafts such as applique and coir products in parts of Orissa. Mahadevia (2001) finds an increase in the informalization of employment and greater participation of women in homebased self-employment dealing with middlemen and contractors in Ahmedabad city of Gujarat, even though the city's role as a major centre of textile export is on the decline. Both the general pressure of industrial capitalist production and the particular external pressures faced by exporting industries which have to respond to international competition, operate to increase this tendency rather than to increase a more regular and secure form of women's involvement in manufacturing work. The tendency to informalization of employment in many sectors including export sectors may also have been encouraged by the complex system of regulation and reservation of certain activities for small enterprises which some observers blame for the lack of dynamism and international competitiveness in these sectors (Mohan, 2002).

This perception of informalization and invisibilization of women's employment is supported by the evidence on increase in subcontracting in Indian industry, especially in terms of export-oriented manufacturing companies and multinational companies operating in India (Suri, ed., 1988; Bose, 1996; Ramaswamy, 1999). One particular estimate of subcontracting intensity for Indian manufacturing (defined as the ratio of the value of goods sold in the same condition as purchased, to value added) found that it had increased from 9.46 per cent in 1970 to 25.3 per cent in 1993–94, for all manufacturing sectors taken together. (Ramaswamy, 1999: 165–6, also for following data) Certain industries, especially consumer non-durable goods, were found to have very high subcontracting intensities in excess of 100 per cent by the early 1990s. These included weaving and finishing of cotton textiles on powerlooms (110 per cent), stationery articles (180 per cent) canning and preparation of fruits and vegetables (178 per cent) and even white goods such as refrigerators and air conditioners (115 per cent). Ratios in excess of 100 per cent indicate that the value of subcontracted production which forms part of the input, is even higher than the value addition involved in the final output.

This particular study by Ramaswamy (1999) identified both technology and labour regulation as factors behind the higher subcontracting activity of factories that used more labour per unit of output. Thus, technological changes that are oriented towards higher labour productivity obviously reduce the requirement of many kinds of unskilled labour in particular, but they also allow a break-up or physical disintegration of the production process which greatly facilities outsourcing. Similarly, labour regulation that puts requirements on worker pay, conditions or safety on employers who gather workers together in factory or workshop settings tends to encourage more use of putting out systems, since these are efffectively free from all such labour regulation and the chances of self-exploitation by home-based workers are greater. So, those activities or parts of production processes that involve more labour use per unit of output are more likely to result in organizational forms dependent upon subcontracting at various levels.

This conclusion is also supported by other work on women workers in 'informal' economic activities. Thus, for example, the well-known case of workers in the *beedi* (local leaf-based cigarette) industry, where approximately 90 per cent of the total work force consisted of women and children working at home (Labour Bureau, 1995). The *beedi* industry is not an export industry, but this suggests that home-based work is already a common manufacturing practice. These are not export-oriented units, but they indicate that such labour practices are widespread and therefore are available for use by export-oriented producers who naturally require even more 'flexibility' in their functioning. Similarly, studies of the export-oriented industries of cashew and coir processing in Kerala found that male workers with higher reservation wages often stayed unemployed while women from the same household worked both at home and in small outside units at very low rates of remuneration (Quoted in Mukhopadhyay, 1999). Moreover a similar pattern of the apprent 'disappearance' of women from the employment statistics during a period when output and productivity in the garments sector was rising has been previously documented for the United Kingdom during the 1970s and 1980s (Mitter, 1986).

If the macro data combined with the micro evidence that is available are accurate representations of current trends, then the feminization of export-oriented employment may have taken a particularly regressive form in India, whereby the marginal utilization of women workers is at the lowest and poorest paid parts of the production chain, and such women are therefore effectively deprived of all the benefits that may accrue from outside employment except for the meagre nominal returns that they receive from piece-rate work.

This in turn constitutes an important challenge for social policy. Thus, if workers are collected at a workplace, then it is likely that there can be greater social control over both general employment conditions and specific factors affecting them. But if the nature of outsourcing is such that it is mediated through a chain of intermediaries, then the final user of the outsourced material – typically a large and even multinational company – can claim that it has no knowledge of the working conditions or remuneration at the bottom of the chain, and need not be responsible for them. Further, even legislation designed to improve conditions of such work, along the lines of the Home Workers Convention of the ILO, is difficult to implement because of the near impossibility of monitoring and ensuring compliance. (These and other issues are discussed in more detail in the section titled 'Measures for social protection of women workers'.)

An important question, of course, is why this is should be so much more the case for Indian women workers. In other words, why is the feminization of work taking this particular form and why is Indian manufacturing so increasingly prone to this type of organizational structure? From the point of view of employers or suppliers of goods, at one level the advantages of home-based production are quite obvious. When industry outsources part or even all of its production processes, it effectively transfers to the workers' households the responsibility for important costs of production: the site, machinery, inputs such as electricity, spare parts, maintenance, health and safety at work, pensions, healthcare and so on. A piece-rate system of payment not only does away with supervision costs because of the worker's tendency for self-exploitation under such circumstances, but it also allows for very low rates of remuneration, often below minimum wage levels. Home-based workers' opportunities for any kind of organization or collective bargaining are limited and therefore they are rarely in a position to demand better contracts from middlemen.

However, these are quite universal features of home-based work, and indeed they have been used to explain its prevalence in countries from Chile to Vietnam. What is probably significant in India is the fact that open employment of women in export-oriented factories, while it is certainly growing and has been quite significant in a number of industries, is less apparent than it was in the Southeast Asian countries during their phase of major export boom. Instead, perhaps a greater role has been played in Indian manufacturing by drawing in women working in very small or tiny units, effectively in the informal sector, or even actually within their own homes. To some extent, I believe this can be explained by the relatively low position of many of India's export commodities in the international value chain, such that there is greater emphasis on very low wages rather than skill and quality considerations. It is noteworthy that even in domestic market-oriented manufacturing, this tendency for outsourcing to home-based work is more pronounced in relatively low value and low skill content goods, in a range of sectors ranging from textiles, garments and leather goods to plastic processing. To that extent this tendency could even be seen as part of a phase of industrial development and export involvement, in which the focus is on maximizing profit through squeezing costs rather than increasing productivity, and supplying low-end goods or low-value parts to the production process.

This hypothesis tends to be quite starkly confirmed by a recent study of the involvement of female labour in the export-oriented knitwear industry of Tirupur, Tamil Nadu (Neetha, 2001). For this reason, it is worth considering the results of that study at some length. Tirupur, a small town in Tamil Nadu, is an old centre of textile production which from the mid-1980s turned into a growing centre for knitwear production for export. It is now actually the largest of the cotton knitwear export centres in India, accounting for 20 per cent of exports directly and nearly half of all such exports if the re-exported sales to Delhi, Mumbai and Chennai are included. Knitwear exports from such centres go dominantly to the developed markets of Western Europe and the United States, and are often sold under famous brand names. The industry is dominated by small and very small producers, who are really subcontracting units for direct exporters and merchant exporters who in turn negotiate with international suppliers. There are also ancillary units and job workers (including home-based workers) all of whom are integral to the aggregate production.

Neetha's study shows that in the early phase of modern industry in Tirupur (1925–70) when organized production was the norm, the mills were mostly composite units carrying out all operations, and employing *only* male workers. In the next phase, between 1970–85, there were the beginnings of the fragmentation and disintegration of production. Production facilities moved to Tirupur as employers fled Calcutta after a series of strikes, and sought to ensure more pliant work forces also using migrant labour. In this period women workers were involved in the production process as 'helpers', in cutting, arranging and folding for the male workers, usually from their own household. (It is worth noting that this was also the period of the decline in the local handloom industry, which left many women workers unemployed or underemployed.) Some of this work would even be done at home as male workers would take the material back with them for the (often unpaid) assistants to work on. The third period from 1985 onwards has been marked by a massive expansion of exports from Tirupur, and this was associated with the rapid acceleration of the processes of subcontracting and informalization. Female workers have been increasingly absorbed into the industry, to the point where they now constitute around 60 per cent of the total work force.

It is interesting to find that by the present time, the division of labour in the Tirupur knitwear industry has become minute and highly specialized, with gender driving most of the changes. The women – typically young women between the ages of 15 and 30 years, and dominantly only 15–20 years – are almost all employed on casual piece-rate contracts which end up providing them with daily incomes which are just above half the official minimum wages in the area. The employment of women is much greater in the lower rungs of the production chain, where uncertainty in production is higher and there is sharp seasonality or volatility in demand. While the horizontal mobility of women workers across units is quite high because of the uncertain employment contracts, upward mobility is close to zero and there is very little chance of moving up the skill ladder to activities like tailoring which remain the preserve of men. Also, the extent of subcontracting varies, but is so extensive that it goes down to the home-based work level, or to production units that are so small that they cannot be called more than very tiny cottage enterprises. What is surprising is that Tirupur is often described as being on the 'high road' of flexible specialization, because of the fact that many former workers have become producers and suppliers, albeit on a small scale. In fact, as can be seen from this very brief description, it is very a much a 'low road' pattern because of its complete depedence on inferior labour contracts using mostly female workers.

This study of Tirupur clearly indicates that feminization of employment has been the direct outcome of the attempt to create a pattern of 'flexible specialisation' to meet shifting international demand requirements and provide the cheapest possible production for international suppliers. Indeed, a similar tendency has also been observed for the small export-production units in certain sectors like garments and plastic processing in Greater Delhi and Ghaziabad (Shah and Gandhi, 1999). It is therefore an accumulation and production strategy which is integral to *a certain phase* of capitalist production for export. It is interesting – if almost predictable – to find that in some more modern units using very recent technology and catering to specific international suppliers on a more stable basis, there has been a shift to time rate wages and also to employing men at the margin. This also suggests that, just as feminization is a response on the part of employers to the need for a more 'flexible' labour force, it may also be a certain stage in a longer evolution, and as production moves up the value chain we may eventually observe the re-masculinization of the export work force, at least to some extent.

Export processing zones

The most visible sign of the link between feminization of paid work and export orientation is of course in EPZs. In India such zones have been both less prominent and less successful than in the Southeast Asian economies, but nevertheless they also bring out the reasons for employers' preference for female workers of a certain age group as well as the need to ensure minimal employment security in such areas.

The idea of an EPZ – which is also known in other countries of Asia as a Free Trade Zone (FTZ), Special Economic Zone (SEZ) and so on, is essentially to provide special incentives to exporters and to allow them to avoid or bypass many of the laws and physical and material constraints which supposedly inhibit export growth in the rest of the economy. As Raman (1989) has pointed out, 'whatever be the terminology, the significance of the Export Processing Zones lies essentially in its physical, social and economic separation from the rest of the country'. Indeed, the latest Exim policy announced by the Government of India declares that the new term will be FTZs to replace EPZs and these are to be treated as outside the country's customs territory.

In India, the first EPZ was established at Kandla in 1960, which was one of the earliest of all developing countries. At present, there are seven EPZs operational within the country, while two more are planned. Of these, the largest three – Santa Cruz EPZ, Noida EPZ and Madras EPZ – employ the bulk of the workers and account for more than 85 per cent of the exports of all the EPZs put together. However, EPZs themselves are still rather unimportant in quantitative terms: over the 1990s they together accounted for less than 4 per cent of the value of all exports from India, and their share has actually stagnated over the past decade despite the increasing number and value of various economic incentives that have been offered to them.

In aggregate they currently employ around 80 000 directly, but some reports suggest that the extent of indirect and unofficial employment is much larger and may be growing. The three large EPZs account for 80 per cent of all EPZ direct employment according to the official data. However, this includes only those workers who are permanent and are entered on the company record books. There are thousands of other workers, who either do not appear on the company records or may be working as contract workers. Thus, for example, the PRIA (1999) study of EPZs found that in Madras EPZ, the MEPZ workers union which is the only union of EPZ workers in India, did not accept the official total employment figure of the zone of 17 000, but rather put the figure around 36 000–38 000 out of which almost 25 000 are women.

The numerical dominance of women workers is a characteristic feature of EPZs across the world, and the Indian EPZs also follow along the same lines. In both Santa Cruz and Madras EPZs, women workers constituted 70–80 per cent of the work force. NOIDA was somewhat of an exception, with only 30–35 per cent women workers, resulting from the predominance of light engineering firms in this EPZ (Mazumdar, 2000). These women are also typically young – the average age is found to be between 20 and 25 years, with around 10 per cent even younger, in their teens, and only around 1 per cent above the age of 30 years (PRIA, 2000).

Officially, EPZs are also governed by the labour laws of the country, but certain distinctions and loopholes have meant that they are honoured only in the breach. Thus, the law states that union activity is permissible. Work hours as per law have been limited to 48 hours per week. Provident fund contributions by the employer, which are limited to just 8 per cent, become applicable after 3 to 5 years. The Bonus law prescribes a minimum of 8.33 per cent and maximum of 20 per cent, which is however, is not obligatory in the first five years if profits are not earned.

However, the critical law which inhibits worker association is that which declares the EPZs to be Public Utilities. Under the Industrial Disputes Act, six weeks' notice is required for a strike in a public utility service. Further, strikes are banned as long as any conciliation proceedings are pending. This makes the use of strikes as a bargaining weapon extremely difficult. It also means that labour laws can effectively be flouted without much resistance from the workers concerned. In any case, the predominant use of young women ensures that tendencies to unionization are already low.

This is probably why it emerges clearly from virtually all the studies on EPZs (PRIA, 1999; Mazumdar, 2000) that none of the provisions of the existing labour laws are actually met in most of the units operating in the major EPZs. Minimum wages are rarely if ever actually paid. (In Madras EPZ, women workers in leather and textile factories were reported to receive Rs. 800 per month in 1999, when the official minimum wage declared by the government at that time was Rs. 1200 per month.) Working hours are typically much longer than the specified maximum without any payment of overtime. The statutory benefits and leave rules are systematically flouted by employers. Basic safety and health precautions are also rarely observed within factories.

According to the PRIA study, 'Women do not get maternity leave anywhere, in fact women generally lose their jobs if they get pregnant. Surprisingly, some companies employ women on the condition that they won't get married or pregnant in near future. As per the factories law, employers are prohibited from allowing women to work in night shifts, but during the survey the contrary was seen women work in night shifts in many places in MEPZ' (PRIA, 1999: 12).

The questionable working conditions are obviously not confined to women workers alone, and it has been found that male workers in EPZs face very similar problems of low pay (typically lower than the official minimum wage) longer working hours and possibility of being fired without justification or compensation. The basic instrument through which all this is achieved is fear, the fear of loss of job as well as that of continuous harassment on the job.

This harassment, which ensures worker acquiescence, is often aided by the overt collusion of various agents of the government. Thus Mazumdar (2000: 6) describes the state of affairs in the NOIDA EPZ: 'even the tenuous rights available to workers ... are rendered further inoperable by a series of restrictions and practices by customs officials in the Zone. Designated a custom bound area, uniformed customs guards at the Gate screen all who enter the NEPZ. Passes are issued to each worker only at the behest of the management of companies. Similarly, they are immediately withdrawn and entry into the Zone is barred, again at management's behest. Illegally dismissed or victimized workers are thus prevented from even approaching the gates of their factories to lodge any protest. In other words, individual managements are able to use the uniformed customs guards as instruments of denial of workers' rights. Even labour department officials cannot take workers who are illegally dismissed into the zone and there is no system of negotiation between the administrators of the zone and the labour department. Workers are deprived of the fundamental right to assembly. Gate meetings and demonstrations are totally banned in the zone. Although technically law and order fall in the purview of the UP Police, the Customs guards act as an extra-constitutional policing authority and have often displayed marked brutality towards workers. A police chowki is located inside the premises of the NEPZ and the factory managements, the zone adminis-tration and the police act in tandem to terrorise the workers.'

The use of piece-rate payment is another common instrument to ensure high rates of production at low rates of wages. Most studies have found that piece-rate strategies of remuneration are increasingly being put into place in all manufacturing activity where this is feasible, and that this has put excessive pressure on workers. In some cases where the wage was not formally piece-rate production targets were arbitrarily increased without any increase in wages. Thus, in Noida EPZ, workers in garment factories found that their production targets had been increased from 300 to 600 pieces per worker per day without any addi-tional labour saving device and certainly no increase in wages.

All the studies report a range of work-related illnesses and disorders, ranging from chronic headaches and stress-related fatigue, to back prob-lems, to disturbances of the menstrual cycle, loss of weight and even more serious complaints. In all such cases, it was found that manage-ment had declared they were in no way responsible for the problems. As a result, dealing with such illness, with the associated absence from work and medical costs, was entirely the burden of the workers.

It is worth noting that these loopholes and strategies which allow for systematic labour exploitation in the EPZs have not made them more efficient or competitive than exporting units within the domestic tariff area which cannot avail of such benefits. Thus, as noted above, the share of EPZs in total value of exports has stagnated at the very low level of between 3 and 4 per cent, while that of EOUs (which get some fiscal and tariff incentives but no concessions in terms of labour laws) has tripled to around 11 per cent over the past decade. While employers of course maintain that the labour 'flexibility' which is *de facto* provided in the operations of the EPZs is crucial in maintaining their profitability, this is questionable. In fact it could be suggested that such laws, by suppressing the cost of labour, actually promote more inefficiency in other aspects of the production process and discourage technological innovations which would enhance productivity.

Measures for social protection of women workers

As most researchers in this area know only too well, it is easy enough to provide a catalogue of woes in terms of the working conditions and wages of women in export-oriented employment. It is much more difficult to work out policies and methods of ensuring some amount of work security and basic living conditions in the current global environment where the need to push for greater external competitiveness is systematically used as the basic argument against the provision of any workers' rights.

In particular, the discussion above leads to certain fundamental questions which are extremely difficult to address. How is it possible to ensure a minimum provision of basic rights and privileges to women workers, and to improve the conditions of their work, without simultaneously eroding their attractiveness to employers and reducing the extent of female wage employment? How can such rights and basic labour standards be assured in the current phase of globalization, in which heightened export competition is actually combined with a phase of aggregate manufacturing employment contraction, as the full force of the adjustment measures is felt in the real economies?

It is probably necessary to define the terms on which such social protection can be ensured. As pointed out by Huber and Stephens (2000), public delivery of a wide range of welfare state services is probably the most significant determinant of the conditions of the citizenry and of women in particular, and is much more significant than what are traditionally seen as straightforward redistributive transfers. Indeed, this argument has resonance in the Indian context, where many of the most basic of welfare state services are untouched by public agencies and expenditure on other has actually declined over the past decade as part of the standard structural adjustment-associated 'belt-tightening'.

It is also true, as they suggest, that there are strong political economy relationships associated with particular patterns of public spending as well as with the delivery of public services. This means that it would be foolhardy to specify certain social policies, without laying the groundwork for their adoption and efficacy through strong social movements which are able to demand these policies of the state. This is why it is necessary, in any discussion of social policy, to note the crucial significance of public pressure and social movements in achieving desired social outcomes, and therefore to realize why the ability to organize and the need to mobilize citizens is essential. Without this, even the most carefully thought out government policies and schemes are likely to have very different actual outcomes on the ground.

With this caveat in mind, let us consider the basic requirements of worker protection in a country like India. The earlier discussion has made it clear that it is futile to expect either decent labouring conditions or viable standards of material income from private employers given the overall context of excess labour supply and low to stagnant employment generation. Thus, a significant share of the burden must necessarily fall upon the state, and it is necessary to generate sufficient social pressure to make the meeting of such requirements a basic political necessity for any government.

In India, it is clear that the dominant notions of how to proceed with the task of 'development' have in turn influenced the measures for social security that have been undertaken by the government (Gayathri, 2001). Thus, in the period of the 1950s and 1960s, the need for welfare dominated policy thinking, leading to social security programmes along the lines of community development programmes and welfare institutions being set up for the most vulnerable groups. In the two decades subsequent to that, that is in the 1970s and 1980s, the emphasis was on equality and equity. This led to the addition of programmes like the Integrated Rural Development Programme which tried to provide basic assets to targeted rural beneficiary households, and the employment schemes under various titles. In the 1990s, when empowerment became the buzzword, there have also been measures such as reservation to political bodies, special financial assistance to vulnerable groups including widows, supplementary nutrition programmes for girls and pregnant and lactating mothers and generally more targeted schemes. As can be seen from this, there has been a related shift from ignoring the issue of social security (based on the earlier prevalent notions of the family or household as an altruistic unit) to one which recognizes the need for specific gender-specific measures.

The most basic requirement for workers – indeed all citizens – in an economy like that of India is food security, that is access to sufficient basic food at prices which are compatible with the actual minimum household nominal incomes. This can and must be a priority of the state, which is why the implicit agenda of the current Indian government, of effectively dismantling the Public Distribution System for food (through inefficient targeting and higher prices) is so dangerous. Also, such a scheme should be universal in nature, which not only reduces administrative costs associated with 'targeting' but also ensures that those who require it actually do have access. Quite apart from the general welfare considerations of such a strategy, it is well known that, given the social construction of gender in South Asia and intra-household consumption distribution, improved access to food for a household disproportionately benefits women and girl children, and the converse is true for reduced food access (Ghosh, 1998).

Similar requirements can be specified for public health programmes, which are not only grossly inadequate in India but are also dramatically underfunded, and have experienced swinging cuts in expenditure over the last decade. As in curative health, preventive health measures and sanitation, which would be considered part of the most basic economic rights of citizens anywhere are also underprovided to an extent that would be unthinkable even in most other developing countries. The need to ensure adequate public provision of such health facilities is so obvious that it probably does not require restating. So also, public housing remains an important domain of development which can be crucially implemented by the state and its various agencies (Mahendradev, 2001).

Of course, the effectiveness of delivery systems in such public goods and services depends upon the degree of transparency and accountability that the system provides. This is why social experiments such as the move towards decentralized planning in the state of Kerala are so significant (Isaac, 2000). It is essential that local people and their elected representatives be given greater control not only in terms of choice of investments in these areas but also over the administration and delivery of such services.

All this being said, it should be noted that at least on paper, the intentions of the Government of India have been blameless – if singularly ineffective – in the past. There is a plethora of laws, as well as of specific schemes, which are designed to improve basic social security in these crucial areas. But mostly they do not have real operational strength, and this is because of a combination of poor and declining public funding and inadequate social participation and accountability.

This relates to the social security of citizens at large, but of course they affect women workers as well. But clearly, given the peculiar and potentially highly exploitative nature of employment in export manufacturing sectors, special measures need to be directed towards those in such employment, especially the more vulnerable category of young women. Once again, formally they are already covered by a range of announced interventions, as described in Table 4.8.

It is evident that at least on paper, there is a whole package of different social security measures. Some states (like West Bengal) have also tried to provide some basic unemployment benefit for urban educated youth and so on. But it is generally acknowledged that the expenditure on such schemes on the whole is not even a small percentage of the requirement. Also, public management of social security and social assistance schemes has been quite inefficient and has not reached very

Table 4.8 Existing models of social security in India

Model	Nature of benefit	Beneficiaries	Admin/financial setup
Employers liability	Workmen's compensation Maternity benefit Gratuity Retrenchment compensation	Workers in the organized sector	Employers manage and pay exclusively
Social insurance I	Medical care Sickness benefit Maternity benefit Occupational injury	Workers in the organized sector	Administered by Employees' State Insurance Corp; financed out of contribution from employers, employees, state governments
Social insurance II	Old age benefit Invalidity benefit Survivor's benefit Provident Fund	Workers in the organized sector and some workers in the unorganized sector	Administered by central board of trustees; financed out of contribution from employers, employees, state governments
Social assistance			
(a) Welfare funds of central govt	Medical care Education Housing Water supply Old age benefit Survivor's benefit	Mine workers Bidi workers Cine workers Construction workers	Administered by departments; financed by special levies in the form of cesses
(b) Welfare funds of Kerala govt	Wide range of benefits including all of the above and housing, assistance for marriage and others	Workers in unorganized sector such as handloom, coir, cashew production	Administered by autonomous boards; financed by contributions from employers, workers and others
(c) Subsidised insurance	Survivor's benefit Invalidity benefit	Vulnerable groups of workers, including handloom, agri. and others	Administered by LIC and GIC; financed by contributions from state and central govts
(d) Other forms	Old age benefit Survivor's benefit Maternity benefit Employment assistance Training, and so on	Persons outside job market and below poverty line, destitutes, orphans, deserted and divorced women, widows, disabled persons, SC, STs OBCs	Administered by departments; financed from general revenues

Source: Jhabvala and Subrahmanya, 2000: 26–7.

many people even when the meagre amount spent is taken account of. There is also evidence that contact with a patronage-dispensing lower bureaucracy can be unpleasant and disempowering for the so-called beneficiaries. And then there is the fact, as was obvious in the discussion on EPZs, that many of these schemes are simply inoperational even when they are officially supposed to exist.

The answer may be to push for making these schemes more participatory and accountable even while increasing both public expenditure in this area and monitoring/control over private spending. Also, there may be a case for combining such schemes with a greater role for similar but more effective schemes run by co-operatives and trade unions such as SEWA and Chhattisgarh Mukti Morcha.

There is another question relating to social policy in the broadest sense, and that has to do with the fact that as long as employment conditions remain adverse in the aggregate or aggregate social levels of productivity remain very low (because of underemployment and so on) it is difficult for any targeted social policy to achieve very much, whether for women workers or any other group. This is a point often missed by those pushing for trade-related labour standards: that even when conditions of work and pay in any particular export industry in any developing country are very inferior, the likelihood is that conditions of work and pay in some other sectors would be even worse. It is precisely the relative absence of productive or more remunerative employment opportunities that makes workers (including women workers) accept terrible conditions of work at low wages in precarious and unstable contracts. So the goal of social policy must be to create more productive employment, which is indeed one of the most basic economic functions of the state given the possibility of generalized market failure that is characterized as unemployment.

This particular expansionary and employment creating role of the state was one of the major contributions of the Keynesian revolution in economic thinking; unfortunately, however, the current dominance of finance means that it is apparently no longer something that can be mentioned in polite circles or serious policy discussion. The standard response to a strategy of using Keynesian policies to take up the existing slack in labour terms and putting it to work in productive ventures which would also ease supply constraints to provide important public goods and services, is that finance capital would not approve and this would therefore lead to capital flight. However, this may be one of the greater misconceptions that currently dominate our thinking. Ultimately finance capital, as all capital oriented to profit making, must be interested in real economic growth and effective utilization of available resources. Whatever the slogans, capital will head to more dynamic economies which show greater evidence of actual or potential expansion, and this in turn is still more likely in countries where state expenditure patterns ensure both higher economic growth and basic conditions of subsistence and work for all workers. In fact, since social policy itself is the result of political economy pressures, as noted above, it can also be changed by public pressure, by social movements and mobilization that demand the more extensive and effective provision of basic public goods and services.

Finally, it is important to note that for social protection regimes for women workers to be truly useful, they have to move beyond the standard model which underlies most public action – that of the male head of household earning wages that provide incomes for all the other members of the household, including all the women, and determining intra-household resource distribution. This is not only because households may not be uniformly altruistic units. As has been seen above, this model may even be irrelevant for many households in which women effectively are the main breadwinners even when they and other household members persist in seeing themselves as supplementary earners. And even when this is not the case, when, for example, women working from the home participate in export oriented activities as part of a complex production chain, measures for social protection of such workers need to take a very different form. However, because participation in export activities often (or even typically) takes place under precarious and inferior conditions and because women may have to deal with the double burden of paid and unpaid work in such circumstances, the employers' preference for such contracts needs to be counterbalanced by effective public recognition of the problem, and by social policy designed specifically for such women workers.

This in turn leads to a larger question: that of the limits of aggregative models of social policy, including Keynesian strategies, in contexts of differentiated populations. Gender concerns are among the most obvious forms of differentiation, and act in more complex ways precisely because the interrelationships *within* households are so important, unlike caste and class-based stratification. This calls for a more nuanced approach to social policy in general as well as to specific schemes and programmes, in order to avoid both the pitfalls of excessive aggregation and of targeting that can lead to error of wrong inclusion for exclusion. And it bears repeating that for social policy to be even moderately successful in this respect, it needs to be combined with mobilization and increased awareness that can only come about through social movements and greater roles for representative institutions.

Note

1. I am grateful to Shahra Razavi, Ruth Pearson and Jomo Sundaram for comments, and to Abhijit Sen, C. P. Chandrasekhar, Amitabh Kundu, Indrani Mazumdar, Madhura Swaminathan, Subhashini Ali and Utsa Patnaik for discussions.

References

Anand, Harjit S. (2001) 'Linkage between Formal and Informal Sectors: Some Findings from Microlevel Studies', in Amitabh Kundu and Alakh N. Sharma (eds) *Informal Sector in India: Problems and Policies*, New Delhi: Insitute for Human Development.

Beneria, L. and M. Roldan (1987) *The Crossroads of Class and Gender: Homework Subcontracting and Household Dynamics in Mexico City*, Chicago, IL: University of Chicago Press.

Bonacich *et al.* (eds) *Global Production: The Apparel Industry in the Pacific Rim*, Philadelphia, PA: Temple University Press.

Bose, A. J. C. (1996) 'Subcontracting, Industrialisation and Labouring Conditions in India: An Appraisal', *Indian Journal of Labour Economics*, 39(1): 145–62.

Central Statistical Organisation (1996) Census of Manufacturing Establishments, Ministry of Planning, New Delhi: Government of India.

Carr, Marilyn and Martha Alter Chen (1999) 'Globalisation and Home-based Workers', WIEGO working paper No. 12.

Chandrasekhar, C. P. (2000) 'ICT in a Developing Country Context: An Indian Case Study', Background paper for *Human Development Report 2001*, New York: UNDP.

Chen, Martha Alter, J. Sebstad and L. O'Connell (1998) 'Counting the Invisible Workforce: The case of homebased workers', *World Development*.

Das, Keshab (2001) 'Wages and Earnings in Informal Manufacturing: Evidence and Issues in Estimation', in Amitabh Kundu and Alakh N. Sharma (eds) *Informal Sector in India: Problems and Policies*, New Delhi: Insitute for Human Development.

Deshpande, Sudha (2001) 'Impact of Emerging Labour Market on Women and their Households: A Tale of Three Slums in Mumbai', in Amitabh Kundu and Alakh N. Sharma (eds) *Informal Sector in India: Problems and Policies*, New Delhi: Insitute for Human Development.

Gayathri, V. (2001) 'Social Security for Women Workers', in S. Mahendradev *et al.* (eds) *Social and Economic Security in India*, New Delhi: Institute for Human Development.

Ghiara, R. (1999) 'Impact of Trade Liberalisation on Female Wages in Mexico', *Development Policy Review*, 17(2).

Ghosh, Jayati (1998) 'Assessing Poverty Alleviation Strategies for Their Impact on Poor Women: A Study with Special Reference to India', *UNRISD Discussion Paper*, Geneva.

Ghosh, Jayati (1999a) 'Macroeconomic Trends and Female Employment: India in the Asian Context', in T. S Papola and Alakh N. Sharma (eds) *Gender and Employment in India*, New Delhi: Vikas Publishing House.

Ghosh, Jayati (1999b) 'Trends in Economic Participation and Poverty of Women in the Asia-Pacific Region', Bangkok: UN-ESCAP also available at website http://www.macroscan.com

Ghosh, Jayati and C. P. Chandrasekhar (2001) *Crisis as Conquest: Learning from East Asia*, New Delhi: Orient Longman.

Heyzer, Noeleen (ed.) (1988) *Daughters in Industry: Work Skills and Consciousness of Women Workers in Asia*, Kuala Lumpur: Asia and Pacific Development Centre.

Horton, Susan (ed.) (1995) *Women and Industrialisation in Asia*, London: Routledge.

Huber, Evelyne and John D. Stephens (2000) 'Partisan Governance, Women's Employment, and the Social Democratic Service State', mimeo.

ILO (1995) 'Women at Work in Asia and the Pacific – Recent Trends and Future Challenges', in *Briefing Kit on Gender Issues in the World of Work*, Geneva.

ILO (1998) 'Labour and social issues relating to Export Porcessing Zones', report for Discussion in Tripartite Meeting of Export Processing Zone Operating Countries, Geneva.

ILO (1999) *Yearbook of Labour Statistics*, Geneva.

Isaac, T. M. Thomas, with Richard Franke (2000) *Local Democracy and Development: People's Campaign for Decentralised Planning in Kerala*, New Delhi: Leftword Books.

Jhabvala, Renana and R. K. A. Subrahmanya (eds) (2000) *The Unorganised Sector: Work Security and Social Protection*, New Delhi: Sage Publications.

Joekes, Susan (1999) 'A gender-analytical Perspective on Trade and Sustainable Development', *Trade, Gender and Sustainable Development*, Geneva: UNCTAD.

Joekes, Susan and Ann Weston (1994) *Women and the New Trade Agenda*, New York: UNIFEM.

Kibria, Nazli (1995) 'Culture, Social Class and Income Control in the Lives of Women Garment Workers in Bangladesh', *Gender and Society*, 9(3) June: 289–309.

Korean Working Women's Network (1998) 'Organisational Strategies of Irregular Women Workers', Seoul, available at http.//www.kwwnet.org.

Labour Bureau (1995) *Report on the Working and Living Conditions of Workers in the Beedi Industry in India*, Ministry of Labour, Shimla/Chandigarh.

Lee, Hyehoon (2001) 'Evaluation and Promotion of Social Safety Nets for Women Affected by the Asian Economic Crisis', Expert Group Meeting on *Social Safety Nets for Women*, Bangkok: UNESCAP.

Lim, Lean Lin (1994) 'Women at Work in Asia and the Pacific: Recent Trends and Future Challenges', *paper for International Forum on Equality for Women in the World of Work*, Geneva: ILS.

Lim, Lin Lean (1996) *More and Better Jobs for Women: An Action Guide*, Geneva: ILO.

Lund, Francie and Smita Srinivas (2000) *Learning from Experience: A Gendered Approach to Social Protection for Workers in the Informal Economy*, ILO and WIEGO.

Mahadevia, Darshini (2001) 'Informalisation of Employment and Poverty in Ahmedabad', in Amitabh Kundu and Alakh N. Sharma (eds) *Informal Sector in India: Problems and Policies*, New Delhi: Institute for Human Development.

Mahendradev, S. (2001) 'Social Security in India: Performance, Issues and Policies', in S. Mahendradev *et al.* (eds) *Social and Economic Security in India*, New Delhi: Institute for Human Development.

Mazumdar, Indrani (2000) 'Workers of the NOIDA Export Processing Zone', New Delhi: Centre for Women's Development Studies, mimeo.

Mejia, R. (1997) 'The Impact of Globalisation on Women Workers', in *The Impact of Globalisation on Women Workers: Case Studies from Mexico, Asia, South Africa and the United States*, Oxfam.

Mitter, S. (1986) 'Industrial Restructuring and Manufacturing Homework: Immigrant Women in the UK Clothing Industry', *Captial and Class* 27 Winter: 37–80.

Mohan, R. (2002) 'Small-Scale Industry Policy in India: A Critical Evaluation', in Anne Kreuger (ed.) *Economic Policy Reforms and the Indian Economy*, Chicago, IL and London: The University of Chicago Press.

Mukhopadhyay, Swapna (1999) 'Locating Women Within Informal Sector Hierachies', in T. S Papola and Alakh N. Sharma (eds) *Gender and Employment in India*, New Delhi: Vikas Publishing House.

Neetha, N. (2001) 'Gender and Technology: Impact of Flexible Organisation and Production on Female Labour in the Tirupur Knitwear Industry', NOIDA, Uttar Pradesh: V. V. Giri National Labour Institute, mimeo.

Pabico, Alecks P. (1999) ' "Invisible" Women Workers Fail to Escape Crisis', Philippine Centre for Investigative Journalism, available at http.//www.pcij.org.

PRIA (2000) Export Processing Zones in India and the Status of Labour, available at website http.//www.pria.org.

Raman, R. Anant (1989) *Review of Free trade Zones in Developing Countries*, New Delhi: Indian Institute of Foreign Trade.

Ramaswamy, K. V. (1999) 'The Search for Flexibility in Indian Manufacturing: New Evidence on Outsourcing Activities', *Economic and Political Weekly* XXXIV(6): 363–8.

Sethuraman, S. V. (2000) *Gender, Poverty and the Informal Sector*, WIEGO, also available at www.wiego.org.

Shah, Nandita and Nandita Gandhi (1992) *Shadow Workers: Women in Home-based Production*, Bombay.

Shah, Nandita and Nandita Gandhi (1998) 'Industrial Restructuring: Workers in Plastic Processing Industry', *Economic and Political Weekly,* XXXIV(22): L12–L29.

Suri, G. K. (ed.) (1988) *Small-scale Enterprises in Industrial Development: The Indian Experience*, New Delhi: Sage Publications.

Standing, Guy (1989) *Global Labour Flexibility: Seeking Distributive Justice*, London; New York: Palgrave/Macmillan.

Standing, Guy (1999) Global Feminization through Flexible Labor: A Theme Revisited, *World Development*, 17(7): 1077–95.

Wee, Vivienne (ed.) (1998) *Trade Liberalisation: Challenges and Opportunities for Women in Southeast Asia*, New York and Singapore: UNIFEM and ENGENDER.

5

Gendering the Debate on the Welfare State in Mexico: Women's Employment and Welfare Entitlements in the Globalized Economy[1]

Viviane Brachet-Márquez and Orlandina de Oliveira

Introduction

With the gender turn in the social sciences, analyses of the Welfare State (WS) have shifted from the assumption of indivisible, solidary and stable households headed by sole male bread earners, which had been implicit in earlier studies, to a perspective that shows how social legislation and the market differentially favour men and women workers, and they, in turn, differentially contribute to the household economy increasingly dependent on multiple bread earners. As a result, scholars who had initially sidestepped the issue of gender have recently begun to include the family dimension within welfare regime typologies (as Esping-Andersen, 1990), or to differentiate welfare regimes on the basis of their gender policy models (as Korpi, 2000). Thanks to these developments, the women-friendly (or unfriendly) side of social and labour policy can be discovered regarding marriage and the family, the protection of children, women's control over their bodies, state protection against male violence, the outlawing or enforcing of the sexual division of labour, or efforts to ensure equal pay for equal work (Orloff, 1993: 307).

However suggestive and fruitful, this debate has remained largely confined to the old democracies and welfare regimes, where the inclusion of women has run parallel to WS development, so that their actions, both as union members and citizens, may well have been instrumental in the creation of gender sensitive legislation (Heclo, 1974; Esping-Andersen, 1990; Hicks and Swank, 1984; Skocpol, 1992; Hicks and Misra, 1993; Huber *et al.*, 1993; Koven and Michel, 1993; Orloff, 1993; Pedersen, 1993; Caroll, 1999; Huber and Stephens, 2000). This leaves open the question of how the more recently legislated WS found in developing countries may have fared regarding women friendly social or labour legislation. Contrary to western democracies, women's entry into the labour market in these countries has occurred decades after male oriented social legislation had been enacted, and was in fact beginning to be retrenched as a consequence of economic downturn. This general downward economic trend, however, has not affected export oriented industries (EOIs), which have represented, since their creation in the 1960s, economic enclaves of relative prosperity in which female employment has traditionally been favoured.

Despite the importance of generating research bearing on these questions, the issues of wage differentials between men and women, or the differential access to social benefits by male and female workers in developing countries are generally little explored. As a result, we do not know if recent economic trends of globalization leading to the expansion of export sectors have resulted in the enhancement of women's position in these countries, especially in EOI enclaves, or if, on the contrary, women workers have been singled out as more attractive to employers in some sectors of the economy precisely because they represent a considerable saving with respect to men in wages and/or social benefits.

This chapter examines this general debate in the context of Mexico, a country whose social legislation history differs from that of developed countries in three important respects: the lateness of large scale industrialization; the involvement in social legislation of a non-democratic, yet pro-worker state; and the lag of some three decades between the introduction of social legislation and the entry of women into the labour force. Moreover, Mexico is a pioneer in the creation of EOIs.

In order to clarify the nature and consequences of these differences we consider two sets of issues: first, we compare access to welfare benefits by Mexican women who are in the labour force with those available to women who are home-makers over the past 90 years; next we compare access to welfare benefits by women working in non-export manufacturing sectors with those available to women who work in export-oriented industries. Our analysis includes both wage and non-wage related benefits. Given the preponderance of the first over the second in Mexico's welfare legislation, however, we emphasize the situation of working women in general compared to those working in EOIs, as conditioned by occupational segregation, wage differentials between men and women, the gender division of labour inside the export sector, and a host of other mostly unwritten rules that either favour or disfavour women in Mexico's labour market. To include all these dimensions, we speak of the *quality of employment* accessible to women, where this concept includes wage level, stability of employment, and *de facto* access to various categories of wage benefits.

In the first part of this chapter, we discuss welfare provisions and labour regulations in Mexico as they relate to women. In the second part, we examine the place of women in the labour market over the past 90 years. In the last, we address the question of women's quality of employment in export versus non-export industries and analyse available secondary data in two export sectors. Given the unresearched state of these questions, we rely, throughout the chapter, on case studies and secondary evidence. Our intention in doing so is less to prove a point than to generate hypotheses and indicate areas for further research.

Welfare provisions and labour regulations in Mexico

Mexico's social legislation: a historical overview

Mexico's social legislation, born out of the first social revolution of the twentieth century (1910–17) was contained, in embryonic form, in the Constitution of 1917, which represented an agenda for the future more than a set of rules for the time.[2] In the decades following the Revolution this agenda was to be slowly and episodically fulfilled, yet never completed. As with many revolutions, rather than ushering in a democratic regime in which the working classes would have participated in the construction of redistributive social legislation, the post-revolutionary period saw the rise and stabilization of authoritarian one-party rule which lasted until 1997 when the victory of opposition parties in Congress was officially acknowledged. This change was sealed in 2000 when an opposition party took the presidency, ending 70 years of one-party authoritarian rule. Nevertheless, as analysts have amply commented (Cornelius, 1975; Eckstein, 1977; Reyna, 1977; Levy and Szekely, 1985), post-revolutionary Mexico was no ordinary authoritarian regime, but a State corporatist regime which divided the population into the worker, peasant and popular sectors, each incorporated into the official party under given conditions, and each with its own set of entitlements to social legislation benefits. Despite the lack of competitive elections, the regime's stability and continued legitimacy depended heavily on the support by the rank and file in these sectors of official party candidates and policies, particularly the better-organized and more pugnacious industrial workforce. The history of social legislation can therefore be read as a series of attempts to preserve the strength and prestige of the official party among the rank and file in officially incorporated unions through the granting of legislation favouring wage (mostly male) workers and their families.

Mexico's welfare regime defined The first important discrepancy from established work on WS development to be noted is that social legislation in Mexico has not followed any single identifiable political philosophy regarding the proper place of the market, or the duty of the State to protect the weak. Although Mexico clearly stands outside of the pre-modern conservative regime defined by Esping-Andersen (1990), it cannot be said to belong to a Christian-Democratic, a social-democratic, or a liberal welfare regime. Rather than reflect a single political welfare orientation, Mexico's social legislation has exhibited elements of different welfare regimes during different historical periods, yet in combination with many continuities from previous periods. The resulting package is a mixture of family-oriented yet socially stratified entitlements, coupled with restrictive neo-liberal reforms introduced in the last decade. Thus, for example, health insurance coverage is, in principle, universal, but in 1995, only some 54 per cent of the population was affiliated, the rest relying on the Ministry of Health's far less generously funded programs, also unable to fully cover the uninsured population.

The general political process behind social legislation Welfare provisions have appeared discontinuously at historical junctures. Although the usual interpretation of this process has been pre-emptive reformism from above (Basurto, 1975; Carr, 1976; Cordova, 1985), an alternative interpretation (Brachet-Márquez, 1994) argues that the enactment of social reforms was almost invariably preceded by political pressure from dissident subordinate groups, mainly independent labour groups or independent tendencies within established groups.[3] In this interpretation, the introduction of reforms (e.g. social security, profit sharing, housing subsidies) is understood as state strategy to retain the loyalty of rank and file party affiliates who may otherwise feel tempted to join such dissident tendencies. Yet, not all social legislation has been prompted by pressures from below. Some, such as family planning or health aspects of environmental protection, have been dictated by international pressures.

This discontinuous process of building social legislation continued until 1982, when import substitution industrialization and debt financing finally became inviable strategies of development. Since then, social reforms have tended to restrict, rather than expand, benefits accessible to the population, either *de jure* or *de facto* (Brachet-Márquez *et al.*, 1996), despite the fact that some programs, such as basic education and public health, have continued their growth in coverage, if not in effectiveness or quality.

A short chronology of social legislation   Three general periods for the construction of Mexico's welfare state may be distinguished: from 1917 to 1942, the major features of today's labour code were elaborated; from 1943 to 1981 social insurance, low income housing subsidies, and special cost of living legislation (such as tax exemptions and controlled prices for basic food products, transportation, drugs, and so on) were created, and a package of programs targeted at the rural and urban 'marginalized' population. Finally, from 1982 to the present, we see the relaxation of employer obligations and the flexibilization of labour practices, the retrenchment of social insurance, the removal of food and transportation price controls and the strict targeting of benefits (such as food subsidies) to the poor. During the first period, corresponding to the initial formative process of Mexico's political regime, principles universally applicable to Mexico's workforce were defined. During the second, corresponding to the crystallization of the corporatist principle, the population was segmented into three distinct benefit groups based and defined by sectors in the Party, with the lion's share going to the labour sector. The last period corresponds to economic decline, the waning of the corporatist principle and the introduction of neo-liberal principles in Mexican politics. Whereas acquired labour and social insurance rights persist *de jure* during this last period, labour laws guaranteeing the stability of employment or workers' access to specific benefits are increasingly disregarded by employers, and social insurance benefits are curtailed via reform.

1917–42   During the first period several welfare programs, such as social insurance and profit sharing, included as basic rights in the 1917 Constitution, were on the agenda, yet decisions were postponed due to lack of resources and consensus (Brachet-Márquez, 1994: chapter 3). The basic conditions for industrial employment, however, were settled by 1932 as the main process accompanying the formation of a disciplined workforce collaborating with the government, and incorporated into the official party. The outcome favoured by the government was a set of rules guaranteeing a minimum wage, the right to unionize and several entitlements above the regular wage, which are *de jure* still obligatory today. Full-time employees, regardless of gender, were to receive paid vacations (with an additional 25 per cent of monthly wage during that period) and an end of year *aguinaldo* equivalent to six weeks' wage. Severance pay was set at three months' wage and an additional 20 days for each year as a full-time employee. Additionally, a paid three months maternity allowance was awarded to women employees.[4] Social legislation for the rural population during this period consisted of a vast program of land redistribution and the creation of an extended network of rural schools and health centres (González-Block, 1989).

None of these measures appear to have any sex bias, as they applied to all workers in principle. In fact, women could have benefited from these measures, had it not been for the fact that their proportion in the work-force, which had been 15.5 per cent in 1910 and 9.5 per cent in 1921 (mainly in pre-industrial craft industries and agriculture) dwindled to a mere 6.9 per cent in 1930, on the eve of the enactment in 1932 of the Labor Code. Thereafter their proportion in the Economically Active Population (EAP) would remain low, until it started rising to 16 per cent in 1970, 35.7 per cent in 1991 and 32.1 per cent in 1995.[5]

1943–81 The first step in the second period was the creation of social insurance. But rather than slowly consolidate different groups of beneficiaries into a unified set with universal social citizenship rights, social insurance in Mexico segmented the population into distinct groups with unequal entitlements.[6] This situation still prevails today despite efforts to propose alternatives (Frenk, 1998). Benefits include protection against work accidents, health and maternity insurance for workers and their families, widows' and orphans' pensions, as well as retirement and free health services for the retired. In these schemes, women were included either as the children, wives or widows of formally employed male heads of households, or as workers themselves. As workers, however, they did not have the same rights as their spouses to entitle the whole family to social security benefits, a restrictive provision that was only repealed in 1998. Missing in all social insurance schemes was unemployment insurance, substituted for by the provision of three months' severance pay. The rural population and non-wage workers were excluded.

Other welfare entitlements geared to the wage economy were to follow during that same period. In 1961, profit sharing was made into law. This meant that in addition to their obligations under the Labor Code and their contribution to social insurance payments, employers now had to set aside some portion of their dividends for distribution to their employees.[7] This measure was followed in 1972 by the creation of the National Institute for Workers' Housing (INFONAVIT), the state's agency responsible for building and financing housing for workers in the private sector, in whose coffers 5 per cent of the payroll had to be deposited for such purpose. FOVISSSTE, a similar, but less generously funded plan, was created for public employees, and a still less generous one (INDECO) for the non-wage population.[8]

Social legislation for the non-wage workforce during this period, principally the rural population and the growing numbers of urban poor, was slow to come and meagre in benefits.[9] Yet from 1970 on, important efforts were made to cheapen basic food products via the creation of CONASUPO, a state agency in charge of buying agricultural produce at guaranteed prices, and distributing them in urban areas throughout the country.[10] Also targeted on the poor was the COPLAMAR package enacted in 1977 to bring free health services, Conasupo coverage and various other benefits to the rural population and the urban poor. Finally, measures to sustain standards of living among the low income population, in the face of growing inflation, were taken from the 1970s on: the prices of some basic food staples, urban transportation and pharmaceutical products were subject to control. Likewise, these products and other unprocessed foodstuff were exempt from value added taxation (Brachet-Márquez and Sherraden, 1994). As a result of these measures, the proportion as well as number of the poor in Mexico diminished steadily until 1981 (Hernández Laos, 1992; Boltvinik, 1999).

During this period, we may also consider three sets of policies destined to facilitate women's role as providers: family planning, child support and child care. The first, adopted in 1974, offers free examination and contraceptive services in all first level health centres, regardless of social insurance affiliation. It also states women's right to choose the number of their children independently of their husbands' preferences, a very important first step in the direction of recovering control over their own bodies.[11] The second, regarding men's obligation to maintain their family, is apparently familistic and maternalist. But the failure to implement it has made it virtually dead letter.[12] Child support is also extremely difficult to obtain from absent/divorced fathers, unless wages can be garnished, which is not always feasible in an economy where a large proportion of workers have no work contracts, or existing work contracts do not reflect actual earnings. Lastly, child care is, in principle, a legal right of working women in the formal sector, and IMSS is supposed to offer facilities for all female workers and widowed fathers.

In fact, however, the supply of day care centres is so far below what would be needed that it cannot even fill the needs of female employees of the social security administrations (Parker and Knaul, 1997). The same applies to National System for the Integrated Development of the Family DIF, the organization in charge of day care centres for women in the informal sector: some centres exist, but only a sprinkle of the demand can be satisfied (ibid.).

On the whole, except for the absence of unemployment insurance, all these programs and laws appear quite progressive, if not always women-friendly. The problem does not lie in the rules themselves, however, but in the laxity with which they have been implemented. For example, from the 1960s on, when women began to be increasingly employed in *maquiladoras*, as we shall see, employers were known to finesse their obligations via the use of short-term temporary contracts and the interdiction for women employees to be married.

1982–2002 This last period opened with the financial debacle of 1982 triggered by a sudden decline in the international price of oil, Mexico's principal export and engine of welfare legislation aimed at the poor. This forced Mexico to declare a debt moratorium and subsequently receive its first international rescue package. Thereafter, welfare reforms resulted from agreements with international financial bodies to reduce public expenditure. Prior to 1982, pro-business policies (mainly high tariffs and low wages) had been tempered by measures aimed at sustaining minimum living standards, as exemplified above. These counteracting measures were gradually replaced by reduced programs targeted first to the poor from 1982 to 1994, and subsequently only to the extremely poor.[13]

Simultaneously the country opened its borders to international competition, while anti-inflation wage controls were left in place to attract foreign investment. The result was a precipitous fall in real wages, the growth of the non-wage economy, a rise in unemployment and under-employment, and a general lowering of living standards throughout the country. To counteract these tendencies, the De la Madrid administration (1982–88) continued the COPLAMAR program despite fiscal constraints, and the following administration (Salinas de Gortari, 1988–94) made it into a multiple program package renamed National Solidarity Program (PRONASOL).[14] From 1994 to 2000, Pronasol was downsized to target only the extremely poor and renamed PROGRESA.

Despite these good intentions, the social consequences of the stabilization and restructuring economic measures launched during this period were unprecedented income polarization from 1989 on, and general pauperization of the bottom deciles of the income distribution (Cortés, 2000). Social expenditures per capita went from $179 to $79 between 1982 and 1986, and health expenditures from 0.4 to 0.1 per cent of the GNP between 1980 and 1983 (Brachet-Márquez, 1994).

Women and labour force participation in Mexico

In this section, we describe with available statistics, the convergence between phases of welfare state development as defined in the first part of the chapter and women's position with respect to the labour market, the availability and stability of employment, wage levels and *de facto* access to benefits, in short, the *quality of employment* as was defined earlier.

Women's labour force participation: a chronology

Women in the first phase of welfare state development, 1910–42   Despite the small size of the industrial proletariat in the first three decades following the 1910 Revolution, anarcho-syndicalism, although repressed before 1910 and systematically discouraged by post-revolutionary leaders, was a force to reckon with. When Madero took office in 1911, no less than 40 strikes broke out, besieging his administration with urgent demands for improvement in the then abysmal quality of employment prevalent in Mexican industry (Ruiz, 1976). In the 1920s, labour–management conflicts continued until the monetary havoc wrought by the Revolution began to give way to relative stability, and the Conciliation and Arbitration courts created since 1911 (and reinforced through federalism in the 1920s) acquired the sufficient clout to impose settlements on workers and employers alike. The enactment in 1932 of the Labor Code institutionalized the new contractual and negotiated relation between employers and their workers, resulting in a reduction in strike activity.

During this initial phase, as noted, the presence of women in the industrial labour force, although sectorally and regionally concentrated, reached around 55 per cent.[15] Despite some improvements in the quality of employment made available to them through the new legislation, women continued to receive less pay than men for equal work, remaining concentrated in the more retrograde pre-industrial manufacturing industries (textiles and mining) with respect to labour management relations. Despite the dearth of quantitative data for this period, we can therefore safely conclude that the quality of employment available to women workers in those days was inferior to that afforded men, at least with respect to wage levels.

Women in the growing phase of welfare legislation, 1943–81   The first three postwar decades of import substitution industrialization and social insurance expansion saw the fast growth of Mexico's industrial workforce. Nevertheless, women's economic participation was initially small. From 1950 to 1970, their share in the labour force increased only from 13 per cent in 1950 to 16 per cent in 1970 (García and Oliveira, 1998). By 1979, women's workforce participation had reached 21 per cent – representing only a modest increase since the 1950s, concentrated in Mexico's three major metropolitan areas (Mexico City, Guadalajara and Monterrey). In these years, women were concentrated in labour-intensive industries (clothing, footwear, food products, appliances and other electrical or electronic firms). They received low wages, and, in some industrial branches, were even used as non-wage home workers with no rights to social benefits (Rendón and Pedrero, 1976; Fernández Kelly, 1982). This period also witnessed rapid demographic expansion, which led to the growth of the service sector, particularly the civil service and health and education services, where women are primarily incorporated as clerks, teachers and health workers.

Another important development in this period, with implications for the future growth of women's labour force participation, was the creation of the *Border Industrialization Program* aimed at stimulating regional development through the direct or indirect generation of employment and foreign investments.[16] At the time, the border region presented clear comparative advantages: it had an abundant workforce and low wage levels; its geographical proximity to the United States facilitated the transportation of inputs and finished products across the border, as well as the supervision of the productive process. Initially, these assembly plants, or *maquiladoras*, were labour intensive and low skill assembly plants that employed mostly young unmarried women with no previous work experience.[17] Production in these units was exclusively oriented toward the export market.

Despite these changes, before the 1980s, although some sectors of the economy were clearly feminized, particularly but not exclusively *maquiladoras*, the majority of women gained access to social benefits mainly as wives, widows or daughters of male breadwinners. Indeed, this is the period when population growth in Mexico reached such alarming proportions that a new law offering free family planning, regardless of social insurance affiliation, was enacted in 1974, with the express purpose of lowering the country's net population growth rate from 3.2 to 1 per cent by 1980 (Brachet-Márquez, 1984). Arguably in these initiatives women are the objects, rather than the subjects, of public policy. This development nevertheless was the first step towards recognizing and legally defining women's reproductive rights – initially the right to choose the number of children they wish to have (as against needing spousal approval for such choices), and subsequently the right to reproductive education and health services.

Women in the declining phase of the welfare state, 1982–2002   The recurrent economic crises experienced since the 1980s in the context of sudden trade and financial liberalization, restructuring of the productive sector, and reduction of public sector employment, have all contributed simultaneously to deteriorating conditions in the labour market.[18] Nevertheless, the impacts on women and men have been different, as we argue below (García and Oliveira, 1998; García, 1999; García and Oliveira, 2000; Oliveira *et al.*, 2002).[19]

Following the 1982 crash of debt-led economic growth, households began to multiply the number of their breadwinners as a strategy against declining real wages and shrinking wage labour opportunities (Cortés and Rubalcava, 1989; González de la Rocha, 1986). This is reflected in the rate of women's labour force participation which nearly doubled from 21 per cent in 1979 to 35.9 per cent in 1999 (ECSO, 1979; ENE, 1999). This increase went hand in hand with important changes in the regional concentration of women workers. Instead of being concentrated, as previously, in large metropolitan areas, large concentrations of women workers were to be found in northern cities, especially on the US–Mexico border which became the fastest growing region in the country, in contrast with previous decades. This trend resulted, in great part, from the economic policies promoting *maquiladoras* since the 1960s. Subsequently, as we shall see, these industries were to expand beyond the northern border while continuing to hire female wage workers, very often poorly paid (Elson and Pearson, 1982; Fernandez Kelly, 1982; Carrillo Hernández, 1985; Iglesias, 1985; Kopinak, 1993, 1995; Contreras, 1998). From the 1980s on, however, the legal principles behind these firms changed, so that they could produce simultaneously as export assembly plants and as manufacturers of finished goods for the domestic market.[20] Simultaneously, important changes were taking place in the technology used by these firms, the ways in which they organized work, and their capacity to generate employment. In particular, they began to favour male over female workers (Carrillo, 1989; Gambrill, 1997; Maclachlan and Aguilar, 1998; Contreras, 1998) as shown in Table 5.1, where the proportion of

Table 5.1 Proportion of female *maquiladora* workers by occupation, 1975–99

Occupation	1975	1979	1991	1999
Total workforce	(67 214)	(111 365)	(467 352)	(1 143 240)
Total per cent	(100)	(100)	(100)	(100)
Women	nd	nd	nd	51.2
Blue collar	67.3	66.3	48.3	45.0
Technical	nd	nd	nd	3.4
White collar	nd	nd	nd	2.8

Sources: INEGI (1988) Estadística de la industria maquiladora de exportación, 1975–86. INEGI (1994) Estadística de la industria maquiladora de exportación, 1989–93. INEGI (2001) Estadística de la industria maquiladora de exportación, 1995–2000.

women blue collar workers declines from 67.3 to 45 per cent between 1975 and 1999.

In the 1990s, women's economic participation rose faster than men's, and concentrated in different sectors of the economy. Available analyses and data for the 1990s illustrate some of the most important changes that have taken place in labour markets, and their gender-differentiated consequences for the workforce. First, the privatization of state enterprises[21] and repeated cuts in the number of civil servants reduced the role of the State as an employer. During the Salinas administration (1988–94), civil servants (among whom women are over-represented)[22] declined from 22.5 to 17.5 per cent of the economically active population (Oliveira and García, 1998). Likewise, the proportion of women employed in health, educational or cultural services went from 15 to 13.5 per cent between 1991 and 1999 (INEGI, 1991, 2000). In Mexico City, Guadalajara and Monterrey, this tendency continued until the late 1990s, with more severe consequences for women than for men (García and Oliveira, 2000). Second, the employment generating capacity of Mexican manufacturing industry declined considerably from 1979 to 1991, following the flooding of the domestic market with imported goods. Women's participation in the manufacturing sector shows a smaller percentage increase from 1991 to 1999 than men's, as shown in Tables 5.2a and 5.2b. This is probably accounted for by the increasing incorporation of male workers into assembly plants and by the gender-differentiated impacts of trade liberalization which destroyed more female than male jobs in the manufacturing sector due to the flooding of cheap imports into Mexico (Carrillo, 1991; Garcia, 1999). Third, the

Table 5.2a   Proportion of men and women workers in manufacturing sector (Mining, Energy and Industry), 1910–99

Sex	1910	1930	1979	1991	1999
Total	18.8	14.1	21.2	17.0	19.6
Men	12.1	12.8	21.0	16.2	19.1
Women	55.2	30.9	21.8	18.6	20.8

Total EAP Figures are:
5 492 215 in 1910, 4 632 817 men; 859 398 women.
5 352 226 in 1930, 4 980 617 men; 371 609 women.
1 907 700 in 1979, 14 483 000 men; 4 594 000 women.
30 534 083 in 1991, 21 256 913 men; 9 277 170 women.
39 069 095 in 1999, 26 049 654 men; 13 019 441 women.

Source: Rendón y Salas (1987).
INEGI, STPS (1979), Encuesta Continua sobre Ocupación.
INEGI, STPS (1991, 1999) Encuesta Nacional de Empleo.

Table 5.2b   Per cent changes in the proportion of manufacturing workers in different historical periods for men and women, 1910–99

Sex	1910–30	1930–79	1979–91	1991–99
Total	−25.0	+50.3	—	+15.3
Men	+5.8	+64.1	—	+17.9
Women	−44.0	—	—	+11.8

Source: Table 5.2a.

tertiary sector (trade and services) as a whole, and the least technologically advanced sub-sectors within the tertiary, expanded considerably. This shift is reflected in the tendency for women to take up small-scale commercial activities, and for men to seek employment in services, especially personal services (García, 1999; Oliveira *et al.*, 2002). Fourth, non-wage work (self-employment and unpaid work) maintained their previous significance, standing at 37 per cent of the EAP between 1991 and 1997, but women's presence in these activities increased from 36.2 to 40.5 per cent in the same period (ENE, 1991, 1997; García, 1999). Fifth, both men and women increasingly worked in small businesses (of up to five workers). In the late 1990s, 57 and 55.9 per cent of the male and female EAP respectively were engaged in small-scale operations (ENE, 1997) (Table 5.3a).

Table 5.3a Proportion of men and women in selected categories, 1991–97

Workers categories	Total		Men		Women	
	1991	1997	1991	1997	1991	1997
Non-wage workers	36.6	37.2	36.8	35.6	36.2	40.5
Small-establishment workers	53.4	56.6	53.9	57.0	52.3	55.9
Unpaid workers	12.2	15.1	10.3	13.2	16.7	18.9
Earning below minimum wage	18.2	21.0	17.1	17.7	20.9	27.4
Workers with no benefits	61.2	66.6	64.3	67.9	54.1	64.2

Source: INEGI (1991, 1997), Encuesta Nacional de Empleo.

The expansion of precarious wage and informal work,[23] according to Tokman (1991), has gone hand in hand with changes in the profile of the female workforce: married middle-aged women with children and low education have markedly increased their economic participation from the 1980s on (García and Oliveira, 1994). Yet unmarried, young and childless women still represent the majority of female workers, owing in part to their higher educational levels and to the increase in some occupational niches that hire mostly women workers. We are here referring to occupations that are socially defined as typically feminine, such as nurses, teachers, receptionists, and secretaries in the private and public sectors, which are also those that very often provide better access to benefits, even though wage levels are relatively low.

For both men and women, these changes have resulted in the deterioration of the quality of employment, defined as access to social benefits, wage levels and employment stability, but with more marked effects for women. Between 1991 and 1997, according to ENE figures, the proportion of economically active men working without any benefits rose from 64.3 to 67.9 per cent, while that for women jumped from 54.1 to 64.2 per cent (Table 5.3a). As for earning levels, the proportion of women earning less than the minimum wage during the same period rose from 20.9 to 27.4 per cent, while corresponding figures for male workers remained around 17 per cent (Table 5.3a). Therefore, women's position proportionately worsened more than men's on all accounts (Table 5.3b).

In sum, during this third period, we witness the accelerated incorporation of women in paid work, but simultaneously the deterioration of work conditions for both men and women, though more severe for the latter. From housewives protected from the market by their husbands' jobs in previous decades, women have increasingly become underpaid

Table 5.3b   Per cent increase in the proportion of the labour force in selected categories, 1991–97

Workers categories	Total	Men	Women
	1991–97	1991–97	1991–97
Non-wage workers	1.6	−3.3	11.9
Small-establishment workers	6.0	5.7	6.9
Unpaid workers	23.8	28.1	13.2
Earning below minimum wage	15.4	3.5	31.1
Workers with no benefits	8.8	5.6	18.7

Source: Table 5.3a.

workers themselves. At the same time, state policies have done little to ease this transition. In particular, the burden of childcare, home care and care of the sick and the aged has continued to fall disproportionately on their shoulders. During the same period, however, the state continued its policy of family planning, which branched into reproductive rights allowing women's access to a broader array of reproductive health services.

Figure 5.1 summarizes the social policies available to the Mexican population during the different periods defined in relation to the position of women in the labour market during these periods. The general impression is that most of these measures are not directly biased against women, but their consequences are either hurting women more than men, or not protecting women to the same extent as men. Nevertheless, given the fragmented nature of the labour market in Mexico, any answer to the question of who loses and who wins must be directed to specific sectors and subsectors. Additionally, we must accept the possibility that some of the existing negative biases found against women may be the result of women's choices when they must balance employment security against benefits and wage levels. Likewise, we must examine whether employers do not use the combination of low wages and adequate benefits as a lure for women workers.

Women in the export sector

In the first part of this section, we review general changes that have taken place in Mexico's export sector since 1982. In the second, we examine the distribution by sex of benefits among *maquiladora* vs *non-maquiladora* workers for a better approximation to the question of

Welfare benefits	Social policy	Quality of life parameters affected	Gender effect
Early period (1917–42)	Minimum wage	Negative when lagging behind inflation	No effect
	Right to unionize	Wage negotiations	Women predominantly hired in non-union shops
	Three-months severance pay and 20 days pay/yr	Dampens unemployment	No effect
	3-month maternity leave	More employment stability	Strong pro-women
Period of WS growth (1943–81)	Social security	Better family health better retirement	Indirect gender effect (women as wives)
	Profit sharing	Higher income	Indirect gender effect (women as wives)
	Worker housing	Higher living standard	Indirect gender effect (women as wives)
	Family planning	Better family health and living standards	Strong direct pro-women effects
	Child care	Better family income	Strong pro-women effect for the few
	Food subsidies	Better family health Nutritional security	No gender effects
	COPLAMAR	Better family health and nutrition for poor	Indirect gender effect
Period of WS decline (1982–)	Withdrawal of food subsidies	Declining family health and nutritional security	Women join labor market
	State employment decline	Declining employment stability	Less stable employment for women
	EOI Growth	More employment	Variable gender effect
	Poverty programmes	Some relief for poor	Indirect gender effect

Figure 5.1   The timing of welfare benefits and women's workforce participation

whether women employed in Mexico's export industries have better access to welfare entitlements than those working in other sectors of the economy. In view of the unavailability of statistics on benefits disaggregated by sex for *maquiladoras*, we have resorted to an indirect method of analysis: we compare men's and women's access to benefits in consumption goods and capital goods industries[24] from two groups of cities: those with high *maquiladora* concentration and those with low maquiladora concentration (henceforth *maquiladora* versus non-*maquiladora* cities).

Women in the export sector: 1982–2000

A critical mass of studies on the possible impact of *maquiladoras* on the national economy, and on the work force nationally, regionally and locally is now available.[25] We also find an abundance of national, regional and local statistics on these plants; nevertheless, they fail to adopt a gendered approach, so that they cannot clarify issues such as sex differentials in wages and access to benefits. Within these studies, some controversies have arisen. Contreras (1998) opposes critical perspectives based on the new international division of labour which emphasize an accumulation model centred on intensive exploitation of labour in the periphery, to analyses that claim a return to Taylorist or neo-Taylorist postures. For some, *maquiladoras* illustrate the principle of interdependence between countries (shared production) and competitive sales, with a focus on gradual modernization and industrial development (see also Stoddard, 1990). Analysts who are most critical of export-oriented policy models emphasize the persistent problems that characterize these industries: their enclave nature, and hence the negligible impact they have on the country's economy; their dependence on imported inputs; and the absence of technological transfers to other national firms. These studies also emphasize the precarious conditions in which workers operate in *maquiladoras*: they pay low wages, and employ low skill labour for routine activities with low union representation (Cobos, 1993; Kopinak, 1993; González-Aréchiga and Ramirez, 1989). By contrast, studies focusing on the more modern *maquiladoras* emphasize the use of cutting-edge technologies and flexible production processes, the creation of new skills and the reasonable wages within the national context (Stoddard, 1987; Brown and Dominguez, 1989; Carrillo, 1989).

Maquiladoras, created in the early 1960s, experienced a boost with Mexico's opening to the international market in the 1980s. By 1999, they accounted for 1 143 240 jobs (Table 5.1). This figure, clearly a large one in the context of employment contraction, is less than the total number of additional jobs required annually in the country as a whole, barely representing 2.5 per cent of the total EAP, yet 21.4 per cent of the wage earning industrial EAP, 21 per cent of total female employment in manufacturing, and 35.5 per cent of wage-earning employment in manufacturing (ENE, 1998; INEGI, 1999).

As they expanded, *maquiladoras* went through a series of transformations that have diminished their capacity to absorb female labour or offer quality employment. With technological change and the shift from exclusive export assembly to internal and external market, these firms have undergone a process of regional de-concentration coupled with an increasing absorption of male labour. By 1998, 34.5 per cent of their total work force (29.3 per cent male and 39.2 per cent female) resided in non-border municipalities (INEGI, 1999). De-concentration has resulted in the relocation away from the border of low-skill, low-wage labour-intensive activities that predominantly employ women, such as garments and textile manufacturing. In 1998, women represented 61 per cent of the labour force in these plants. By contrast, border *maquiladora* employment in 1998 was concentrated in the manufacturing of electrical and electronic accessories, and in the assembly and production of vehicles, employing 55 and 41.9 per cent of women respectively (MacLachlan and Aguilar, 1998; INEGI, 1999). This sectoral change has led to comparatively higher wage levels in the border region (Carrillo, 1989; Catanzarite and Strober, 1993; Marchand, 1994; MacLachlan and Aguilar, 1998), coupled with increasing gender stratification within border *maquiladoras*: women are over-represented among workers, and men in technical positions; 56.6 per cent of the workers, but only 28.8 per cent of the production technicians are women (INEGI, 1999). This occupational stratification is said to partly result from skill differentials, but also from wage discrimination within the same skill levels (Contreras, 1998).

Women's quality of employment in *Maquiladora* vs non-*Maquiladora* activities: an empirical test

To obtain the contrast between high and low *maquiladora* activity, we compare employment conditions for men and women in two groups of cities: Ciudad Juarez, Matamoros and Tijuana on the northern border, which jointly generated 41.4 per cent of *maquiladora* employment in 1998, on the one hand, and Mexico City, Guadalajara and Monterrey on the other, which jointly accounted for 51 per cent of the GNP in manufacturing, trade and services in the same year, yet occupied 1.4 per cent of the national industrial labour force in *maquiladoras* (thereafter high and low *maquiladora* cities respectively).[26] The data presented in Table 5.4 show the higher feminization of *maquiladora* cities with 56.9 per cent of women employed in manufacturing, as compared to 43.3 per cent for men in Matamoros, for example.

Table 5.4 Per cent wage-earning workers in consumer goods and capital goods industries by sex in *maquiladora* and non-*maquiladora* cities, 1998

Selected cities	Women			Men		
	Total manufacturing	Consumer goods	Capital goods	Total manufacturing	Consumer goods	Capital goods
Maquiladora *cities*						
Cd. Juárez	58.5	5.1	48.5	56.0	7.2	45.3
Matamoros	56.9	7.1	47.9	43.3	9.0	28.4
Tijuana	44.6	7.7	28.2	35.1	12.2	16.9
Non maquiladora *cities*						
Mexico City	20.4	11.6	3.0	29.0	14.0	7.1
Guadalajara	25.8	14.4	5.4	35.8	16.5	9.4
Monterrey	28.7	10.6	9.3	37.9	9.1	15.8

Source: INEGI, Encuesta Nacional de Empleo Urbano (ENEU), México, 1998, second quarter.

Wage levels   Contrary to Southeast Asia (Gereffi, 1997), EOI development in Mexico has been spurred by the repeated wage contractions and currency devaluations experienced since the 1980s, which have had the effect of continuously deepening the gap between US and Mexican wage levels, and therefore attracting foreign investment. The question debated among Mexican scholars has been whether the decline in real wages in the *maquiladoras* is equal to, or more severe than, the general wage decline in Mexican industry as a whole. Nationally aggregated figures show, according to Gambrill (1997), that real wage decline between 1975 and 1993 is no worse for *maquiladoras* than for other manufacturing firms, but that wage levels in the manufacturing sector as a whole are, on average, twice as high as in *maquiladoras* for the same period. This, she claims, is because in *maquiladoras* the majority of women employees are poorly unionized, low-skilled and young.

Yet a different picture emerges from the analysis of more disaggregated data. Wage differentials within the *maquiladora* industry appear to be a function of manufacturing sectors, technology and the cities where plants are located (Carrillo and Ramirez, 1990). Figures for 1992 show that wages paid in the more 'feminized' *maquiladoras* (garments, footwear and electronics) are in fact higher than those paid in equivalent non-export domestic firms (Maclachlan and Aguilar, 1990). Also belying the thesis of lower wage levels in *maquiladoras* are statistics showing an important relative wage increase for *maquiladoras* in the 1990s (STPS, 2000). The latter is confirmed in the present comparison: hourly wages in consumer goods and capital goods firms are somewhat higher in *maquiladora* than in non-*maquiladora* cities (Table 5.5). In Matamoros the presence of more militant unions may account for the better wages paid to workers (Gambrill, 1997). Even then, women are clearly at a disadvantage in comparison with men (Table 5.5).

Access to wage-related benefits   Some analysts point out that *maquiladoras* have increasingly offered better social benefits as a strategy to retain their workers, thereby reducing the comparative disadvantages these firms had suffered in the past. Available evidence indicates that, in effect, the basic benefits established by Federal law (*aguinaldo*, paid vacations and social security) are more prevalent in these firms. In specific subsectors such as electronics, however, no important differences between *maquiladoras* and non-*maquiladoras* have been reported (Gambrill, 1997). On the other hand, the extra benefits reported, such as on-the-job private medical attention, transportation to and from work, restaurant tickets, bonuses or

Table 5.5 Median real hourly income in consumer goods and capital goods industries by sex in *maquiladora* and non-*maquiladora* cities, 1998

Selected cities	Manufacturing industries			
	Consumer goods		Capital goods	
	Women	Men	Women	Men
Maquiladora *cities*				
Cd. Juárez	8.8	10.0	8.4	9.2
Matamoros	8.1	9.2	13.6	16.5
Tijuana	11.1	12.2	10.4	11.5
Non-maquiladora *cities*				
Mexico City	6.7	8.0	8.1	9.4
Guadalajara	6.7	8.3	6.9	8.8
Monterrey	7.5	10.0	8.3	9.6

Source: INEGI, Encuesta Nacional de Empleo Urbano (ENEU), México, 1998, second quarter.

study scholarships, are restricted to high-skill workers in large capital goods *maquiladoras*, so that they can by no means be said to characterize the *maquiladora* industry as a whole (Contreras, 1998).

Table 5.6 shows the relatively privileged situation of workers in *maquiladora* cities in relation to those employed in non-*maquiladora* cities, especially in the capital goods industries.[27] In effect, the proportion of those without access to wage-related benefits is higher in non-*maquiladora* than in *maquiladora* cities for both consumption goods and capital goods.[28] As for differences by gender, we find that women in capital goods industries have a better situation relative to men in that fewer are working without benefits in all six cities (Table 5.6). These results suggest that the participation of women in border EOIs has somewhat improved their access to basic legally mandatory welfare benefits, but not fully so, and probably not in all industrial sectors. This does not change the fact that by law, all employees, men and women alike, should have access to such benefits, so that we are only talking about gender-specific differences in the degree to which labour laws are routinely violated in Mexico. Women's relative advantage is more than offset by the move toward the regional de-concentration of low technology and low pay assembly plants in which they outnumber men. Moreover, even within the border *maquiladoras*, male worker participation is concentrated in the more skilled occupations.

Table 5.6 Per cent wage-earning workers with no benefits in consumer goods and capital goods industries by sex in *maquiladora* and non-*maquiladora* cities, 1998

Selected cities	Manufacturing industries			
	Consumer goods		Capital goods	
	Women	Men	Women	Men
Maquiladora *cities*				
Cd. Juárez	7.3	20.1	0.5	1.9
Matamoros	8.9	19.6	0.4	2.8
Tijuana	7.8	6.7	1.0	2.7
Non-maquiladora *cities*				
Mexico City	27.4	31.1	13.2	17.4
Guadalajara	33.1	26.6	4.2	18.2
Monterrey	17.1	11.4	2.6	7.2

Source: INEGI, Encuesta Nacional de Empleo Urbano (ENEU), México, 1998, second quarter.

Employment stability   The relative advantages of workers in *maquiladora* cities are even more apparent when we look at employment stability. A higher proportion of those employed in these cities enjoy employment stability than in equivalent firms in non-*maquiladora* cities. As Table 5.7 shows, verbal and temporary contracts (i.e. with no benefits) are far more frequent in the second than in the first group of cities. Likewise, women are more likely to enjoy employment stability in *maquiladora* than in non-*maquiladora* cities.

Women-friendly non-wage benefits versus discriminatory practices   Despite better access to benefits in border cities, high turnover constitutes a serious problem in the *maquiladora* industries, especially so in the garment and electronic sub-sectors (Contreras, 1998). According to Carrillo and Santibañez (1993), the preponderance of young unmarried labor accounts for this situation. If this is so, we should find that firms with higher percentages of women employees are more likely to use women-friendly policies in order to reduce labor turnover. Although the present sample of cities cannot answer this question, other evidence indicates that this is not the case. Although some incentives are offered by *maquiladoras*, in general they are not particularly women friendly. For example, we do not find a high prevalence of childcare facilities or subsidies offered for childcare, and these mostly apply to workers with

Table 5.7 Per cent wage-earning workers with temporary or verbal contracts in consumer goods and capital goods industries by sex in *maquiladora* and non-*maquiladora* cities, 1998

Selected cities	Manufacturing industries			
	Consumer goods		Capital goods	
	Women	Men	Women	Men
Maquiladora *cities*				
Cd. Juárez	10.8	17.4	0.4	1.7
Matamoros	29.3	34.7	4.4	7.0
Tijuana	12.3	16.0	7.5	12.6
Non-maquiladora *cities*				
Mexico City	52.3	52.4	43.0	38.0
Guadalajara	53.8	38.2	13.4	39.0
Monterrey	26.6	20.1	15.4	16.9

Source: INEGI, Encuesta Nacional de Empleo Urbano (ENEU), México, 1998, second quarter.

higher skill levels (Carrillo and Hernández, 1985). Additionally, many analysts report the use of discriminatory hiring practices for women, including pregnancy tests, educational requirements, marital status or recommendation letters (Carrillo and Hernández, 1985; Barrera Bassols, 1990; Corona Guerrero, 2001).

In sum, the situation of relative advantage of employment found among firms in *maquiladora* cities, in comparison with those in *non-maquiladora* cities, is evident for both men and women, where employment stability and access to benefits is concerned. As for wage levels, differences are less marked (except in the capital goods industries of Matamoros), due to the fact that Mexico's export strategy is based on wage compression. Moreover, we have to take into account the higher cost of living in the border *maquiladora* region, and consequently the higher minimum wage for this region, which partly explains the higher wages paid in manufacturing industries in *maquiladora* cities.[29]

As for gender differences, it is mostly in *maquiladora* cities that women enjoy more employment stability and better access to benefits than men. Yet their wages are lower than men's in all six cities, partly, but not wholly as a result of skill differences, as we have seen.[30] While these results partially substantiate the hypothesis that employment in EOIs represents an improvement for women, we must also emphasize the heterogeneity of Mexico's manufacturing industry (Carrillo, 1989, 1990;

Gambrill, 1997; Contreras, 1998) which makes any generalization difficult to sustain across industrial sectors. As we have seen in this sample, for example, capital goods industries offer better employment stability and better access to benefits than consumer goods industries overall, although for wage levels the results obtained are not so clear-cut. The faster expansion of non-border in relation to border *maquiladoras* also raises further questions. Therefore, the relatively better position of women in border cities capital goods *maquiladoras* is representative of the more labour- and women-friendly sub-sectors of the export economy only, and therefore unrepresentative of the entire export-oriented sector.

What is also clear, is that whatever advantages women workers may enjoy in border industries cannot be attributed to their higher participation in unions. The northern border is precisely the area where union membership is the lowest, with the exception of Matamoros (Barrera Bassols, 1990). Finally, given that the female labour force in *maquiladoras* represents only 4.4 per cent of the country's female labour force, the general statement that the majority of women workers in Mexico (64.2 per cent in 1997) have very low or no access to benefit remains entirely valid.

Conclusions

In this chapter we have examined the Mexican scenario in the light of major debates regarding the role of women in the construction and access to welfare state benefits. We have also gathered what evidence could be gleaned from various sources of the changes undergone by women workers at various historical stages of the construction of Mexico's welfare regime, particularly in the wake of Mexico's entrance into the globalized market since the 1980s. In this search, we have emphasized employment in assembly plants for export, or *maquiladoras*, presently the more dynamic sector in the economy.

In general, we have noted the stronger presence of women in the labor market from the 1980s onwards, but also a decline in the quality of employment available to all workers (in terms of wage levels, employment stability and access to benefits), although available evidence indicates that overall, female workers have suffered more from these negative trends than male workers. This has been so first because secure and high benefit public employment (in civil service, health services and education) has been cut; second because manufacturing jobs for women have become scarcer; and third because male workers have increasingly been incorporated into better-quality jobs in the *maquiladoras.* The decline in women's quality of employment is also due to their increased presence in low-pay and low-benefit sectors such as small-scale commercial activities, non-wage work and self-employment in marginal activities (street vending, home work, etc.).

In the *maquiladora* industry, understood to cover a highly heterogeneous set of activities, we have noted two trends. First the displacement of women workers from border cities where wage levels have been relatively high and the benefits more substantial, to low-skill labour-intensive *maquiladoras* in other parts of the country, and their gradual replacement by men in border cities, due in part to a shift in manufacturing activities spurred by technological change. Second, a comparative lowering of wage levels for women, even in the supposedly more 'women-friendly' border *maquiladoras*, represented by capital goods industry, despite the availability of better benefits in these firms.

In sum, the evidence gathered indicates that the benefits for women from export industries, as represented by *maquiladoras*, are extremely thin: first, they do not apply to all *maquiladoras*; second, they do not apply to all manufacturing activities within the *maquiladora* sector, and third, they do not apply to wage level differentials. Even in terms of benefits, where it does apply, it merely consists of the implementation of some (not all) *de facto* benefits to which all workers are, in principle, entitled. It does not include such benefits as childcare provision or maternity leave, both major necessities for women workers, and *de jure* mandatory entitlements for all women employed in the formal sector.

Given these findings, we definitely cannot speak of an overall association between export industry and better welfare benefits for women. Some branches of exports, where women workers outnumber men are under-protected, while others are relatively protected. On the other hand, some remaining nonexport subsectors, such as public employment in teaching and nursing do far better than export industries in the protection of women's quality of employment.

Given the overall picture of economic decline, employment contraction and generalized low wage levels, one may wonder how Mexican families have managed to survive. Since the 1980s, the major buffer against market forces in Mexico has not been public welfare, but the family. Families have multiplied the number of their earners and pooled their incomes to make ends meet, thus resorting to self-exploitation in order to survive (Cortés and Rubalcava, 1989; González de la Rocha, 1994). As Mexico's population ages, and family patterns evolve, this compensating mechanism may weaken, thereby exposing important sections of the population to even harsher economic conditions, on a scale that the State will not be able to tackle with the very limited targeted poverty funds presently available.

Notes

1. This paper was prepared for and financed by the UNRISD project on Globalization, Export oriented Employment for Women and Social Policy.
2. Section VI of Article 123 of the Constitution which deals with rules and benefits for employers and workers contained the promise of a Labor Code that would be created in 1932, and of social policies that could have to wait for decades to be enacted.
3. This interpretation is similar to Korpi's idea of considering the disruptive capacity of the working class as a political resource (Korpi, 1983).
4. For details on these processes, see Clark (1932), Carr (1976), Basurto (1975).
5. These statistics have been elaborated by Oliveira *et al.*, 2002, based on official and historical sources.
6. In 1943, the Mexican Institute of Social Security (IMSS) was created for private sector workers (although at first benefits were restricted to those working in Mexico City), followed by similar institutions for petroleum workers, electricity workers (later incorporated into IMSS), the armed forces and finally (in 1959), public servants, each with separate installations and different benefit levels. Only few worker categories outside of the manufacturing sector, such as sugarcane workers in 1963, were included.
7. For a detailed study of the creation of this policy, see Kaufman (1975).
8. Other housing initiatives had been launched in the 1950s, but too circumscribed to have any national impact. For a detailed analysis of housing policy, see Aldrete Haas (1991).
9. Also, rural health centers, which had empowered politically the rural population, were dismantled (González-Block, 1989), and the collective farming ejidos left to perish slowly.
10. See Grindle (1977) for an analysis of the creation and functioning of Conasupo, and see Fox and Gordillo (1989) for the sequel in the rural population of this policy.
11. We must note, however, that sterilizations have been performed without informed consent in many rural regions where female illiteracy is still prevalent, especially among indigenous groups, where family planning is least needed due to record high infant mortality rates.
12. For example, the presence of male heads of households in their home is automatically presumed to mean that they maintain their families, so that no lawsuits can be undertaken against improvident male household heads as long as they are present. Also, the definition of 'abandoning the home' is different for men and women: for the former, absence can only be legally ascertained after six months of consecutive absence (Brachet-Márquez, 1996a), while for women it is immediate.
13. For example, instead of the controlled prices for tortillas and milk, 'tortibonos' (tortilla tickets) and milk cards were issued to the poor. Other control prices on basic foods (sugar, rice, eggs and beans) were removed. From 1994 on, subsidized food distribution networks were downsized or

phased out: Conasupo stores disappeared in urban centers, and 577 milk distribution centers servicing 1 132 000 people were closed (Jusidman, 1999: 6).
14. For an analysis of Pronasol see González Tiburcio (1991).
15. For more detail on this phase, see Clark (1932), Basurto (1975) and Oliveira *et al.* (2002).
16. For a brief history of *maquiladoras*, see, Carrillo (1989), Gambrill (1995), Contreras (1998).
17. In some *maquiladoras* it was even informally forbidden at the time for women to marry for as long as they worked in these units.
18. First the debt crisis of 1982, followed by the IMF intervention; then the financial panic of 1994–95 which shook the whole region generating the so-called 'Tequila effect', and prompted the 25 billion dollar international rescue; and last, the 1998 Banking and Savings Protection Fund scandal (Fobaproa) whose destruction by irresponsible and dishonest bankers cost the Mexican taxpayer 65.6 billion dollars, to be paid over the next twenty years. For a detailed analysis of Mexico's experience of stabilization and restructuring policies in the 1980s and 1990s, see Aspe (1993) and Cárdenas (1996).
19. There is an ongoing debate regarding the different consequences for men and women of adjustment and restructuring processes in developing countries. As summarized by García (1999), it has been argued that technological change, reductions in public employment, the masculinization of export industries, and the expansion of informal work associated with such processes have negatively affected women more than men (Feldman, 1992; Bakker, 1994; Kerr, 1994). Others focus on the general decline in the quality of employment for men as well as women associated with restructuring and adjustment policies (Standing, 1989). In the case of Mexico, both processes have been observed simultaneously.
20. The legal principles defining the *maquiladoras* have undergone important changes over the last three decades. Initially, they were considered transitory assembly industries whose products had to be exported; beginning in the 1980s, they were redefined as part of the national industrial development and therefore could also engage in manufacturing; in the late 1980s, they were re-defined as instruments of technological transfer and promoters of competitiveness in relation to national manufacturing industries (Contreras, 1998). Yet, while these industries are now considered national, according to NAFTA, their products are only gradually allowed into the domestic market without tariffs (Gambrill, 1995).
21. Between 1990 and 1994, banks that had been nationalized in 1982 were re-privatized. All remaining public firms except petroleum and electricity were also sold. The product of these sales was the source of financing of Pronasol, the antipoverty program.
22. Figures for men vs women are unavailable in this case. Where they are, civil servants are merged with armed forces, where men are predominant, thereby masking the higher presence of women among civil servants.
23. Including in this category small businesses, self-employment and unpaid work.
24. Capital goods include electrical and electronic accessories, repair tools, and the production and assembly of machinery and motor vehicles. Consumption goods refer to food production and packing, clothing and textiles, leather and shoes, furniture and wood products.

25. See Oliveira (1989); Carillo (1989, 1991); Carrillo and Santibañez (1993); Oliveira and García (1996); Gambrill (1997); Contreras (1998); Zenteno (1999).
26. The data were taken from INEGI, 1999, García and Oliveira 2000, Garza, 2000.
27. In 1998, the proportion of men in capital goods industries in the border municipalities was 64.1 per cent as against 13.8 per cent in the consumption good industries. The figures for women are: 64.1 and 17.4 per cent respectively (INEGI, 2000).
28. Workers without benefits, according to the ENEU survey (on which our tables are based), are those who receive none of the following benefits: *aguinaldo*, profit-sharing, paid vacations, housing credit, private medical attention or private health insurance, affiliation to IMSS or ISSSTE or other types of unspecified benefits.
29. We must also keep in mind that border cities are deficient in housing quality and availability, and in urban services (water, drainage), as pointed out by Sánchez (1990).
30. To have a more accurate idea of the consequences on the quality of life of women workers and their children, we should also consider the effect on their health (Denman, 1990; Kopinak, 1995).

References

Aldrete Haas, José Antonio (1991) *La Desconstrucción del Estado Mexicano. Políticas de Vivienda 1917–1988*, México, DF: Nueva Imagen.

Amenta Edwin and Drew Halfmann (2000) 'Wage Wars: Institutional Politics, WPA Wages and the Struggle for US Social Policy', *American Sociological Review*, 65(4): 506–28.

Aspe, Pedro (1993) *El camino mexicano de la transformación económica*, México, DF: Fondo de Cultura Económica.

Bakker, Isabella (1994) 'Introduction: Engendering Macro-economic Policy Reform in the Era of Global Restructuring and Adjustment', in Isabella Bakker (ed.) *The Strategic Silence. Gender and Economic Policy*, New Jersey: Zed Books/The North-South Institute, 1–29.

Barrera Bassols Dalia (1990) *Condiciones de trabajo en las maquiladoras de Ciudad Juarez*. México, DF: Instituto Nacional de Antropología e Historia.

Basurto, Jorge (1975) *El Proletariado Industrial en México (1850–1930)*. México, DF: Universidad Nacional Autónoma de México.

Boltvinik, Julio (1999) 'Condiciones de vida y niveles de ingreso en México, 1970–1995', in José Antonio Ibañez Aguirre (ed.) *Deuda Externa mexicana: ética, teoría, legislación e impacto social*. México, DF: Instituto de Análisis y Propuestas IAP/Universidad Iberamericana/Plaza y Valdés.

Brachet-Márquez, Viviane (1984) 'La planificación familiar en México: proceso de elaboración de una política pública', *Revista Mexicana de Sociología*, 46(2).

Brachet-Márquez, Viviane (1994) *The Dynamics of Domination: State, Class and Social Reform in Mexico (1910–1993)*, Pittsburgh: University of Pittsburgh Press (also published in Spanish as *El pacto de dominacion: estado, clase y reforma social in Mexico (1910–1995)*, Mexico, DF: El colegio de Mexico, 1995).

Brachet-Márquez, Viviane (1996) 'Poder paterno, poder materno y bienestar infantil: el papel de la legislación familiar', in Claudio Stern (coord.) *El Papel del trabajo materno en la salud infantil*, México, DF: El Colegio de México/The Population Council.

Brachet-Márquez, Viviane and Margaret Sherraden (1994) 'Political Change and the Welfare State: the Case of Health and Food Policies in Mexico (1970–1990)', *World Development*, 22(9): 1295–1312.

Brachet-Márquez, Viviane, Andrew Beveridge, Lorne tepperman and Jack Veugelers (1996) 'Social Trends in North America: Rising Inequality, Shrinking Safety Nets and Social Fragmentation', Intergovernmental Commission on the Environment, Montreal, Québec, Canada: NAFTA.

Brown, F. and L. Domínguez (1989) 'Nuevas tecnologías en la indústria maquiladora de exportación', *Comercio Exterior*, 39: 215–23.

Catanzarite, Lisa M. y Myra H. Strober (1993) 'The Gender Recomposition of the Maquiladora Workforce in Cd. Juárez', *Industrial Relations*, 32: 133–47.

Cárdenas, Enrique (1996) *La política económica en México 1950–1994*, México, DF: El Colegio de México/El Fondo de Cultura Económica.

Carr, Barry (1976) *El Movimiento Obrero y la Política en México 1910–1929*, México, DF: ERA.

Carrillo, Jorge (1989) 'Transformaciones en la Industria Maquiladora de Exportación', in B. González-Aréchiga and R. Barajas Escamilla (eds), *Las Maquiladoras. Ajuste Estructural y Desarrollo Regional*, Tijuana: Fundación Friedrich Ebert, 37–54.

Carrillo, Jorge (ed.) (1991) *Mercados de trabajo en la Industria Maquiladora de Exportación*, Tijuana, Secretaría de Trabajo y Previsión social (STPS) and El Colegio de la Frontera Norte (COLEF).

Carrillo and Hernández (1985) *Mujeres fronterizas en la indústria maquiladora*, México, DF: Sep/Cefnomex.

Carrillo, Jorge and M. Ramírez (1990) 'Maquiladoras en la Frontera Norte: Opinión sobre los Sindicatos', in *Frontera Norte*, 2(4): 121–52.

Carrillo, Jorge and J. Santibáñez (1993) *Rotación de Personal en las Maquiladoras de Exportación en Tijuana*, México, Secretaría del Trabajo y Previsión social-El Colegio de la Frontera Norte.

Carroll, Fero (1999) *Emergence and Structuring of Social Insurance Institutions: Comparative Studies on Social Policy and Unemployment Insurance*, Stockholm: Swedish Institute for Social Research.

Clark, Marjorie Ruth (1932) *Organized Labor in Mexico*, Chapel Hill, NC: University of North Carolina Press.

Cobos Pradilla, Emilio (1993) 'The Limits of the Mexican Maquiladora Industry', *Review of Radical Political Economics*, 25(4): 91–108.

Contreras, Oscar F. (1998) *Las Maquiladoras en Tijuana: Mercado de Trabajo, Producción Flexible y Aprendizaje Industrial*, PhD dissertation, México: Centro de Estudios Sociológicos, El Colegio de México.

Córdova, Arnaldo (1985) *La ideología de la Revolución Mexicana*, México: UNAM/Era.

Cornelius, Wayne (1975) *Politics and the Migrant Poor in Mexico City*, Stanford: Stanford University Press.

Corona Guerrero, Pedro (2001) 'Repercusiones inmediatas del TLCAN en la indústria manufacturera de México y su impact en la fuerza de trabajo femenina', in González Marin Maria Luisa (ed.) *Globalización en México y desafíos del empleo femenino*, México DF: Unam/Porrúa.

Cortés, Fernando (2000) *La distribucikón del ingreso en México en épocas de estabi-lización y reforma económica*. México DF: CIESAS/Porrúa.

Cortés, Fernando and Rosa María Rubalcava (1989) *Autoexplotación forzada(y) equidad por empobrecimiento. La distribución del ingreso familiar en México*. San Diego, CA: US-México Center.

Denman, Catalina (1990) 'La Salud de las Obreras de la Maquila: El Caso de Nogales, Sonora', in G. De la Peña *et al.* (eds), *Crisis, conflicto y sobrevivencia*, Guadalajara: CIESAS, Universidad de Guadalajara, 229–58.

Eckstein, Susan (1977) *The Poverty of Revolution*, Princeton, NJ: Princeton University Press.

Elson, D. and R. Parson (1981) 'Nimble Fingers make Cheap Workers: An Analysis of Women's Employment in Third World Export Manufacturing', *Feminist Review*, 7 (Spring): 87–107.

Esping-Andersen, Gösta (1990) *The Three Worlds of Welfare Capitalism*, Princeton, NJ: Princeton University Press.

Feldman, Shelley (1992) 'Crises, Poverty and Gender Inequality: Current Themes and Issues', in Lourdes Benería and Shelley Feldman (eds), *Unequal Burden. Economic Crises, Persistent Poverty and Women's Work*, Boulder, CO: Westview Press, 1–25.

Fernández Kelly, Patricia (1982) 'Las maquiladoras y las mujeres de Ciudad Juárez, México: paradojas de la industrialización bajo el capitalismo integral', en Magdalena León (ed.), *Sociedad, subordinación y feminismo*, vol. 3, Bogotá, Asociación Colombiana para el Estudio de la Población, pp. 141–65.

Fox, Jonathan and Gustavo Gordillo (1989) 'Between State and Market: the Campesinos' Quest for Autonomy', in *Mexico's Alternative Political Futures* (eds) Cornelius Wayne Judith Gentleman and Peter H. Smith, Research Monograph Series No. 30. La Jolla: Center for US-Mexican Studies, 131–72.

Frenk, Julio (1998) *Economía y salud*. México DF: Funsalud.

Gambrill, Mónica (1995) 'La política Salarial de las Maquiladoras: Mejoras Posibles bajo el TLC', *Comercio Exterior*, 44(7): 543–9.

Gambrill, Mónica (1997) *La Política Laboral de las Maquiladoras antes del Tratado de Libre Comercio: El Caso de Tijuana, Baja California*, PhD dissertation, México: Centro de Estudios Sociológicos, El Colegio de México.

García, Brígida (1999) *Reestructuración Económica y Feminización del Mercado de Trabajo en México*, México: Centro de Estudios Demográficos y Desarrollo Urbano, El Colegio de México.

García, Brígida (2000) 'Evolución de la Población Económicamente Activa en las Principales Ciudades de México, 1990–1998', in Gustavo Garza (coord.), *Atlas demográfico de México*, México: Consejo Nacional de Población (CONAPO).

García, Brígida and Orlandina de Oliveira (1994) *Trabajo Femenino y Vida Familiar en México*, México: El Colegio de México.

García, Brígida and Orlandina de Oliveira (1998) 'La Participación Femenina en los Mercados de Trabajo', *Trabajo*, 1(1): 139–62, January–June.

García, Brígida and Orlandina de Oliveira (1999) 'Reestructuración Económica, Trabajo y Familia en México: Los Aportes de la Investigación Reciente', paper presented at Primer Congreso Nacional de Ciencias Sociales, Consejo Mexicano de Ciencias Sociales A. C. (Comecso), 19–23 April.

García, Brígida and Orlandina de Oliveira (2000) 'Recent Trasnformation in the Metropolitan Labor Markets of México', in *Work, Family and Women's empower-ment in Mexico*, Final Report, Mexico: El Colegio de México.

Garza, Gustavo (1999) 'Monterrey en el Contexto de la Globalización Económica en México', in Esthela: Gutiérrez Garza (coord.) *La Globalización* en Nuevo León, México: Universidad Autónoma de Nuevo León, Ediciones-El Caballito, 19–50.

Garza, Gustavo (2000) 'Tendencias de las Desigualdades Urbanas y Regionales en México, 1970–1996', *Estudios Demográficos y Urbanos*, 15(3): 489–532.

Gereffi, Gary (1997) 'Las maquiladoras de México en el Contexto de la Globalización Económica,' in *Estudios Sociales* 7(14): 73–98.

González-Aréchiga, Bernardo and José Carlos Ramírez (comps.) (1989) 'Productividad sin Distribución: Cambio tecnológico en la Industria Maquiladora Mexicana', *Frontera Norte*, 1(19): 97–124.

González-Block, Miguel Angel (1989) 'Economía política de las relaciones centro-locales en las instituciones de salud de México', unpublished doctoral thesis, México: El Colegio de México.

González de la Rocha, Mercedes (1986) *Los recursos de la pobreza. Familias de bajos ingresos en Guadalajara*, México, El Colegio de Jalisco/Centro de Investigaciones y Estudios Superiores en Antropología Social (CIESAS)/Secretaría de Programación y Presupuesto.

González Tiburcio, Enrique (1991) 'PRONASOL: hacia la nueva síntesis', *Cuadernos de Nexos*, October: X–XIII.

Grindle, Merilee S. (1977) *Bureaucrats, Politicians and Peasants in Mexico*, Berkeley and Los Angeles, CA: University of California Press.

Hamilton, Nora (1982) *The Limits of State Autonomy: Postrevolutionary Mexico*, Princeton, NJ: Princeton University Press.

Heclo, Hugh (1974) *Modern Social Politics in Britain and Sweden*, New Haven, CT: Yale University Press.

Hernández-Laos, Enrique (1992) *Crecimiento económico y pobreza en México. Una agenda para la investigación*, México, DF: UNAM.

Hicks, Alexander and Joya Misra (1993) 'Politics Resources and the Growth of Welfare in Affluent Capitalist Democracies, 1960–1982', *American Journal of Sociology*, 99: 668–710.

Hicks, Alexander and Duane Swank (1984) 'On the Political Economy of Welfare Expansion: A Comparative Analysis of 18 Advanced Capitalist Democracies, 1960–1971', *Comparative Political Studies*, 17: 81–118.

Huber, Evelyne and John D. Stephens (2000) 'Partisans Governance, Women Employment and Social Democratic Service State', *American Sociological Review*, 65(3): 323–42.

Huber, Evelyne, Charles Ragin and John D. Stephens (1993) 'Social Democracy, Christian Democracy, Constitutional Structure and the Welfare State', *American Journal of Sociology*, 99: 711–49.

Iglesias, Norma (1985) *La flor más bella de la maquiladora: historias de vida de la mujer obrera en Tijuana, B.C.N.*, México: Centro de Estudios Fronterizos del Norte de México.

INEGI (1991) *Encuesta Nacional de Empleo* (ENE), México: INEGI-Secretaría del Trabajo y Previsión Social.

INEGI (1997) *Encuesta Nacional de Empleo* (ENE), México: INEGI-Secretaría del Trabajo y Previsión Social.

INEGI (1998a) *Encuesta Nacional de Empleo* (ENE), México: INEGI-Secretaría del Trabajo y Previsión Social.

INEGI (1998b) *Encuesta Nacional de Empleo Urbano* (ENEU), México: INEGI-Secretaría del Trabajo y previsión Social (STPS).

INEGI (1999) *Estadística de la Industria Maquiladora de Exportación 1993–1998*, México: INEGI.

Jusidman, Clara (2000) 'La política social en las grandes urbes', paper presented at the Simposium of the Instituto Tecnológico de Estudios superiors de Occidente, March 15.

Kaufman, Susan (1975) *The Mexican Profit-Sharing Decision: Politics in an Authoritarian Regime*, Princeton, NJ: Princeton University Press.

Kerr, Joanna (1994) *Final Report of The Expert Group Meeting on Women and Global Economic Restructuring*, Ottawa: The North-South Institute, 20–22 June.

Kopinak, Kathryn (1993) 'The Maquiladorization of Mexican Economy', in Ricardo Grinspur and Maxwell A. Cameron (ed.), *Political Economy of North American Free Trade*, USA: Macmillan Press, 141–61.

Kopinak, Kathryn (1995) 'Gender as Vehicle for the Subordination of Women Maquiladora Workers in Mexico', in *Latin America Perspectives*, 22: 30–48.

Korpi, Walter (1983) *The Democratic Class Struggle*, London, UK: Routledge.

Koven S. and Sonia Michel (eds) (1993) *Mothers of the New World: Maternalist Politics and the Origins of the Welfare State*, New York: Routledge.

Levy, Daniel and Gabriel Szekely (1985) *Estabilidad y cambio. Paradojas del sistema político mexicano*. México, DF: El Colegio de México.

MacLachlan, I. and A. Aguilar (1998) 'Maquiladora Myths: Locational and Structural Change in Mexico's Export Manufacturing Industry', *The Professional Geographer*, 50(3): 108–28.

Marchand, Marianne H. (1994) 'Gender and New Regionalism in Latin America', *Third World Quarterly*, 15(1): 63–76.

Oliveira, Orlandina de (1989) 'La Participación Femenina y los Mercados de Trabajo en México: 1970–1980', *Estudios Demográficos y Urbanos*, 4(3): 465–93, September–December.

Oliveira, Orlandina de and Brígida García (1996) 'Cambios Recientes en la Fuerza de Trabajo Industrial Mexicana', *Estudios Demográficos y Urbanos*, 11(2): 229–62, May–August.

Oliveira, Orlandina de and Brígida García (1998) 'Crisis, Reestructuración Económica y Mercados de Trabajo en México', *Papeles de Población*, 15: 39–72, January–March.

Oliveira, Orlandina de, M. Ariza and M. Eternod (2002) 'La Fuerza de Trabajo en México: Un Siglo de Cambios', in José Gómez de León and Cecilia A. Rabell Romero (coords.), *Cien años de Cambio Demográfico en México*, México: Fondo de Cultura Económica.

Orloff, Ann (1993) 'Gender and the Social Rights of Citizenship: The Comparative Analysis of gender Relations and Welfare States', *American Sociological Review*, 58: 303–28.

Parker, Susan W. and Felicia Knaul (1997) 'Day Care and Female Employment in Mexico: Descriptive Evidence and Policy Consideration', Documento de Trabajo, CIDE.

Pedersen, Susan (1993) *Family Dependence, and the Origins of the Welfare State: Britain and France, 1914–1945*, Cambridge, England: Cambridge University Press.

Rendón, Teresa and Mercedes Pedrero (1976) 'Alternativas para la mujer en el mercado de trabajo en México', en *Mercados regionales de trabajo*, México: Instituto Nacional de Estudios del Trabajo, 205–39.

Reyna José Luis (1977) 'Redefining the Authoritarian Regime', in *Authoritarianism in Mexico*, (eds) José Luis Reyna and Richard S. Weinert, Philadelphia: Institute for the Study of Human Issues.

Ruiz Ramón, Eduardo (1976) 'Madero's Administration and Mexican Labor', in *Contemporary Mexico* (eds) James Wilkie, Michael C. Meyer and Edna Monzónde Wilkie, Berkeley, CA: University of California Press.

Sánchez, Roberto A. (1990) 'Condiciones de Vida de los Trabajadores de la Maquiladora en Tijuana y Nogales', in *Frontera Norte*, 2(4): 153–81.

Secretaría del Trabajo y Previsión Social (STPS) (2000) *Situación del Mercado Laboral*, México: STPS, Estudios Estadísticas del Trabajo.

Skocpol, Theda (1992) *Protecting Mothers and Soldier*, Cambridge, MA: Harvard University Press.

Standing, Guy (1989) 'Global Feminisation Through Flexible Labour', *World Development*, 17(7): 1077–95.

Stoddard, Ellwyn R. (1987) *Maquila: Assembly Plants in Northern Mexico*, El Paso: Texas Western Press (University of Texas at El Paso).

Stoddard, Ellwyn R. (comp.) (1990) 'Maquiladoras Fronterizas e Interpretaciones de Investigación: Un Simposio Internacional', in *Frontera Norte*, 2(3): 139–67.

Zenteno, René (1999) 'Tendencias y Perspectivas en los Mercados de Trabajo Local en México: Más de lo Mismo?', México: Instituto Tecnológico de Estudios Superiores Monterrey (ITESM), mimeo.

6
Globalization, Export-oriented Employment and Social Policy: The Case of Mauritius

Sheila Bunwaree

Introduction

Women in Mauritius are relatively late entrants to the paid labour market. The establishment of export processing zones (EPZs) in the 1970s changed the Mauritian labour market scenario significantly, absorbing a large pool of female labour. However, the current rapid changes in the global economy and the relocation of production to cheaper sites as well as the import of cheap female labour, mostly from China, is impacting dramatically on the Mauritian labour market. In the 1970s the incorporation of married women across quite a wide age range into the industrial labour force heralded opportunities for women's paid work to make substantial contributions to household income and well-being. The 1970s scenario, however, has radically changed in recent years. The feminization of employment of the 1970s and 1980s is now leading to a feminization of poverty.

This chapter attempts to analyse the dynamics between social policy and industrialization in the Mauritian context. More particularly, it examines the linkages between globalization of production, women's labour market participation as well as social policy design and delivery. The chapter is divided into three parts. The first part provides a brief history of the country and outlines the state-led development model. The role of an autonomous bureaucracy and the political elite as well as their relationships with those holding economic power is emphasized. How local sugar capital was attracted into the EPZ and the different marketing arrangements that the state engaged in at the international level

159

are discussed. The way that the Mauritian EPZ evolved shows that this development was more the result of statist intervention rather than a *laissez-faire* strategy.

The second part examines the history of welfare in Mauritius. It explains how the leaders of the time were inspired by Fabianism and how revenues from the sugar export tax were largely used to fund the social programmes until mid-1980s when the sugar export tax was abolished. The reasons for the continued commitment towards the welfare state, and the ways in which it was funded after the abolition of the sugar tax, are analysed. It also discusses some of the challenges that the welfare state confronts in this new era of jobless growth.

The third part of the chapter looks at women's participation in the labour force particularly in the EPZ. The 'male biased' politics of employment is also examined. Women continue to be disproportionately represented in low-skill, low status and low paid jobs. The displaced Mauritian workers as well as the foreign workers are given a voice. The challenges facing the Mauritian economy and the sustainability of the EPZ are discussed.

The concluding section looks at the travails of success particularly the implications of poverty in a highly inegalitarian context. Although Mauritius made persistent efforts to sustain its social policies and its welfare state as evidenced by its refusal to abide by some of the conditionalities of the IMF, there seems to be a growing asymmetry in the distribution of entitlements. Global competition for cheap labour as well as liberal trade regimes and flexible labour market policies have particularly affected the employment and welfare entitlements of both local and foreign working-class women, as well as large segments of the marginalized Creole population. The chapter concludes by arguing that the trends of flexibility, liberalization and feminization combine to pose a historical challenge to social and labour market policy in Mauritius.

Mauritius in the post-colonial period

Independence and state legitimacy

Pluri-ethnic Mauritius located in the South Western part of the Indian Ocean gained its independence in 1968 after having experienced successive waves of colonization, by the Dutch, the French and the British. Mauritius had no indigenous population. Its population represents processes of deterritorialization from across the globe, including Africa, India, China and the White settlers. Unlike many former colonies which achieved their statehood by fighting wars of national liberation against the metropolitan powers, Mauritius gained its independence by concession from the parent country. No nationalist sentiment existed in Mauritius. Anti-colonial feelings were expressed by the Hindu majority, but the other ethno/religious groups preferred to retain ties with the mother country. Fear of Hindu hegemony was prevalent.

Violence flared in May 1965 with riots between Creoles (Mauritians of African descent) and Hindus. Several people were killed and the British sent in troops, which remained until the end of the year. To reduce tensions and dampen fears of the different communal parties, the British brought forward a plan to establish a new electoral commission to deal with issues of representation. The proposals that emerged continue to shape Mauritian elections today. Single member constituencies were scrapped on the grounds that they tended to overrepresent the Hindu community. They were replaced by 20 constituencies with three members each. In addition eight seats were to be allocated after the elections to the 'Best Losers' representing communities under-represented in the main election. The politicians had woven a political spoils system which ensured that each ethnic group had an established stake in the system, thus ensuring its legitimacy for all the ethno-religious communities (Mukonoweshuro, 1991; World Development Report, 1997).

The concern with recognition and representation of different social groups did not, however, ensure equal treatment for all. Women, in particular, continued to be under-represented and excluded from political institutions. The Task Force on Women in Mauritius Report, (2001) observes that: '[W]omen are in the minority in parliament despite the fact that they compose the majority of the electorate.' Since women in Mauritius remain largely invisible in decision-making positions, women's concerns and interests are not adequately represented at policy levels. They have very little or no influence in key decisions regarding social, economic and political areas that affect society as a whole. Mauritius has for a long time been regarded as a success story in terms of both the development of the economy and of welfare policy, but there is a silence about the ways in which women's interests or contributions are reflected in policy. Whist the society and the economy rely directly on women's labour power both in the reproductive sphere as well as in the productive sphere, they are given scarce recognition and representation in real terms. Although the question of identity as related to rights is becoming increasingly important in the multiethnic mosaic of Mauritius as highlighted by the 'malaise Creole' ("Malaise Creole" refers to the deplorable conditions in which some segments of the Creole population live in. The accumulated frustration and alienation of these groups contributed to the 1999 riots) of 1999 and its aftermath, gender is not sufficiently contested in the political domain. Needless to say, identities are not fixed and static, they are fluid and dynamic. Women in Mauritius, like in many other parts of the world, do not form an undifferentiated group or a homogenous block and therefore do not share the same interests. This in turn minimizes the possibility for the emergence of a collective identity which they can use to defend their particular interests. Even where they could unite to face a common problem (such as the women who are losing their jobs in the EPZ), they are often unable to defend their interests because of lack of awareness and prevailing repressive legislation.

State legitimacy was also strengthened by the consolidation of democracy and the welfarist orientation of successive governments. Mauritius has regular elections by the ballot, a lively civic culture, a vibrant free press and relatively impressive economic growth. In addition to making its people feel politically represented and secure, the state also focused on consolidating the economy and improving the quality of life of its people.

In the late 1960s and early 1970s, Mauritius had to grapple with massive unemployment, huge balance of payment problems, rapidly rising population, soaring prices and a stagnating mono-crop economy. Yet in less than a decade, it gained the status of a small 'tiger' economy. It created an EPZ, developed a strong tourist industry and, more recently, a financial and offshore centre. Parallel to these developments, Mauritius provides free health, free education and old age non-contributory pensions to all its citizens irrespective of sex, ethnicity and race. Social policy thus proved to be one of the most important prongs of the country's development model. This consolidated the legitimacy of the Mauritian developmental state (Brautigam, 1999).

Three core elements are attached to the understanding of developmental states. The first centres on the autonomy of the government. In other words, the government can operate freely and independently from the pressures of particular interest groups. The second is the capacity of the state to steer the country's development. Capacity here refers to the cooperation and agreement between a bureaucratic and a political elite to move with the same developmental objectives in mind. And the third element is the development of an industrialization strategy which is home grown and to a large extent a nationalistic one. Here cooperation between the state and the local private sector is emphasized.

The bureaucracy is the prime mover in Mauritian society (Bunwaree, 1994). In addition to diversifying the economy, the government spared no efforts to provide more social services to the population. The state also used its intellectually trained elite to develop a host of institutions to help consolidate the economy. Expansion of educational opportunities and the 'grand morcellement' (parcelling of land through sale of small plots of fairly poor and marginal land) contributed immensely to the social mobility of the working class, particularly people of Indian descent. This mobility has also contributed to a political class and a bureaucracy which, with time, gained increasing political power.

Mauritius has managed to juggle different policies in order to minimize trade-offs that often exist between economic dynamism and social justice. In short, Mauritius has achieved some sort of 'democratic corporatism'. In his study of small European countries, Katzenstein (1998: 32) describes democratic corporatism as:

> ... distinguished by three traits: an ideology of social partnership expressed at the national level; a relatively centralised and concentrated system of interest groups, and voluntary and informal coordination of conflicting objectives through continual political bargaining between interest groups, state bureaucracies, and political parties

What Katzenstein calls an ideology of social partnership is equivalent to what is often referred to as 'social dialogue' in Mauritius; this is in fact an ideology based on the twinning of economic and social policy which is considered to be vital for the maintenance of social harmony in an ethnically diverse and class ridden society such as Mauritius.

But unlike class and ethnicity, gender as a category does not command the same kind of attention from the state. Absent from this 'social dialogue' are voices representing women's interests. Both local and expatriate female labour remain on the margins of the labour market. In a letter addressed to the Minister of Finance (le Mauricien, 17 June 2000), the Mouvement Liberasyon Fam (MLF) writes:

> In your budget speech you state that unemployment is 4% for men and 11.3% for women. As if this is something that is reassuring. Why this differentiation? What is the point that you are making? Is it that you regard the unemployment of women as being less serious than that of men ... We were expecting the government to take measures to counter growing unemployment yet the government has chosen to do the contrary – it is leaving job creation and training entirely to the private sector ... We demand that you take measures to create public employment, prevent delocalisation and job loss.

The delocalization referred to is particularly that of factories in the EPZ which are moving to countries such as Madagascar where labour is cheaper. Job loss is due to this as well as to sudden closures. Many firms have been declared bankrupt over the last couple of years. Existing legislation does not require that the employer give notice to the workers before it closes down.

The Mauritian EPZ

The idea of an EPZ in Mauritius originated from Professor Lim Fat, an academic from the University of Mauritius. Professor Lim Fat, a Mauritian of Chinese origin, was familiar with the experience of Taiwan, and believed that the East Asian Tigers possessed a surplus of capital that could be invested in Mauritius. In 1971 the Export Processing Zones Act was launched. Investors were provided with a series of incentives such as duty-free entry of capital goods and raw materials, tax holidays on corporate profits and dividends, free repatriation of capital and dividends, infrastructure and credits (Latham-Koenig, 1984: 171). The package also included relief from income taxes for the first ten years, with further concessions if profits were reinvested in the island; subsidized rates for water, electricity and plant construction; and a labour force that would be compliant, competent and less costly. The Export Processing Zones Act also provided firms with favourable labour laws for dismissal and overtime (Madani, 1999). These incentives, although helpful in getting the EPZ off the ground, were not enough to sustain its early development. It was only from 1983 onwards, with the coalescing of new fiscal incentives and fortuitous external developments that the EPZ took off.

In terms of the package of incentives provided under Mauritius's Export Processing Zone Act of 1970 (and subsequent modifications) the concessions and incentives offered to export-oriented industries are very similar to other EPZs around the world. However it is important to emphasize that in Mauritius, the EPZ is not confined to a single restricted enclave zone or industrial estate as is the case in many Central American and East and South East Asian countries. The EPZ is scattered throughout the island and includes any location or factory where goods are produced for export (Anker *et al.*, 2001).

Although sometimes regarded as an example of the merits of the 'invisible hand', export-led industrialization in Mauritius must be attributed to the visible hands of the state. In short, it was the political elite and the local bureaucrats who recognized the potential of export-led industrialization for economic growth and thus helped to develop an enabling environment for it to grow. The island's already negotiated markets in Europe were used as a lure to attract potential investors. Through the Lome Convention Mauritius received export concessions from the EC countries and the major advantage in Mauritius has been its exemption from the quantitative restrictions imposed by the European Economic Community under the Multi Fibre Agreement. Government policies in education and social services also contributed to the pool of readily available, cheap and adaptable labour, so crucial for the success of the EPZ.

The local bureaucrats also recognized that the thriving sugar sector had resulted in significant local capital accumulation, which could be attracted to the EPZ. Producers were beginning to realize that investments in the sugar sector had attained their optimum profitability and were on the lookout for new investment opportunities. The state reacted by giving the right signals. State policies, guarantees and concessions acted as a pull factor, thus causing a substantial amount of local sugar capital to be invested in the EPZ. Around 50 per cent of capital in the EPZ was local, coming mostly from the sugar oligarchy. The rest came from the local commercial banks and foreign partners.

EPZ and foreign investment

A decision was taken in 1983 to reduce corporate income taxes from 66 to 35 per cent and personal income taxes from 70 to 35 per cent. With the sharp drop in tax rates, the government attracted new investment into the EPZ. Ironically, with the lower tax rates, tax revenue has actually trebled (Watson, 1988: 23). The EPZ attracted investment from overseas (including South Africa, France, Switzerland, West Germany, the United Kingdom, United States, India and Hong Kong; the latter is the major investor) as well as locally. The substantial commercial presence of the local Chinese community makes Hong Kong industrialists feel more comfortable; thus capital withdrawn from an uncertain and transitional Hong Kong has found its way to the safe haven of Mauritius (Harden, 1988).

In 1985, the government established the Mauritius Export Development and Investment Authority (MEDIA) to promote EPZ investment and exports around the world. Financial benefits and low domestic wages have been central components of the attractiveness of Mauritius to foreign investors, but other advantages such as political stability should be noted too.

The EPZ in Mauritius is largely designed, directed and subsidized by the state and this contributed to its annual expansion of about 30 per cent in the 1980s. By the end of the 1990s, however, the situation had changed drastically. The pronounced job loss in this sector contributes to an increasing feminization of poverty. The latter is dealt with in the third part of the chapter but prior to this, an analysis of Mauritian social policy design and delivery is required.

The construction of the welfare state

Welfare states in many parts of the world are increasingly under strain. In some parts of the developing world they are simply not sufficiently developed and elsewhere they have been dismantled as a result of the rolling back of the state under the aegis of structural adjustment policies. Mauritius can in some ways be regarded as an exception. It resisted various pressures, including policy conditionalities for the abolition of free education, free health services as well as the abolition of subsidies on food that the IMF attempted to impose as part of the structural adjustment programme. Until today, Mauritius provides free health, free education and old age non-contributory pension to all its citizens irrespective of gender, ethnicity and race. There also exists some form of social aid, subsidized low cost housing and subsidies on rice and flour.

Central to the 'country's social scaffolding' is the relatively large portion of the budget that goes to social expenditure. The latter absorbs about 40 per cent of government spending today. And in spite of the various pressures to downsize the welfare state, various governments have remained committed to it. Mauritius is a country where wealth is highly concentrated in the hands of a few families and political parties are well aware of the extent to which government social expenditure legitimizes the state. The popularity of the party in power depends heavily on the continued financing of the welfare state. The important role of a strong welfare state in supporting the economic growth of the country is fully captured in the government's Vision 2020 report (1996: 5) which states:

> Some people marvel that we have achieved so much economic success despite the burden of our welfare state. It can well be argued that in reality it was the other way round. We achieved economic success because of the strength of our welfare system.

The history of concern for social welfare has its roots in Fabianism. The first Prime Minister of the island, Sir Seewoosagur Ramgoolam, and a number of other leaders had studied at the London School of Economics where they were influenced by the model of gradual socialism advocated by Fabianism. The leaders of the Labour Party at the time visualized a public–private partnership to build a modern welfare state. The challenge they faced was to find the resources necessary to build this new type of state.

Financing of the Mauritian welfare state

The Beveridge report of 1942 published in England had an impact on Mauritius. Simmons (1982) argues that a newly empowered British Labour government passed the Colonial Development and Welfare Act of 1946, allocating a budget for social programmes in the colonies. An economic commission was established by the colonial government in Mauritius with the view of making recommendations regarding the utilization of these funds.

Mauritius was at the same time undergoing political liberalization. The end of oligarchical rule was imminent. A final blow to the political monopoly of the French elite came after a constitutional reform was implemented in 1948 and an election was held the same year. Simmons (1982) argues that the Labour Party members were 'caught between a desire to pass social measures and an equally strong desire to balance the budget'. Although Ramgoolam did not become a Labour Party member until 1950, he was elected to the council, where he continued to insist on the need for welfare benefits.

Mauritius saw the birth of the social security system in 1950. Non-contributory pensions were established for Mauritians over 60. In an initial phase the government applied a means test but in 1957 pension entitlements became universal. Funded by the Colonial Development and Welfare Act budget, the government increased spending on public health, including a malaria eradication campaign that halved the infant mortality rate (from 155 per thousand to 67 per thousand) in a little more than a decade (Titmuss and Abel Smith, 1968: 234). Mauritius did not have a free national health service but prices for medical services were kept low through price controls and some groups received free health care, including labourers working for the government, police and prison officers (Titmuss and Abel Smith, 1968: 200).

The sugar export tax

The base for the development of the welfare state was already set during the latter part of the British colonial period (i.e in the second half of the twentieth century). After independence, the government intensified its efforts to consolidate the welfare state. A couple of years after independence, from 1971 to 1975, the price of sugar on the international market was very high leading to a sugar boom. The latter encouraged and facilitated the introduction of a sugar export tax.

This tax provided the revenues needed to consolidate the welfare state. The idea of a sugar tax was not new; the Mauritius Labour Party programme of 1949 had already mentioned it (Seegobin and Collen, 1976). Its advocates were convinced that the sugar marketing arrangements being negotiated by the state, guaranteed planters a healthy and substantial profit, which justified the tax. The relatively independent nature of the Mauritian state bureaucracy explains the effective implementation of this sugar levy.

This policy decision marked perhaps the beginning of an articulation between social engineering and the economics of the day. The decision to tax sugar exports was made – and perhaps could have only been made – by a relatively autonomous state bureaucracy within a developmental state. The sugar tax was seen to be central to the ability of the government to support its social and welfare policies:

> The tax allowed government to fund its social programme, health, education and food subsidies, and ... rural electrification ... The expenditure was a way of meeting important consumption needs so that social peace could be maintained while wages were low. (Dommen, 1996)

Contrary to the advice offered by Meade (a British academic who was invited by the colonial government in 1961 to submit a report on the economic and social conditions of the island), the sugar tax adopted was a progressive tax, applied most harshly to the large estates, while small cane growers were assisted and subsidized by the state. This reversal of the agricultural priorities of the colonial state was in part due to the new Mauritian government's need to be responsive to its own constituencies and electoral supporters.

The issue of the sugar export levy was so controversial that the PMSD, which represented the oligarchy, left the coalition with the MLP when the tax was agreed; the tax itself has remained contentious and was re-debated every time the levy was raised. The large planters consistently opposed the sugar tax and any increase in its terms. But the state showed its autonomy by implementing it, increasing it and maintaining it for a good number of years.

As the 1970s were drawing to an end, world sugar prices fell, cyclones hit the country and the soaring price of oil had a negative impact on the economy. Meanwhile, the state's continuing social welfare programmes led to larger debts and public deficits. By the end of the decade the state was experiencing recession and rising unemployment. The state had no option but to adopt a structural adjustment package. The sugar export tax was finally abolished in 1984, two years after the Mouvement Militant Mauricien (MMM) led by Paul Berenger, a Franco-Mauritian, came to power. The reasons for the abolition of the tax were the fall in international sugar prices and the need to modernize and make the sugar sector more efficient. Fiscal policy was readjusted with the introduction of a sales tax. This, coupled with other forms of direct and indirect taxes, international loans and the various forms of aid and grants that the Mauritian government obtained from its two former colonial powers (England and France) as well as other countries such as India and China helped to sustain the welfare state. Some of the aid and grants were used for the building of more schools and hospitals. In spite of pressures from the IMF the MMM government was committed to the maintenance of social expenditure and free health and education services on which its pre-election campaign had been based.

Main components of the welfare state

Free education, free health services and universal old age pensions and some forms of social aid are central to the welfare state. The country takes great pride in stating how it resisted the IMF/World Bank conditionalities to abolish free health and free education as well as subsidies on rice and flour. But although there are to this day no user-fees on state-provided education and health services, there has been a parallel and growing private sector providing educational and health services. These services, particularly health, are usually of much better quality and only the rich can afford them. Although education is free, other related educational costs such as textbooks, school uniforms, transport and most importantly private tuition disadvantage the already disadvantaged. Given the highly competitive nature of the education system, those who cannot afford private tuition tend to do less well. Some families also privilege their sons' education over that of their daughters, especially when confronted with economic difficulties (Bunwaree, 1997).

Primary education was free and almost entirely public even before independence. Free secondary schooling and university education were made free in 1976. But to access secondary education one has to pass the end of year primary school examination, a highly competitive examination, which usually eliminates some 40 per cent of the student population at the age of 10 plus (Bunwaree, 2001). Out of these only a rather small percentage can access vocational and training schools. Girls remain largely invisible in these sectors. Free education at secondary level had unintended benefits on girls but subtle discriminatory mechanisms still exist in the education and training system. Women and girls remain largely under-represented in the scientific and technical fields and therefore unable to access jobs in the newly emerging sectors of the economy.

Free health services exist in the country. Although provision of health care seems to be gender neutral, it is in reality gender blind. There are inadequate services for women-specific conditions and the nature of regulation of employment, particularly in the EPZ, makes it very difficult especially for working-class women to obtain adequate health care. Legislation, for example, in the Occupational Health and Safety Act, tends to privilege men in the sense that men tend to occupy positions which are more prone to accidents which are covered by the legislation. But women who might be suffering from repetitive strain injury resulting from very long hours of work on the same job are not entitled to any form of compensation.

The work conditions within the export processing enterprises can also adversely affect the worker's health, but often there is little access to appropriate public health or medical attention. The Clean Clothes Campaign report (2002: 33) writes:

> There is free public health care in Mauritius. Workers reported health problems because of the dust inside factories; most workers don't get protection. Some factories are very hot and lack appropriate ventilation. Workers in some factories mentioned that they do not get time to go to the doctors, and that often the factory does not approve the required medical certificate. This results in workers not being paid for sick leave.

EPZ and the National Pension Fund

Apart from the universal non-contributory old age pension, the government has also established a National Pension Scheme. In 1975 the government invited two academics (Professors Abel Smith and Tony Lynes from England) to advise on the feasibility of implementing a national pension scheme for workers not covered by the public sector and the sugar industry pension programmes. Their report became the foundation of the National Pensions Act of 1976.

In July 1978, the national pension scheme based on a principle of contributions by the employer and the employee became operational. Employers had to contribute 6 per cent and employees 3 per cent. This was also applicable to EPZ workers, but in practice the contributions were not always made. This was reported by a number of workers especially those from small units of the EPZ who have lost their jobs as a consequence of sudden closures. However, this remains a rather under-researched area. Moreover, due to the absence of gender disaggregated data it is difficult to know whether it is a phenomenon that affects men more than women. However, given the fact that women form the majority of employees in the EPZ, it is not unreasonable to argue that women may be disproportionately affected by low levels of employee contribution to the pension scheme.

The other major component of the social security system was the Social Aid Act of February 1983. This came during the period that Structural Adjustment Programmes were in full swing in Mauritius. Assistance provided to widows, orphans and the disabled was revised under this act. Joynathsing (1987: 137) argues that the accompanying Hardship Relief Act of 1983 provided minimal, means-tested payments to 'heads of households below the age of 60 who have family responsibilities and whose resources fall short of their minimum needs'. The question we should pose is how are the heads of households defined? Are they mostly male?

Joynathsing, quoting the Social Aid Act, argues that 'any person who as a result of any physical or mental disability, any sickness or accident certified by an approved medical practitioner, abandonment by her spouse, any sudden loss of employment which has lasted continuously for not less than six months, and being temporarily or permanently incapable of earning his livelihood and having insufficient means to support himself and his dependents, shall be qualified to claim social aid'. In reality very few people receive benefits under this scheme when they suffer from sudden loss of employment. Some people argue that the amount of social aid allocated is so low that it is not worth applying for, while others refer to the complicated bureaucratic procedures and/or stigmatizing nature of the procedures for application as major disincentives.

Moreover, as is evident from the above quotation, the language of the Social Aid Act is loaded with sexist assumptions: the Act speaks of someone being incapable of earning 'his' livelihood and having insufficient means to support himself and his dependents. This is tantamount to saying that women are 'dependents'. In reality, however, many households in Mauritius have women as their sole 'breadwinner'. (Burn, 1996)

Challenges to the welfare state

Given the demographics of the island and the rapidly ageing population, the Mauritian state is bound to face difficulties in sustaining its
welfare state. According to the Battersby Report of 1998, the country will
experience a steep decline in the pensioner support ratio. This implies
that a greater part of the wealth produced by those working will need to
be transferred to the pensioner population and overall productivity
would decline as a consequence of too few people working.

Pressure from the World Bank to cut public expenditure on social
services persists. In 1998 the World Bank's country director for Mauritius
visited the country and made a speech highlighting the need for
Mauritius to revisit its welfare state.

> Public resources should target only the genuinely needy. The welfare
> state needs streamlining not only to reduce fiscal imbalances, but
> also to ensure that public resources are not wasted and that incentive
> frameworks are not distorted. (Sarris, 1998)

This brings us back to debates about means testing and targeting. The
above presupposes that the 'needy' can be easily identified, and yet as
the third section will argue, the 'needy' often fail to access different
forms of welfare entitlement. Mauritius, as indicated above, has both a
system of contributory and non-contributory pensions. The latter covers
all citizens over 60 years irrespective of gender. But many women who
are losing their jobs in the EPZ are way below 60 age limit and are therefore not entitled to pensions from the non-contributory scheme; and it
would seem because of lack of contributions from employers, have no
entitlement to the contributory benefits provided under the National
Pensions Act of 1976.

The issue of how best to optimize resources coming into the pension
funds with the view of raising more revenues is currently under debate
in Mauritius. Some argue that the retirement age should be raised from
60 to 65 years, while others argue that retirement should be kept low to
create space for new entrants into the labour market, given the limitations in the economy's capacity to create new employment. In the face
of rising unemployment and the absence of any kind of unemployment
benefit, reform of the welfare system is increasingly urgent. The 'Social
Aid' safety net continues to provide minimal income support for some
although, as indicated in the next section, the delivery systems have
been criticized as stigmatizing and de-humanizing. But the dehuman-
ization does not stop with the welfare state. The work conditions in

certain sectors, particularly the EPZ, are very dehumanizing as well. In recent years Mauritius has allowed the entry of cheap imported labour to work in manufacturing and other sectors. Not only do foreign workers suffer from lack of access to social policy benefits, they also have to face very exploitative work and living conditions, as we shall argue below.

Local female labour, imported labour and sustainability

Expatriate labour in Mauritius

The international migration of labour, and in particular of female labour is a prominent feature of contemporary globalization (Sassen, 1984, 1988). However much of the literature has focused on South–North migration, and the employment of migrants in the global cities and services of advanced economies (Sassen, 1990).

Since the mid-1980s Mauritius has played host to migrant female labour from other parts of the global South. Due to alleged labour shortages in the manufacturing sector, the government began to issue permits mainly to large- and medium-sized companies to import workers for the EPZ. Whereas in 1985 there were no foreign workers employed in export manufacturing, by 1996 there were nearly 2000 recorded, and in 1996, 6771 out of 79 793 (or 8.5 per cent) employed workers in the EPZ were foreign workers. In 1997 foreign labour accounted for nearly 9 per cent of total EPZ employment, and the numbers have continued to rise (Kothari and Nababsing, 1999: 26–9). At the same time total employment in export processing contracted from a peak of 90 861 in 1991 to 79 793 in 1996 (ibid: 29).

These figures reflect contradictory trends and pressures. First the labour shortage in manufacturing reflected not so much the absolute shortage of Mauritian women in the target demographic groups, but the increasing unwillingness of such women to accept the conditions of work in the EPZ, particularly the requirements to undertake shift work and overtime. Interestingly the employment of foreign workers is concentrated in larger establishments which are partly or wholly owned by foreign nationals. The majority of the foreign labour force is employed in the garments and textiles sectors.

Over half of these workers came from mainland China, and a substantial share from South Asia (India, Bangladesh and Sri Lanka). Neighbouring Madagascar supplied only 3.2 per cent of the total. While the origins of migrant workers reflect geographical and cultural proximities, the nationality of ownership of establishments also seems to play a role (Kothari and Nababsing, 1999: 47).

The gender composition of migrant workers reflects that of employment in Mauritian EPZ as a whole, which has fluctuated between 65 per cent and 75 per cent women at different times. However there is a much higher percentage of women amongst the Chinese and Sri Lankan migrant labourers (98.2 per cent and 100 per cent respectively of the Mauritian Research Council's sample). A high percentage (48 per cent) of the migrant women workers were married, mostly under 30 years old, and 70 per cent of the married workers had at least one child. This is interesting given the widespread perception that most EPZ workers are young, single and childless.

However in spite of falling demand for labour in the EPZs many employers have voiced a preference for employing foreign workers who they claim are 'readier to perform overtime and are more disciplined and productive' (ibid: 44). This view is apparently shared by Mauritian workers surveyed by the World Bank (1998). This study reported that over 70 per cent of the workers surveyed thought that foreign workers worked harder than local workers. Over 80 per cent of the workforce, predominantly women, said they did not perform night shifts, though they reported that all or most foreign workers did engage in such work. Employers also claim that foreign workers have lower levels of absenteeism, do not absent themselves from the production line at the end of the shift, and are willing to meet even tight deadlines when necessary; this was attributed to workers' need to maximize earnings in order to be able to remit savings to their families.

There are of course costs to employing foreign workers, including a lengthy process to obtain permits, the provision of accommodation, health checks and travel. However in spite of this industrialists continued to express – and to act upon – a preference for foreign labour throughout the 1990s, driven by the need to maintain competitiveness in global markets by achieving higher productivity levels and greater labour flexibility without increases in labour costs and other administrative constraints at the level of industrial relations. However, as Gibbon (2000: 42) observes 'Long before 1999, ... Mauritian producers faced clear problems of stagnant productivity, increasing dependency on foreign labour, low and stagnant profitability and rising debt.'

The Clean Clothes Campaign (2002: 33) reports that foreign workers were attracted by the opportunity to earn high wages. However, what the foreign workers saw as 'high wages' was the kind of wage that the Mauritian worker is not willing to accept. Apart from low wages, it is the lack of job security, overtime work, the work being too hard and absence of career prospects which are put forward as reasons for not accepting work in the EPZ (Author's Survey on attitudes of workers towards the EPZ, 2001: 7). As the President of the Mauritius Export Processing Zone Association, commented, 'The problem is that people have decided not to work in the EPZ ... thank God that foreign workers exist since they help to solve the problem' (*Le Defi-Plus*, 2001).

Dependency on foreign labour changes the dynamics of the Mauritian labour market but views diverge on the question. On the one hand, the capitalist and private sector argue that Mauritian workers are unproductive and unwilling to work whilst on the other workers and trade unions suggest that the working conditions are becoming unbearable (*Le Defi-Plus*, 2001: 22).

The Mauritian labour market

Part of the complex reasons for the hiring of imported foreign over local labour lies in the ethnically segmented and gendered nature of the Mauritian labour market. The labour force in the private sector is mostly comprised of Whites, Mulattos and very few Creoles; the Franco-Mauritians remain the country's wealthiest group and have invested in the manufacturing sector and tourism; they are followed by the Chinese dominating this sector, though there are wealthy Muslim textile and grain traders as well. At the bottom of the socio-economic scale are the Hindu plantation workers, Muslims working in low-paid jobs within the informal sector and Black Creole factory workers, dockers and fishermen. Women continue to be over-represented in low-skilled, low-status and low-paid jobs. Some 38.7 per cent of women of working age are considered to be economically active whilst male participation rate is approximately 78.7 per cent. The highest proportion of women's employment is in the EPZ. However the sex-based occupational segregation is striking in Mauritius. Except for the EPZ, and the category 'community, social and personal services' women have a marginal presence in most occupations.

Table 6.1 shows that 39 per cent of females employed are in the EPZ whilst only 7.6 per cent of males are in this sector.

By 1990 nearly 568 EPZ firms were employing approximately some 90 000 workers, almost one-third of the island's total work force (Table 6.2). Unemployment fell drastically and the country was considered to have reached almost full employment around the mid-1980s. Just before the mid-1990s however, the EPZ sector started experiencing

Table 6.1 Sector-wise analysis of female and male employment 1995 – percentages

	Females	Males
Manufacturing		
EPZ	39.0	7.6
Other	5.2	14.7
Total	44.2	22.3
Agriculture		
Sugar	6.8	7.8
Other	4.8	6.4
Total	11.6	14.2
Trade, restaurants and hotels	12.8	14.7
Central and local government	8.7	15.6
Community, social and personal services	17.5	7.8
Financial and business services	3.1	3.0
Transport, storage and communication	1.8	8.2
Construction	Negl.	11.7
Miscellaneous	0.3	2.5
Grand total	100.0	100.0

Source: Economic Indicators n°. 245 – MEPD, 2002.

Table 6.2 Number of enterprises and employment in the EPZ, 1970–94

Year	Enterprises	Employment
1970	10	644
1976	87	17 403
1979	92	20 742
1984	195	37 532
1988	591	89 080
1990	568	89 906
1994	494	82 176
1995	481	80 466
1996	481	79 793
1997	480	83 391
1998	495	90 116
1999	512	91 374
2000	518	90 682
2001	522	87 607
2002	506	86 949

Source: Central Statistical Office, Employment statistics, 1995. Economic and Social Indicators Issue No. 397, 16 December 2002.

a setback. A large number of workers started losing their jobs. The number of enterprises started dwindling. It reached the figure of 495 in 1998. After 1998, the number of enterprises increased again. But the increase did not mean an increase in the absorption of local labour.

Given that the loss of jobs is greatest in the EPZ sector, women are the worse hit since they form the largest component in this sector; this adds to the labour market exclusion of many women. Given the profile of the EPZ workers (see below), it is difficult to envision how the displaced female workforce could be integrated in the emerging sectors such as the financial services, offshore and tourism sector or other more technologically advanced sectors of the EPZ. The latter demands skills and aptitudes that these women often do not possess. Very often, women who suffer job loss go back to domesticity as their gender identity.

Profile of the EPZ workforce

Variables such as age, gender, educational level, marital status and ethnicity are important in understanding the profile of the EPZ workforce. There have been some changes in the composition over time. Women constituted 70 per cent of the workforce in 1994, and in the case of the apparel sub-sector the female share was 75 per cent. The available data indicates that the numbers and proportion of married women in the EPZ have been rising over time. At the start of the MEPZ, women factory workers were mainly young, single women who had completed their primary education (Hein, 1984). Afterwards, more married women took up employment in EPZ factories and also many women continued working after marriage. In their survey on women workers in the MEPZ, Heeralall and Lau Thi Keng (1993) report a tendency towards the ageing of the female population in the MEPZs; the age group of under 25 years which made up of 70 per cent of the female workforce in 1977 only represented 30 per cent of the workforce in 1993. In the 1970s women tended to marry at a much younger age than they do now. Strong family planning campaigns, legislation that permits no more than two paid maternity leaves per woman in the EPZ, and the very difficult economic conditions of the 1970s help explain how women stayed on in the EPZs.

A large proportion of the EPZ workers possess primary schooling only. Less than 60 per cent passed the certificate of primary education (CPE), 36 per cent have secondary education, with only 5.8 per cent having passed the school certificate. Only 10 per cent have had vocational training. It is sometimes argued that free educational services have contributed to making a pool of adaptable labour available. Adaptability here perhaps means being docile, punctual, dexterous, having nimble fingers to do the jobs required.

The ethnic distribution of the EPZ labour force reflects the ethnic distribution in the country but this is different from the early days of the EPZ. At that time, a greater proportion of Creoles were employed in the EPZ. Currently the gender breakdown for each ethnic group shows differences, with the Creoles having a higher share of women in the EPZ (79 per cent) compared to Hindus (66 per cent) and Muslims (61 per cent). Similar proportions of single and married women are found across ethnic groups, whereas among men a smaller proportion of Creoles are married.

Factors affecting women's entry into the labour market

Changing fertility patterns in the country made it possible for women to enter the formal labour market. While the conventional explanations for fertility decline have been the success of family planning programmes and improvements in women's health and educational status, economic conditions may have played a more important part in triggering such dramatic changes in fertility behaviour. The coping mechanisms and survival strategies of women in the face of worsening economic conditions in the 1960s, which led them to defy norms of gender propriety, morality and identity, to risk gender conflict over fertility, bear striking parallels with the later entry of women in export manufacturing factories in the 1970s. In fact, the first phase of the EPZ in the early 1970s coincides with the most rapid period of fertility decline, between 1962 and 1972. Birth control and factory employment were adjustments to increasing poverty in a context of rising social aspirations.

The dispersed/non-enclave nature of the Mauritian EPZ makes it quite atypical. That the EPZ is not localized in one particular region but rather scattered around towns and villages of Mauritius reflects a conscious policy choice, of taking 'work to the worker' rather than 'worker to work', which facilitated women's employment in export processing. This formed part of a deliberate strategy of dispersal and rural industrialization initiated in 1983. The rural factories tend to be smaller and newer compared with the urban factories, whose workers are better paid; survey data (1992) indicate that 71.5 per cent of rural workers compared to 57.9 per cent of urban workers had a wage below 900 rupees per month in 1987. This in some senses echoes Hart's (this volume) argument about the forces pushing for rural industrialization.

In contrast to the Chinese expatriate workers who sleep in appalling dormitory conditions either on top or close to the factories, Mauritian women commute to work from their homes on a daily basis and can therefore juggle their reproductive and productive roles. Traditional and conservative gender ideologies concerning the role of men as breadwinners and women as homemakers were also challenged by the massive entry of women into the labour market, particularly into paid factory work. However, in Mauritius as elsewhere very few men took up reproductive work (Pearson, 2000), while women working in the factories depended largely on other women for help with their reproductive tasks. Although the extended family has been replaced by the nuclear family, the fact that families often live in the same compound especially in the rural areas provides the possibility for exchange and interdependence, thus easing women's multiple burdens and responsibilities.

The establishment of the Mauritian Export Processing Zone Welfare Fund (MEPZWF) – a body which was created in the early 1980s to improve the welfare of women workers – may have also been an incentive for at least some women to remain in the EPZ. The MEPZWF helped to provide women with soft loans to purchase labour-saving domestic appliances, and jointly with the private sector, set up crèches/nurseries in the vicinity of some factories. Recreational activities for women workers were also organized. The extent to which all this has contributed to Mauritian women's welfare, however, has not been adequately studied. There is some evidence that in spite of efforts to facilitate the lives of women, much remains to be done. Referring to a study carried out by the Ministry of Economic Planning and Development in 1994, the National Gender Action Plan (2000: 7) highlights the fact that husbands provided very little help in household chores and that utilization of electric appliances was minimal. Although efforts were made to improve the plight of EPZ women by the setting up of the MEPZWF, large numbers of women especially in the rural areas were unaware of its existence or the services offered.

Politics of employment and the male bias

It is interesting to note that the Mauritan government created the EPZ to alleviate the unemployment problem which was perceived to be a male one. Nevertheless, despite high unemployment among men, about 80 per cent of EPZ employment has been feminine throughout the 1980s (Hein, 1984).

Although unemployment affected both men and women in a very significant manner in the 1970s, no efforts were made to create jobs for women and there was complete silence about the issue in public debates. The *Travail Pour Tous* (Work For All) programme which was a government-sponsored work scheme, created some 20 000 jobs for men throughout the public sector; despite its name, women were excluded. Designed specially for men, it reflected and reinforced the government's view that men are the 'breadwinners'. In stark contrast to the silence that pervaded the issue of female unemployment, much public concern has been expressed about the gender imbalance in employment patterns in the EPZs. The policy attempt to correct this supposedly discriminatory situation against men is an important indicator of the anxiety generated by the impact of adjustment on employment patterns. The 1983 Census on Economic Activity (Volume 4: 17), for example, notes

> [T]he creation of the textile and wearing apparel industries (which) have not only provided relatively low wage jobs to females, possibly to the detriment of males, but have even attracted women who would otherwise be inactive, into the labour market to compete for jobs. The recent abolition of differential wages for men and women in the EPZ has enhanced the chances of male employment in textile industries and will ultimately lead to a more equitable sex-wise distribution of jobs in the manufacturing sector.

Professor Lim Fat signalled the lack of specialized personnel in the EPZ as a major constraint on expansion. He advocates an increase 'in the government subsidy towards training costs to 75% for male trainees only, from 40%. Such a differential assistance would induce the subsequent employment of more male labour – where unemployment is more acute' (Lim Fat, PROSI, 1985).

The second measure proposed by Professor Lim Fat was advocated well after the December 1984 liberalization of male wages, which abolished the minimum wage for men in the EPZ but not for women. Previously, the minimum wage for women with one year's experience was 63 per cent of the male minimum wage and only 76 per cent of the minimum wage of a young man under 18 years of age. The numbers of men absorbed in the EPZ after wage liberalization increased. Although the differential assistance proposed for training was not adopted, the discrimination between men and women persisted in that the minimum wage for men was abolished but not for women. The impact of this abolition was that male employment grew by 135 per cent from 3836 to 9040, whilst female employment grew from 23 473 to 31 710, an increase of only 35 per cent. Given that a higher relative wage for men generally discriminates against their employment the fact that wage liberalization led, albeit temporarily, to growth in employment of men in the EPZ requires further scrutiny.

Up to 1984, the EPZ sector and the clothing sub-sector were dominated by the knitwear industry. In 1983, the share of knitwear in terms of employment in the wearing apparel sector was 70 per cent, and garments represented 24.6 per cent. The share of knitwear employment had fallen to 29.62 per cent in 1994 and that of garments rose to 70.37 per cent. Between 1983 and 1986, over three years, the share of other garments had risen from 24.6 per cent to 49.6 per cent, and in 1988 the peak year for male employment in the EPZ, the share of garments had risen to 56 per cent. Knitwear employs relatively more women than garments. After the abolition of the gender differential in wages in 1985, the share of women in wearing apparel fell to 74 per cent from 94.6 per cent in 1983. In 1988, the share of women in wearing apparel fell to 67 per cent, rose to 75.5 per cent in knitwear and fell to 60 per cent in garments. By 1994, the share of women in wearing apparel had risen to 75 per cent, risen to 81.6 per cent in knitwear and 72.1 per cent in garments (Burn, 1996). The female bias in the EPZ had reasserted itself.

These disaggregated figures suggest that the increase in men's share of employment in wearing apparel is also due to the relative decline of the knitwear industry. It also highlights the sensitivity of the gender composition of employment to the product composition of the industry. The share of women in textiles decreased from 51.2 per cent in 1983 to 47.1 per cent in 1984, 38.4 per cent in 1986 and 29.5 per cent in 1994. The increased employment of men with the expansion of this sector, which is partly vertically integrated with the wearing apparel sector, is due also to changing technology and the utilization of continuous shift production which is generally regarded as more appropriate for men. The higher average daily earnings for employees on daily and hourly rates of pay in the textile compared to the wearing apparel sector were also likely to attract male workers. The absence of gender-disaggregated data on earnings in Mauritius, except for ad hoc survey data, makes it difficult to undertake more refined gender analyses.

The dynamics of the Mauritian labour market are quite complex and the lack of data, particularly disaggregated by gender, makes analysis and interpretation even more difficult (Burn, 1996; Du Mee de Chazal, 2001). Political factors, especially the influence of unions and political parties have often been much more important than market forces in determining wage increases. With rising employment in the mid-1970s, there was mounting pressure on the government to relax the repressive conditions facing unions and re-instate general elections. The Parti Mauricien Social Democrate (PMSD), which had been responsible for the establishment of the MEPZ and for assembling the incentive packages for investors and the related repressive legislation regarding unionization, had in the mid-1970s started contributing to the mobilization of women workers in unions (Oodiah, M., 1988). On the other hand, the increasingly popular political party, MMM, tried to use the EPZ workers to its own advantage. Union activity in the EPZ was largely manipulated by the political parties and was neither an indicator of the militancy nor of the class or gender consciousness of women workers (Hein, 1988). The strong political involvement of the different parties in the EPZs as the country moved towards the 1976 elections led to the setting up of a greater number of unions in the MEPZ and to a substantial rise in minimum wages reflecting the dominance of political factors over pure market forces in the determination of wage levels in Mauritius.

The increase in men's employment in the EPZ coincided with the boom in clothing exports. The influx of capital from Hong Kong contributed to an important expansion in the production of clothing in the EPZ and, as access to European markets was facilitated through the Lome Convention at the time, large amounts of foreign earnings were brought to the island. This is referred to as the 'clothing boom' comparable to the sugar boom that Mauritius experienced in the 1970s. However, the impact of structural adjustment was still being felt in other sectors, especially the construction industry, which was having a negative effect on other related sectors, and hence on men's employment opportunities. There was a time lag before investment picked up again and buoyancy of the other sectors was re-established. The expansion and revival of the other sectors coincides with the decline in male employment in absolute and relative terms since 1988 in the EPZ.

The assumption that men would be attracted to the EPZ as a result of higher wages can perhaps hold true only in circumstances when there is no preferable option; but when alternative employment possibilities exist, the situation is different. The masculinization of the EPZ labour force in Mauritius was therefore reversed in the early 1990s but this may change again either because of the shift towards capital-intensive industries which demand skills that Mauritian women do not have or feminization may continue but predominantly made up of migrant workers.

Labour importation, job loss in the EPZ and the welfare of women

In spite of the reestablishment of the 'female bias' in EPZ employment after the late 1980s, in the late 1990s Mauritian women face different kinds of pressures including the threat and the actuality of losing their jobs to female migrant workers.

In 1999 unemployment rates for women and men stood at 11.3 per cent and 4 per cent respectively; the comparable figures for 1991 were 2.2 per cent and 3 per cent respectively. Female unemployment has increased by more than fivefold over the period 1991–99, compared to a 1 per cent rise for their male counterparts (see Table 6.3).

Undoubtedly the slowdown of employment in the EPZs as well as the continuing importation of foreign labour partly explains the rise in female unemployment. Understanding what is happening to employment levels and workers in the Mauritian EPZ is becoming increasingly complex, and there is widespread anxiety about maintaining current levels of demand for women's industrial labour (Frisen and Johansson, 1993). This does not necessarily mean that there are increased employment opportunities for Mauritian women.

It is clear that the trend towards employment of migrant labour will continue. Although government initially saw this as a transient phenomenon, industrialists see it as a long-term strategy which offers an alternative to relocation to 'cheap labour' countries, and even as an

Table 6.3   Unemployment by gender 1990–99

Year	% rate of unemployment	
	Male	Female
1990	3.1	2.3
1991	3.0	2.2
1992	3.2	3.6
1993	3.5	4.9
1994	3.8	6.0
1995	4.1	7.3
1996	3.9	9.0
1997	3.9	10.2
1998	3.9	10.4
1999	4.0	11.3

Source: Central Statistical Office, Labour Force Statistics, 1999.

alternative to further mechanization and technological upgrading of production to higher value added processes (Kothari and Nababsing, 1999: 112).

Implications for women's empowerment: voices of Mauritian and foreign women workers

By the beginning of the twenty-first century there are fears that women's advancement will be hampered because large numbers of women are unable to access alternative employment opportunities either due to age barriers and/or lack of appropriate skills. Some initial studies carried out by undergraduate students at the University of Mauritius indicate that women feel dis-empowered as a consequence of job loss. This is supplemented by an exploratory study that I carried out on EPZ women workers (both local and Chinese) in 2002 (Bunwaree, 2002).

Mauritian women face increasing insecurity and vulnerability as a result of the loss of employment which they have enjoyed for more than a generation. One women reported that

> All my life practically, I have worked in the EPZ, now that they are closing I have nothing to do. I am 50 years old. I still have children at school. I do not know what to do. There is not much else I can do. I have worked on the same kind of machine through and through ... (Mantee)

Their household coping strategies also affect other household members including children whose access to free education service is impeded when they are needed to contribute to household income:

> Now that they have asked us to leave, I have had to leave. The company has changed its name and there are many young Chinese workers there. Since I have lost my job, I cannot find another one ... I am currently rearing some animals but I have had to make my eldest son leave school ... he is looking for a job ... . (Josee)

What is clear from these accounts is that retrenched workers from the EPZs are not in a position to command financial assistance from either the contributory or the non-contributory pension schemes on the island. In spite of the notion that citizenship implied economic entitlements earned through work, former factory workers have been excluded from such benefits:

> I do not even understand why we lost our jobs … one good day, on my arrival at work, I found huge padlocks in the gates … Overnight we found ourselves without jobs … There is no one to defend our rights … we were not given the possibility to be unionised … there was a kind of threat from the boss all the time …. (Ghislaine)

Expectations that the welfare state would deliver assistance to retrenched women workers has proved unfounded:

> It has been over 8 months since I have lost my job, my family has asked me to go to the ministry of social security and to get a pension. I have been there many times, more than 7 times and each time I go there, they ask me for some kind of paper, first it was, the marriage certificate, then the birth certificates of my children and then the water and electricity papers. I do not have some of these papers … . (Daniele)
>
> Branches of the Ministry of social security are found everywhere – not far from where I live, there is one office … When I lost my job, I went there for some 'social aid' – it's been more than 8 months and nothing is happening … My husband does not work, he had an accident some years back and I have 3 children …

Unemployment has also provoked resentment towards Chinese and other foreign workers who are perceived to have taken jobs rightly belonging to Mauritian women.

> These Chinese girls are contributing to our job loss. If they did not come in, it would have been easier. Our employers would not have had a choice, they would still be needing us. The Chinese girls spoil everything. They are prepared to do overtime and work harder … I can't stand them … Moreover, they are prostituting themselves. (Geeta)

But in spite of the privations of unemployment Mauritian women still express a sense of their own place in the hierarchy and as yet have not been prepared to adopt the working practices, conditions and attitudes of temporary migrant workers:

> I cannot understand this. If the Chinese girls are willing to work like slaves, we are not prepared for this. They come here just for the

money. In addition to work in the EPZ, they prostitute themselves. This is all very bad ...

The stories of the Chinese female workers are no less poignant than that of the Mauritians. The only difference perhaps is that they have a job, albeit temporarily and they can earn and remit money to their families, although in many cases their earnings are often much less than what they were expecting. The deceitful aspects of their contracts bring a sense of disillusionment to these workers:

> We have been cheated. When we were contacted, we were told that we would be earning a certain amount of money. We signed a contract in China and when we came here, we signed a different contract. The latter is in English and we often do not understand what we are signing for

In spite of the perception by Mauritian management and workforce alike that Chinese and other foreign women are enthusiastic about their working conditions and opportunities, the migrant workers do not necessarily see it that way:

> It is true that we can work very hard but the conditions are not good, we do not get any rest and moreover we sleep in very unhealthy conditions. There are many of us in this long shelter and the toilets and showers are too few. We have to wake up very early to be able to use the facilities. I would much rather go back but then I have to think of my son, it is because of him that I have come so that I can save to educate him ...

Another Chinese worker being interviewed by the press had this to say:

> If this is paradise, I prefer going back to hell in China. (News on Sunday, 10–16 May 2002)

The Clean Clothes Campaign Report (2002) draws attention to other ongoing problems that the expatriate workers confront.

> The problems with foreign workers came to a head in the Spring of 2002, when 2 women workers both Chinese died. One worker died of pneumonia and the other of brain haemorrhage. Spontaneous protests erupted as expatriate workers went on strike and marched to

the Chinese embassy ... The Mauritius Employers Federation and the Mauritius Export Processing Zone Association have responded to the critics with drafting guidelines for employment of Guest workers in the EPZ sector in Mauritius, in July 2002 ...

But, as Kothari and Nababsing reported some years ago even when problems are detected and warnings issued, enforcement of standards has proved to be difficult and the conditions of some of the living quarters of foreign workers remain unacceptable (1999: 41). However, in spite of their disillusionment and the various exploitative conditions they face, most of migrant workers stay in Mauritius until their contracts expire (which is usually 2–3 years). Their difficulties do not prevent them from achieving high productivity which is reflected in the continuing preference of management for migrant over local women workers.

> Managers praised the skill and speed of foreign workers, preferring them to local workers who with their social and family obligations seem 'demanding, lazy, and overall less productive' in the eyes of management. It seems that for management, the ideal situation would be a workforce that was available 24 hours a day (Clean Clothes Campaign, 2002: 33)

Sustainability of the EPZ: implications for gendered social policy

Although the Mauritian EPZ has been an important engine of growth, it is not necessarily sustainable in the long term. The EPZ remains vulnerable to exogenous shocks and its dependence on external raw materials and on a limited number of markets, and lack of linkages to the domestic economy are of concern to both the public and private sectors (Matthew, 1992). The sustainability of the EPZ is also affected by the rising costs of production and the emergence of cheaper sites of production such as in Madagascar, Sri Lanka and Vietnam, not to mention China. Mauritian textile exports have been a major source of foreign exchange but it is feared that they are now becoming uncompetitive in the global market (*The Economist*, 28 February 1998).

This is highlighted by the prospect of the expiry of the Multi Fibre Agreement (MFA) in 2005. The MFA has offered Mauritian textile and clothing exports preferable entry to European and American markets, but in a couple of years' time Mauritian exports will have to compete on the same terms as other countries.

Moreover, there has been little diversification of Mauritius' industrial production, and apparel and clothing still represent over 80 per cent of its industrial exports. The Africa Growth and Opportunity Act which offers advantaged access to US markets for Sub-Saharan African countries on condition that they enact certain domestic measures is a double edged sword: while it may offer increased market access in the future, some observers argue that in order to benefit from such opportunities, workers would have to become more flexible, productive and competitive, which may lead to a further undermining of workers' rights and entitlements; this can increase the incentives for importing foreign workers rather than employing Mauritian women. Whilst policy makers have expressed the desire to upgrade the technology of production to attract a different kind of foreign investment, the lack of trained skilled labour, particularly among women, is seen to be an obstacle for this strategy (De Chazel Dumee, 2001).

Conclusion

The export industrialization strategy pursued in Mauritius, in the context of a developmental state committed to an inclusive welfare system, would seem to have offered women in Mauritius access to the economic entitlements derived from formal sector employment, as has been the case in industrialized countries in the twentieth century. But this study indicates that two factors have impeded such an outcome; first the trajectory of deregulation and global reach of world markets has meant that Mauritian industrialists have to compete against a range of lower cost locations and are therefore committed to continually reducing the unit cost of labour. The changes in the international regulation of trade and markets, and particularly the demise of privileges granted under the MFA, have removed any relative protection the Mauritian state might have had for retaining even a minimal range of workers' entitlements to pensions, redundancy payments and social assistance. In spite of the fact that the Mauritian government resisted the IMF's request to abolish free education, free health and subsidies on rice and flour, there is evidence that recent economic reform has resulted in the impoverishment of low-income groups.

Given the structure of ownership in Mauritian export factories, and the concentration of clothing and apparel products, the importation of Chinese and other labour has served as a useful strategy for industrialists to confront what was perceived as a growing lack of competitiveness. First it has been able to access cheaper labour in situ – without relocation.

Although this involves some costs for the enterprises, Government regulation ensures that such workers remain with their 'importing employer', have a limited right to remain and therefore do not represent a high cost in terms of employer pension contributions, and other benefits. The dispersed nature of the EPZ in Mauritius was a factor which facilitated the incorporation of married women into the export labour force whilst allowing them to retain the possibility of fulfilling their reproductive roles in their households. Migrant labourers in contrast are separated from their own households, are housed in enclave dormitories, are able and expected to work shifts and regular overtime, do not join trade unions and have little expectation of social benefits from their temporary host state.

Labour importation also highlights the ways in which the conditions of women workers' incorporation into Mauritian industrialization is also changing. Reluctance to work shifts or overtime, expectations of work-related benefits and pensions, assumptions about redundancy pay and unemployment benefits have all been shaken by the current adjustments in the export sector. Existing employees have been made redundant and it is unlikely that any future increase in women's employment will be on the same terms as that enjoyed in previous decades.

The second issue is the trajectory of the developmentalist welfare state itself. As this chapter has demonstrated, the apparently universal welfare entitlements of the Mauritian state were deeply gendered, built on the assumption of a male 'breadwinner' and 'dependent' female. The much heralded free health and education services have remained but entitlements to other benefits such as income support in the face of loss of employment have not materialized over recent large-scale retrenchment of women workers from export production.

These recent events highlight the in-built tension between economic growth within the confines of the current global economy, and the resource implications of generational and social reproduction. One way of avoiding the costs of reproduction is to employ migrant labour. But in order to redress the lack of gender equity in social and welfare provision for Mauritian women workers in the export sectors it is necessary also to safeguard the rights of migrant women; if not the current trends which point to continuous erosion of women's work-related entitlements will continue well into the twenty-first century.

References

Africa Competitiveness Report (1998), cited in PROSI magazine, February 1998, no. 349, Mauritius.

Anker, R., R. Paratian and R. Torres (2001) *Mauritius: Studies in the Social Dimensions of Globalisation*, Geneva : ILO.

Battersby Report (1998) Mauritius National Pensions Fund – Actuarial Review as at 30 June 1995, London: Government Actuary's Department.

Brautigam, D. (1999) 'The "Mauritius Miracle": Democracy, Institutions and Economic Policy', in *State, Conflict and Democracy in Africa* R. Joseph (ed.), Boulder, Co: Lynne Reiner.

Budget Speech 1991–1997, Ministry of Finance, Government Printing.

Bunwaree, S. (1994) 'Mauritian Education in a Global Economy', *Editions de L'ocean Indien*, Mauritius: Rose-Hill.

Bunwaree, S. (1999) 'Gender Inequality – The Mauritian Experience', in *Gender, Education and Development* (eds) C. Heward and S. Bunwaree, London: Zed Books.

Bunwaree, S. (2001) 'The Marginal in the Miracle: Human Capital in Mauritius' *International Journal for Educational Development*, 21: 257–71.

Bunwaree, S. (2002) Livelihoods of women workers in the Mauritian Export Processing Zone, unpublished study.

Burn, N. (1996) 'Mauritius', in *Gender and Industrialisation* (eds), U. Kothari and V. Nababsing, editions de L'Océan Indien, Mauritius: Rose-Hill, pp. 33–79.

Clean Clothes Campaign report (2002), South Africa.

De Chazal DuMEE Report (2001) 'Patterns and Trends in the Feminisation of Poverty in Mauritius', Internal report to De Chazal Firm.

Dommen, E. (1996) 'Meade's Sugar Export Tax Saved Mauritius' in Week-end, Mauritus: Port-Louis, 10 March.

Economic Indicators No. 245, 1996, Ministry of Economic Planning and Development, Mauritius.

Elson, D. (1996) 'Appraising Recent Developments in the World Market for Nimble Fingers', in Confronting State, Capital and Patriarchy: Women Organizing in the Process of Industrialization, A. Chhacchi and R. Pittin (eds), Basingstoke: Macmillan.

Frisen, L. and H. Johansson (1993) 'Export Processing Zones and Export Led Industrialization: The Case of Mauritius', Minor field study series no. 44, Department of Economics, Sweden: University of Lund.

Gibbon, P. (2000) 'Back to the Basics Through Delocalisation: The Mauritian Garment Industry at the End of the 20th Century', working paper subseries on globalisation and economic restructuring in Africa, Copenhagen: Center for development research.

Harden, B. (1988) 'Offshore Jobs Dynamo Offers Model for Africa', Washington Post, 9 October.

Hazareesingh, K. (ed.) (1980) Selected speeches of Sir Seewoosagur Ramgoolam.

Heerallall, P. and J. C. Lau thi Keng (1993) Impact of Industrialisation on EPZ Women and their Families, Mauritius: CEDREFI.

Hein, C. (1984) 'Jobs for the Girls: Export Manufacturing in Mauritius' *International labour review*, 123(2) March–April.

Hein, C. (1988) 'Multinational Enterprises and Employment in the Mauritian Export Processing Zone', working paper no. 52, World Employment Programme Working Paper, Geneva: ILO.

Heyzer, N. (1997) 'Integration of Gender Concerns in Multilateral Trade Organizations', presentation to the 1997 Women Leaders network meeting: The economic impact of women in the APEC region, UNIFEM: www.undp.org/unifem

Joynathsing, M. (1987) 'Social Welfare in Mauritius', *Social Welfare in Africa*, John Dixon, (ed.), London: Croomhelm, pp. 121–63.

Katzenstein, P. T. (1998) *Small States in World Markets – Industrial Policy in Europe*, Ithaca and London: Cornell University Press.

Kothari, U. and V. Nababsing (1996) Gender and Industrialisation, *Editions de l'ocean indien*, Mauritius: Rose-Hill.

Kothari, U. and V. Nababsing (1999) 'Foreign Migrant Workers in Mauritius', Mauritius Research Council, unpublished study.

Latham-Koenig, A. (1984) Mauritius: Political Volte Face in the 'Star of the Indian Ocean' Round Table, 290.

Le Defi-Plus, 4–10 August 2001, Mauritius, p. 22.

Le Mauricien, 17 June 2000, Mauritius.

Le Mauricien, 25 November 2000, Mauritius.

Madani, D. (1999) 'A Review of the Role and Impact of Export Processing Zones' in policy research working paper 2238, Washington, DC: The World Bank Development Research Group.

Matthew, W. R. (1992) *Export Processing Zone in Jamaica and Mauritius: Evolution of an Export Oriented Development Model*, World Bank, Washington DC.

Mauritius Research Council Study (1999) 'New Industrial Strategies: A Study of Gender, Migrant Labour and the EPZ in Mauritius', Mauritius.

Meade, J. E. (1968) *The Economic and Social Structure of Mauritius*, London: Frank Cass.

Ministry of Economic Planning and Development (2002) Economic and Social Indicators, No. 397, 16 December.

Ministry of Finance, Budget Speech 1991–97, Government Printing, Mauritius.

Ministry of Women, Family Welfare and Child Development (2000) National Gender Action Plan, Port- Louis, Mauritius.

Mukonoweshuro, E. G. (1991) Containing Political Instability in a Poly-Ethnic Society, *Ethnic and Racial Studies*, 14(2): 199–224.

National Gender Action Plan (2000) Ministry of Women, Family Welfare and Child Development, Port- Louis, Mauritius.

News on Sunday, 10–16 May 2002, Mauritius.

Oodiah, M. (1988) *Histoire du syndicalisme Mauricien, une esquisse*, published by Federation des travailleurs unis, Mauritius.

Pearson, R. (2000) 'All Change? Men, Women and Reproductive Work in the Global Economy', *European Journal of Development Research*, December, 12(2): 219–37.

PROSI Magazine, 1985, no. 4, Mauritius.

Ramgoolam (1998) 'Achieving Economic Growth In Africa: The Mauritian Experience', Address at Harvard University, 25 September.

Ringadoo, Hon. Sir Veerasamy, Minister of Finance, 1976 Budget Speech, 25 May 1976.

Ringadoo, Hon. Sir Veerasamy, Minister of Finance, 1977 Budget Speech, 26 April 1977.

Sarris, M. (1998) Presentation Round Table with the Government of Mauritius, Maritim Hotel, Balaclava, Terre Rouge, 25–27 March, 8.

Sassen, S. (1984) Notes on the Incorporation of Third World Women into Wage Labour Through Immigration and Offshore Production, *International Migration review*, 18(4): 1144–67.

Sassen, S. (1988) The Mobility of Labour and Capital: A Study in International Investment and Labour, New York: Cambridge University Press.

Seegobin, R. and L. Collen, (1976) Mauritius: Class Forces and Political Power, *Review of African Political Economy*, 8, pp. 109–18.

Simmons, Adele Smith (1982) *Modern Mauritius: The Politics of Decolonization* Bloomington: Indiana University Press.

Task Force Report to the Ministry of Women's Rights (2001) Port-Louis, Mauritius.

The Budget Speech (1983–84) Ministry of Finance, Port-Louis, Mauritius.

The Economist (1998) 'Miracle in Trouble', London, 28th February.

Titmuss, Richard M. and Brian Abel-Smith, assisted by Tony Lynes (1968) *Social Policies and Population Growth in Mauritius*, London: Frank Cass and Co. Ltd.

Uppiah, S. (1999) 'Globalisation and Women Workers in the EPZ in Mauritius', unpublished undergraduate thesis.

Vision 2020 (1996) The National Long Term Perspective Study, Government Printing press, Mauritius.

World Development Report (1997) Oxford University Press, New York.

7
Reworking Apartheid Legacies: Global Competition, Gender and Social Wages in South Africa, 1980–2000[*]

Gillian Hart

Introduction

In the early 1980s, the apartheid state offered some of the most generous incentives in the world for labour-intensive industries to locate in 'industrial decentralization points' either in or adjacent to former bantustans. Light industries – many of them from Taiwan and employing mainly women – mushroomed in these spaces of apartheid. At the same time, there was a sharp contraction of heavy capital-intensive industries in the main urban centres. Responding to a fierce neo-liberal critique from powerful South African business interests, the de Klerk government slashed subsidies in 1991.

Since the mid-1990s, the post-apartheid state has embraced foreign direct investment and export production as the centre-piece of its neo-liberal thrust, and the key to a prosperous global future. Yet to date these promises have remained radically unfulfilled. Under pressure from cheap imports, employment in labour-intensive industry has shrunk dramatically, foreign direct investment has been minimal and neo-liberal imperatives have placed sharp constraints on redistributive social policies.

In this chapter I examine changing relationships between labour-intensive industrial production and the conditions of reproduction of labour in South Africa since 1980. I draw both on secondary evidence and my own intensive research in two former industrial decentralization points in northwestern KwaZulu-Natal that are deeply connected with sites in East Asia to advance three related arguments:

- First, the conditions of reproduction of labour power are central to understanding peculiarly South African forms of articulation with the global economy. Yet these conditions are not only a matter of social policies (or lack thereof!), but also a much longer and deeper history of racialized dispossession and expropriation. More generally, histories of agrarian social property and power relations have played a central role in shaping regionally specific trajectories of labour-intensive production and social wages not only in South Africa but also in other parts of the world – including, most notably, key regions of East Asia.

- Second, a gendered perspective is crucial to understanding the relationships among industrial production, social policy and the conditions of reproduction of labour power. Yet an approach that focuses on the 'impact of globalization' on women is severely limited. Instead, attention must be given to how gendered relationships and identities articulate with race, ethnicity and other dimensions of difference; and how these, in turn, shape and inflect the forms and dynamics of industrial production. The ways in which Taiwanese industries have taken hold in South Africa provide vivid illustrations of the inextricable connections among class, gender and race; and of the complex histories that enter into the making of the social wage.

- Third, I will underscore the importance of the politics of place, showing how dispossession and industrial production played out quite differently in two seemingly similar towns in South Africa during the apartheid era; how the (very limited) social policies set in place after apartheid have filtered through configurations of local state power in strikingly different ways; and how strategies to attract foreign investment are provoking intense, but locally differentiated forms of struggle.

These local divergences provide further illustration of deep interconnections between workplace and community politics, and how these overlap with struggles in other social arenas to shape the social wage. Taken together with the other two arguments, they underscore the contradictions and unsustainability of the neo-liberal project in conditions of profound deprivation and inequality.

The argument unfolds in three parts. First I outline the emergence of labour-intensive forms of industrial production based predominantly on women's labour in decentralized regions of South Africa in the 1980s, and how Taiwanese investment took hold in these areas. In the second section I draw on comparative connections to focus on the question of why East Asian investment in decentralized regions of South Africa has been so socially explosive. These comparative insights are deeply revealing of how gender, race and other dimensions of difference shape the dynamics of industrial accumulation. They also illuminate connections between production and the conditions of reproduction of labour power – in particular, how agrarian histories have played into the formation of the social wage, and shaped the conditions of global competition. The third section discusses the ANC government's embrace of neo-liberalism in the mid-1990s, and shows how the local state has become a key site of contradictory imperatives of redistribution and accumulation.

In extending the definition of the social wage beyond employment-based entitlements or even conventional social policy to encompass agrarian questions, my purpose is simultaneously political and analytical. This broader conception not only allows for a fuller understanding of how historically specific relationships between production and reproduction of labour have shaped divergent trajectories of low wage industrialization. In addition, in the context of post-apartheid South Africa, this extended definition helps thrust histories of racialized dispossession to the forefront of attention. In the process, it holds open the possibility of broadly based claims for redistributive justice based on citizenship rights, and for linking struggles in multiple arenas as well as across the rural–urban divide.

The apartheid era: dispossession and industrial decentralization

The rapid expansion of labour-intensive industrial production in South Africa in the 1980s is inextricably bound up with two key thrusts of apartheid spatial and racial engineering that intersected in complex ways with capitalist imperatives as well as with gendered livelihood strategies. One is the displacement of millions of black South Africans from the land as well as from urban areas in the preceding 20 years, and the formation of huge townships with urban-like densities in predominantly rural areas designated as bantustans. In the country as a whole, according to the Surplus Peoples Project, between 1960 and 1983 some 3.5 million people were displaced from rural and urban areas in 'white' South Africa to settlements in the former bantustans; about half were from rural areas, 65 per cent from white-owned farms and 35 per cent from African freehold land (Platzky and Walker, 1985). Yet this figure is almost certainly an underestimate if one takes account of ongoing and accelerating evictions of African tenants and workers from white-owned farms. Simkins (1983) calculated that the percentage of Africans living within the borders of bantustans grew from 4.2 million in 1960 (39 per cent of all Africans) to over 11 million in 1980 (52.7 per cent). Between 1980 and 1986, according to Simkins' more recent estimates, an additional

1.6 million black South Africans disappeared from rural 'white' South Africa.

Massive agglomerations of population within bantustan borders defy conventional rural–urban categories. Colin Murray (1988) coined the term 'displaced urbanization' to describe these huge, densely packed settlements in desolate patches of veld, many of them separated from former white towns and smaller cities by what apartheid planners (in appropriately militarist language) called buffer zones. The industrial estates that popped up during the 1980s were located either within relocation townships or, more often, in the buffer zones. Invariably they were within commuting distance of former white towns, where industrialists had access to the appurtenances of white privilege.

Rapid growth of decentralized industrial estates in the 1980s represented the culmination of more than 20 years of efforts by apartheid state functionaries to lure industries to the borders of bantustans. The so-called border industrialization policy formed a key element of Hendrik Verwoerd's grand apartheid vision of stemming the flow of Africans to urban centres and containing them in 'independent' bantustans. In addition to exemption from minimum wages under the industrial council system, border industry incentives included tax concessions, low interest loans, transport subsidies and tariff protection. Over the course of the 1960s the extent of industrial decentralization was quite limited, and did little to stem the pace of African urbanization. Towards the end of the decade, the apartheid state intensified its efforts to reconfigure industrial geography and mesh it with 'self-governing' bantustans where forced removals and farm evictions were producing massive concentrations of dispossessed people. The Physical Planning and Utilization of Resources Act of 1967 placed strict controls on industrial expansion in the main metropolitan areas, while stepping up incentives for industrialists to relocate in bantustan and border areas. During the 1970s a number of relatively large-scale heavy industries with a predominantly male workforce were established in areas adjacent to rapidly expanding bantustans. These efforts to reconfigure the industrial space economy found ready legitimation in the discourse of scientific regional planning in ascendance at the time.

In 1981, just as spatial policies were becoming discredited in most of the capitalist world by the rise of neo-liberalism, P. W. Botha's 'reformist' administration unveiled a new regional strategy. The so-called Good Hope plan dramatically increased incentives for industrial decentralization, with the emphasis shifting from tax concessions to direct cash subsidies. Under this new Regional Industrial Development Programme

(RIDP), subsidies were graded according to location, with 'industrial development points' in more distant bantustan locations receiving higher levels than 'deconcentration points' on the peripheries of major urban areas. Some bantustan administrations such as the Ciskei added extra incentives such as extended tax holidays, thereby creating what was widely seen as the most generous package of incentives in the world. At the national level, the huge increase in incentives was financed by windfall revenues from the sharp increase in the gold price in the early 1980s.

Over the decade of the 1980s, predominantly female employment in decentralized industries expanded in the context of stagnation of the national economy and poor performance of the manufacturing sector as a whole. During the 1970s, total manufacturing employment grew by over 35 per cent; over the 1980s it stagnated, and by the early 1990s there were 89 000 fewer jobs in manufacturing than there had been in 1982 (Joffe *et al.*, 1995: 6). Yet in the five-year period between 1982 and 1987, according to the industrial census, 147 000 new jobs were created in decentralized areas; by the early 1990s, this figure had risen to over 250 000 (Urban Foundation, 1990). Nearly 30 per cent of employment growth in decentralized areas was concentrated in KwaZulu-Natal where evidence on shifts in the gendered structure of employment are also most comprehensive, thanks to a study by Posel, Friedman and Todes (1993) who assembled data from a variety of different sources. Between 1980 and 1991, the total number of economically active people in manufacturing in KwaZulu-Natal rose by 10 per cent, largely as a consequence of expansion of the clothing industry. African women accounted for virtually all of this increase, and their share of manufacturing employment jumped from 26 to 33 per cent. In the country as a whole, national industrial census data indicate declining investment and employment in male dominant sectors such as chemicals, metal and machinery over the 1980s, and the concomitant growth of female- and labour-intensive industries – notably clothing and textiles, many of them concentrated in industrial decentralization areas.

Taiwan formed by far the single largest source of foreign direct investment under the RIDP during the 1980s. By the end of the decade, between 300 and 400 Taiwanese industries were operating in decentralized areas of South Africa. The predominance of Taiwanese investment was partly a reflection of diplomatic links between Taiwan and South Africa in a period when both were relatively isolated from international circuits. Changes in the trajectory of industrial accumulation in Taiwan were also important. By the early to mid-1980s, rapid industrial growth driven by extremely small-scale enterprises – many of them in rural and peri-urban regions – was beginning to run out of steam as a consequence of rising wages and exchange rate appreciation. At precisely the point that the apartheid state was offering massive subsidies, many Taiwanese industrialists were searching for alternatives and the Taiwanese state was actively fostering their moving out (Hart, 1996a). There was, in short, a peculiar conjuncture in which a small but significant segment of the highly competitive global economy relocated to peripheral regions of South Africa just as male-intensive heavy industries were going into decline.

On the face of it, these patterns seem to signify the same sort of shift from import substitution industrialization (ISI) to export-oriented industrialization (EOI) that happened in other parts of the world during this period – albeit in the context of aggregate decline. The most common interpretation is that South Africa in the 1980s represented an extreme form of a Latin American ISI economy, with excessive state support for heavy industry inhibiting the more efficient deployment of scarce capital resources (Joffe *et al.*, 1995). In similar vein, the RIDP was widely portrayed as yet another instance of the heavy hand of the state distorting the optimal allocation of resources – an argument to which we shall return below. Yet the picture is more complicated. In the first place, as Fine and Rustomjee (1996) have argued quite compellingly, the South African manufacturing sector does not adhere to the conventional model of ISI derived from Latin American experience. Instead, it is part of what they call the minerals–energy complex (MEC), which is linked in turn with the highly concentrated character of South African corporate capital; a symbiotic but changing relationship between state corporations and private capital around the MEC; the limited capacity of the MEC to promote diversification out of the MEC core industries; an overbloated financial system, and a proclivity to channel resources abroad. In addition, they argue, export-orientation does not necessarily shift industrialization away from the MEC: 'Most new manufacturing sector investment [in the 1990s] is taking place in mega-projects within the established MEC core, which as a whole has historically been export-oriented' (Fine and Rustomjee, 1996: 232). By the same token, the primary beneficiaries of export incentives set in place during the 1980s were core MEC industries, including the iron and steel corporation (Iscor), armaments manufacturers and industrial chemicals.

In short, the conventional ISI/EOI dichotomy is problematic in the South African context, and certainly does not map on to male- and female-intensive industries. The more useful distinction, perhaps, is between MEC and non-MEC industries. The latter include clothing and textiles, food processing, metal fabrication, printing, furniture making and the like – which were precisely the industries that sprang up in industrial decentralization areas in the 1980s under the aegis of the RIDP. Partly as a consequence of sanctions, much of their output was directed to the domestic market during the 1980s (Pickles, 1991: 81). In addition, the domestic market for clothing was relatively protected by tariffs through most of the 1980s; at the same time, Altman (1995) argued, even with extremely low wages in decentralized areas, South Africa could not compete with low-cost producers in other parts of the world.

In the early 1980s when P. W. Botha launched the Good Hope strategy – and with it the RIDP – a major rapprochement between the state and large-scale corporate capital was in train. While the latter were hardly enamoured of the RIDP, they were willing to turn a blind eye. By the mid-1980s the rapprochement was falling apart in the midst of escalating protest, the fusing of militant labour and community organization to form what has been called social movement unionism, growing international opposition to apartheid and the imposition of sanctions by the United States in 1986. It was in the context of this political and economic crisis that powerful business interests launched a major critique of the RIDP. Sponsored initially by the Urban Foundation (UF), the think-tank of big business, the critique was subsequently taken up by a Panel of Experts (PoE) appointed by the Development Bank of Southern Africa. Under pressure from this critique the de Klerk government slashed RIDP subsidies in 1991, and made the reduced package available throughout the country, not just in designated decentralization areas as in the past.

On one level, critique of the RIDP was both easy and capable of unifying the left and the (neo-)liberal right. The link with apartheid and its institutions was palpable; wages were extremely low and bantustan authorities frequently sought to ban union activity; the incentives were absurdly large and easily abused; and some of the decentralization areas were patently incapable of surviving without subsidies. Yet the UF/PoE critique went much further, invoking neo-liberal logic to argue that the RIDP was not only wasteful, inefficient and politically motivated, but also represented a hopeless effort to fly in the face of 'natural tendencies' for industry to agglomerate in major urban centres. Thus, some critics maintained, the RIDP bore much of the blame for slow industrial growth in South Africa as a whole during the 1980s (e.g. Tomlinson and Addleson, 1987). Flat assertions that industrial decentralization didn't work in South Africa and had never worked anywhere in the world were rife. In short, the critique conjured up images of crazed apartheid spatial engineers seeking to turn back the tides of economic logic by locating factories in the middle of nowhere. It went hand in hand with arguments that South Africa's future lay in the large metropolitan centres and that, with the lifting of influx control restrictions on mobility – which in fact happened in 1986 – large numbers of black South Africans who had been confined to relocation townships in the bantustans would simply pack their bags and move to the cities.

In the face of this total onslaught, dissenting voices were few and far between. Yet those that arose made extremely important points. First, Trevor Bell (1983, 1986) argued that the movement of labour-intensive industries to peripheral regions since the early 1970s was not simply the result of apartheid policies that distorted incentives, but was driven in large part by industrialists' search for lower production costs in the face of intensified global competition. Neo-liberal critics of the RIDP either dismissed or underplayed what Bell termed 'spontaneous decentralization'. They also ignored tendencies towards industrial dispersal in many different parts of the world – including not only Taiwan and China, but also the much-vaunted 'Third Italy'. Yet, while industrial dispersal became a characteristic feature of global capitalisms in the late twentieth century, its multiple forms, dynamics and trajectories cannot simply be deduced from an abstract capital logic (Hart, 1998).

A second set of dissenting arguments came from feminists who called for a more finely grained understanding of the complex and contradictory ways in which women's entry into the industrial wage labour force was reconfiguring power relations within and between households (Ardington, 1984; Pudifin and Ward, 1986; Jaffe, 1988, 1991; Bonnin et al., 1991; Posel et al., 1993; Posel and Todes, 1995). These interventions reflected broader debates in the literature on women's industrial labour (e.g. Elson and Pearson, 1981), but were firmly situated in the context of South African racial capitalism. While pointing to appalling wages and working conditions in decentralized industries, feminists also called attention to the contradictory character of these jobs – how, for example, they provided women with more room to manoeuvre in the context of influx control restrictions on mobility; how access to industrial wage employment enabled women to maintain somewhat more independent lives; and how industrial jobs provided an alternative to what were often even worse alternatives, namely domestic labour and work on white farms.

In addition to endorsing these arguments about the contradictory implications of the RIDP for women in relocation townships, Laurine Platzky (1995) added a third layer of complexity to the simplistic neo-liberal critique. On the basis of detailed studies in three decentralization areas in the late 1980s, she called attention both to the diversity of local dynamics and to the unanticipated consequences of industrial dispersal. These included, very importantly, the emergence of labour organizing in some – although not all – areas: 'Whereas trade union organisation may have stunted the growth of low paid employment, such that plants paying less than R100 per month have been eliminated, trade unions have ensured higher wages for some IDP workers' (Platzky, 1995: 286). On the basis of more complete evidence than that deployed by either the UF, or the PoE, Platzky also argued that, in a decade of severe economic recession, the RIDP had contributed to the survival of certain highly competitive manufacturing sectors, and to the entry of new manufacturing products and processes.

It was in the context of these debates that I commenced research in 1994 in two decentralization areas in northwestern KwaZulu-Natal, Ladysmith-Ezakheni and Newcastle-Madadeni. Like many such areas, they comprise former white towns located within 15–25 km of huge black relocation townships formed through dispossession. In 1994–95 I worked collaboratively with Alison Todes in Newcastle, where we conducted an industrial survey to trace trends in industrial employment since 1991 when RIDP subsidies had been slashed. My interest during this period was focused on Taiwanese investment, which was substantial in Newcastle. Alison Todes' work grew out of her observation that female migration into Madadeni had increased during the second half of the 1980s – precisely the period in which influx controls had been lifted, and people were supposed to be flocking into the main metropolitan centres. Our joint research in 1994–95 engaged directly with the debates over industrial decentralization and employment during the 1980s, and carried them in some new directions.

First, our research illuminated sectoral and gendered shifts in employment in Newcastle during the first part of the 1990s, a period of industrial decline in the economy as a whole (Hart and Todes, 1997). We documented a sharp decline – in the order of 30 per cent – in employment in male-oriented employment between 1990 and 1994. Much of this contraction was in classic MEC industries – iron, steel and industrial chemicals – that had located in Newcastle in the early 1970s. The other large sector in Newcastle – clothing and textiles – registered a decline in employment of about 4 per cent – far below that in metropolitan areas in the same period. Yet most of the contraction came from the closure of two relatively large South African firms. Between 1990 and 1994, the number of very small clothing firms – the large majority Taiwanese – rose from 34 to 58 (Hart and Todes, 1997). What had happened was that, despite sharply lower subsidies, small-scale Taiwanese knitwear producers continued to move into Newcastle as part of a tightly integrated network of small firms very similar to the system of satellite production in Taiwan (Hart, 1996a).

These patterns flew in the face of confident predictions by RIDP critics that industries would bleed away from decentralized areas once subsidies were lifted. While there have reputedly been large-scale factory closures some of the more remote areas in other provinces, this was not the case in KwaZulu-Natal in the first half of the 1990s. An evaluation of the 1991 RIDP in the province conducted in 1996 suggested remarkable stability in the other two main decentralization areas – Ezakheni and Isithebe (Harrison and Todes, 1996). This study also documented how, in the face of intensifying competition, small clothing and textile firms were moving into other peripheral parts of the province in search of lower costs. At a general level these patterns are, of course, consistent with Bell's argument about the importance of competitive pressures rather than just apartheid subsidies as key forces driving decentralization of labour-intensive industries. We argued that these industries are indeed fragile, but that the fragility derives less from the lifting of subsidies than intensifying competition and escalating labour conflict, particularly in Taiwanese firms (Hart and Todes, 1997).

A second broad contribution of the Newcastle study was to illuminate the reworking of transnational connections through which industrialists from Taiwan – and increasingly other parts of Asia as well, most notably Mainland China – were coming into South Africa. Through the 1980s, Taiwanese industrialists were typically channelled through bantustan investment corporations. Newcastle was the exception. In the mid-1980s the white local government officials in Newcastle set up their own recruiting system in Taiwan. Essentially, this was a competitive response to actions by the KwaZulu bantustan investment corporation, which had allocated the bulk of resources to the industrial estate in Ezakheni adjacent to the town of Ladysmith, 100 km to the south. Over and above RIDP incentives, Newcastle local authorities offered prospective Taiwanese industrialists cheap luxury housing left empty when the planned expansion of a branch plant Iscor (the Iron and Steel Corporation) fell through in the late 1970s. Through the 1980s, Newcastle became what was probably the single largest area of

Taiwanese settlement in South Africa. By the early 1990s, the Newcastle model was being adopted by a number of other white local governments in towns all over South Africa. In short, despite the dramatic decline in subsidies, there arose a system of spontaneous transnationalism, with white local governments bypassing the national government and reaching directly into the global economy. I shall return in the latter part of the chapter to talk about further changes in transnational connections in the post-apartheid period, as well as the insights that emerged from these connections in Newcastle as well as in Ladysmith.

The third part of the Newcastle study consisted of in-depth interviews that Alison Todes conducted with members of 31 households, and a survey of a further 354 households in the Newcastle townships. These interviews helped to clarify why, contrary to widely held expectations, people in relocation townships adjacent to industrial decentralization points were not simply moving into the main metropolitan centres with the lifting of what in the apartheid lexicon was known as 'influx control'. Todes showed how relocation townships had assumed the role often described for rural areas as a 'home base' of social security from which selected household members – predominantly men – make forays in search of employment and income elsewhere, while women perform reproductive labour as well as generating income:

> Newcastle emerged as this kind of home base in the context of influx control when the movement of families to cities was difficult and accommodation hard to find. Children were left with grandmothers while daughters worked in the city, and wives returned home on marriage – or at least after they had children. When household members living in cities became unemployed or unable to find jobs, they returned 'home' to Newcastle. As in rural areas, pensioners retired there after working elsewhere for much of their lives. Newcastle also served as the place where the sick or disabled were looked after. Although the end of influx control has eased access to urban centres, lack of accommodation, violence, and the absence of secure employment has meant that Newcastle has retained its 'home base' functions (Todes, 1997: 317–18; see also Hart and Todes, 1997).

Yet, Todes goes on to note, these areas are emphatically not rural. On the one hand, they were formed out of a process of dispossession and less than 4 per cent of households had access to land. On the other, most households derive some income locally, and access to service and infrastructure is higher than in most rural areas. In fact, as we shall see, the apartheid state channelled fairly substantial subsidies into services in relocation townships like those outside Newcastle. One of the great ironies of the post-apartheid era is that these subsidies are being cut in the name of neo-liberal austerity.

While relocation townships assumed the functions of a home base in the context of apartheid restrictions on mobility, such functions persist in the post-apartheid era. Apart from sharp contractions in employment in the main urban centres, other limitations on mobility became evident in the first half of the 1990s. Todes shows how residents of relocation townships have not only put years of effort and considerable resources into building and improving houses in relocation townships; in addition, particularly for women, place-based social networks nurtured over the years are a deeply meaningful and centrally important part of their lives. In short, many residents of what were widely labelled the 'dumping grounds' of apartheid have painstakingly woven together a fabric of everyday life that provides at least a modicum of security.

Todes' research also sheds light on some of the complex relations between women's reproductive work and their access to extremely low wage, often harshly exploitative forms of industrial employment in industrial decentralization areas. The household survey revealed that the only 25 per cent of women workers in the Newcastle clothing industry were married, and that the largest single category (over 40 per cent) were daughters living with at least one parent, usually the mother, in three-generational households. Yet most were not young girls. In fact, the majority of women industrial workers in the sample were in the 26–50 age group. Todes' work revealed powerful constraints on women's mobility, arising not only from lack of options elsewhere but also their centrality to maintaining a base of social security. Evidence from life histories suggested that, in the past, a large proportion of men and smaller numbers of younger unmarried women had engaged in circular migration, sending back remittances to Newcastle that were often tied to housing improvements. Women who remained in the townships formed the lynch pin of social security in extremely complex, spatially extended networks and flows of people and resources. Although the study was not a finely grained inquiry into the operations of power and gender within and across spatial and social arenas, it pointed clearly to growing pressure on women arising out of the collapse of male employment both within and beyond Newcastle. With the decline in remittances, local sources of income assumed additional importance. At the same time, a growing proportion of employment in the clothing industry was in the segment dominated by Taiwanese industrialists where wages were extremely low and labour relations particularly fraught with conflict.

The socially explosive character of East Asian investment in these regions of South Africa signifies far more than just an unpleasant episode in a turbulent history of labour relations. How East Asian forms of low wage, labour-intensive production are refashioned when they are transplanted to South Africa is deeply revealing of the operation of gender, race and ethnicity in relation to class processes. These transnational connections also shed new light on the relationships between production and the conditions of reproduction of labour power. In particular, they bring questions of the social wage to the forefront of attention, but in a way that links it directly to sharply divergent agrarian histories. These connections, in turn, illuminate the contradictions inherent in the neo-liberal project, particularly in the context of the deeply racialized material inequalities that remain a pervasive feature of the post-apartheid era.

East Asian connections: gender, race and the social wage

A growing body of feminist research in Asia and elsewhere – much of it based on participant observation on factory floors and in the communities where workers live – has shown how even the seemingly most despotic and coercive low-wage factory regimes are to some degree negotiated orders – albeit highly asymmetrical ones. While workers are certainly subject to a powerful array of disciplinary forces, they often construct alternative interpretations and definitions. Such 'cultural struggles' (Ong, 1991) do not necessarily have direct political effects; in some circumstances they may indeed become part of a process of accommodation or partial consent to industrial work discipline and familial pressures. A key point, however, is that these processes can and do vary markedly, even in conditions that on the surface appear quite similar. A great deal depends on *how* cultural and symbolic resources are deployed and reconfigured through everyday practice not only on the factory floor, but also in other social arenas.

A particularly interesting example of this type of approach is Lee's (1995) comparative study of management practices and worker strategies in two factories owned by the same company, one in Hong Kong and the other in Shenzhen (just over the border in China). Lee shows how gendered practices on the shopfloor were very different, and how this in turn reflected differences in the historical constitution of the workforce, as well as in the everyday conditions and practices of social reproduction. Most of the workers in China were young, unmarried women migrants, whereas those in Hong Kong were mainly older married women. Participant observation enabled Lee to illuminate the varied ways that the local communal institutions within which workers were situated became incorporated in shopfloor practices:

> Localistic networks in Shenzhen and family and kin in Hong Kong mediated the supply of labor and provided resources that neither the state or employees offered to women. Incorporating localism and familialism into the respective factory regimes reduced management's financial burden, legitimized management control, and satisfied workers' mundane interests. (Lee, 1995: 394)

While management manipulated the gendered hierarchies of localism and familialism to exercise greater control, workers invested them with their own understandings and used them to temper and mitigate managerial domination. These practices also reflected a set of meanings which, while contested, were sufficiently shared to provide the basis for negotiation – as well as worker acquiescence.

Another important example is Hsiung's (1991, 1996) research based on participant observation in unregulated small-scale factories in Taiwan, which provides a finely grained understanding of paternalism as an ongoing product of constant struggle and negotiation on the factory floor. In many of these factories, married women from the local community have come to constitute a large proportion of the workforce. In the course of working in such factories, Hsiung observed considerable conflict between workers and employers. Workers' resistance was, however, informal, individualized and clandestine, and articulated in the idiom of paternalism: 'because pre-existing family/kinship systems are intertwined with the production unit, the conflict of interest between the factory owner and waged workers often takes the form of familial disagreement. The construction of paternalism illustrates the constant struggle between those who own the means of production and those who sell their labor ...' (Hsiung, 1991: 148–9). Both owners and workers were deeply invested in personalistic constructions. Workers invoked the concept of 'help' to drive home that they were not simply selling labour, but also providing a personal commitment in return for which they expect a variety of favours; employers for their part engaged in petty acts of 'goodwill', which doubled as personal debts that were reclaimed when owners made excessive demands on workers (ibid.: 186–7). Rather than simple coercion, labour relations were constantly renegotiated in the idiom of familial obligation. Some employers also deployed appeals to ethnic pride. In short, gender, kinship, local community and ethnic identity provided the cultural raw materials from which production relations and work experiences were fashioned in satellite factories.

The centrality of kinship idioms as the currency of negotiation between male managers and women workers is a consistent theme in the ethnographic literature. Some of these studies also yield insights into very different articulations of racial/ethnic and sexual/gender difference. Ong (1987) for example describes how managers of Japanese firms in Malaysia emphasized their racial and national superiority vis-a-vis Malay women workers. At the same time, they invoked a familial discourse that defined women workers as 'children' who should 'obey their parents'.

These insights offer some important clues into dynamics at play when Taiwanese industrialists moved to South Africa. As I argue more fully in my book (Hart, 2002), the depth and intensity of conflict derived at least in part from the way racial and gendered difference were being constructed in relation to one another. The majority of Asian industrialists, who had come from a setting in which negotiations with women workers are conducted in the idiom of family and kinship, constructed African women workers as *so* different that they had no means of invoking and deploying these idioms.

The anger and resentment that workers experienced is captured very precisely in the phrase I heard repeated a number of times – namely, their sense of being treated 'just like animals'. Virtually all the workers with whom I met spoke bitterly of their sense of ill-treatment in Taiwanese factories. All complained about low wages and of being driven to work unreasonably hard through the 'score' system – a minimum level of production that workers have to meet. In almost all of these discussions, however, workers talked most fully and eloquently about everyday practices and conditions in the factories that they found demeaning – one of the most consistent complaints being about poor toilet and kitchen facilities which, many of them said, showed their employers' lack of concern about them as people. One woman provided a particularly interesting example of how she had gone about trying to shame her employer. She described how she had complained about respiratory problems caused by fluff from acrylic yarn. When her employer ignored her complaint, she wore a surgical mask to work not only to facilitate her breathing; her purpose, she made clear, was to demonstrate the level of pollution in the factory, and to assert her humanity. In one way or another, all of the workers with whom I spoke expounded on this theme of inhumanity, expressing a profound sense of affront at being 'treated just like animals'. Their bitter complaints about harsh treatment by Taiwanese industrialists resonated with how industrialists frequently constructed workers in terms such as their having 'not yet entered civilization'.

In short, I suggest, the particular ways in which most Taiwanese industrialists produced understandings of racial difference undermined their capacity to engage with workers on anything other than openly coercive terms. Yet these dynamics were neither uniform, nor cast in stone. The exceptions were in some ways just as revealing. In the course of conducting the industrial survey in Newcastle, Alison Todes and I were struck by how a small group of Taiwanese industrialists actively distanced themselves and their labour practices from those of their compatriots, and declared themselves quite satisfied with worker productivity. They also waxed eloquent in describing their own ingenuity. Unfortunately it was not possible to elicit workers' experiences of and reactions to the strategies these industrialists described. Even so, the origins and representations of these self-proclaimed 'good bosses' are quite revealing of their strategies to recreate paternalism.

With one key exception, all were former technicians who came to South Africa to work for the first round of industrialists, and had considerable experience on the factory floor. All started on a very small scale, and since expanded – in sharp contrast to their original bosses, most of whom had contracted the scale of their operations. In several cases they were engaged in direct competition with their former bosses. Nevertheless, as we shall see, their capacity to expand their scale of operations appeared limited by precisely the strategies they deployed to elicit worker consent.

Several common threads run through the stories these industrialists told about their methods of coping with workers. First, they claimed a familiarity with workers' living conditions in the townships, together with careful selection of workers. Some claimed that they have visited workers' homes, and one described how he selected his workers from different townships; that way, if there was trouble in one of the townships he would be assured of workers from the others. The question of the conditions in which workers live is a crucial issue to which we shall return below.

Second, they portrayed their relations with workers in the language of generosity, paternalism and keeping workers happy: 'If you help these people you can help yourself', declared one; 'we're very free here'. Often quite explicitly, they contrasted their generosity – encompassing higher wages, as well as parties, loans, sick pay, leave pay and other 'gifts' – with the tight-fistedness of their compatriots from whom they actively distanced themselves. As is typically the case in clientilistic relationships, gifts often came with surveillance and other strings attached to them. For example, one industrialist explained how, if worker said she was sick, he sent a driver to her house to check that she really was sick; if so, he sent her to hospital and paid the bills. Compassion and familialism also had its limits. While declaiming that everyone in the factory was like a family, and his willingness to grant leave to workers for family crises, one industrialist stipulated 'one father, one mother dead only once!'

Wages and work effort were also described in terms of gift-giving: 'I give you the right money, you give me the right job.' But the carrot of higher wages was combined with the stick of enforcement built into the forms of work organization common to all these factories. In all cases, workers were organized into mutually competing groups that were presented with a daily or weekly production quota. Group monitoring was the key enforcement mechanism: if a group failed to meet the quota, all workers were penalized even if only one or a subset of individuals failed to perform to the required standard. If they met the quota, they could either leave early or earn bonuses for additional production.

What was emerging, in short, was a paternalized system of piece rates through which these self-styled 'good bosses' were able to produce a modicum of worker consent. Yet this strategy was also subject to sharp limits – in particular, none of these industrialists were able to expand the scale of their operations beyond about 30 workers.

Just as some industrialists began to discover ways of recreating paternalistic strategies of labour control, a new source of instability appeared in the form of identical knitwear produced in China. The competitive threat appeared suddenly and without warning. In the second half of 1994 when Alison Todes and I did our first round of research in Newcastle, imports were not an issue at all. When we returned in mid-1995, the Newcastle knitwear industry was in a state of siege. Most industrialists blamed the influx of knitwear on corrupt customs officials, but they also conceded that it was a portent of things to come as trade liberalization took hold. Even the most enthusiastic proponents of free markets were adamantly opposed to the lifting of tariff barriers whose protection they had enjoyed. 'If this government opens up the gates they kill all business', declared one; jumping out of his chair, he demonstrated vividly how 'they take a big wire and tie it around our neck; they take a big rock and drop it on our foot!'

Perhaps the ultimate irony was that the competition came from compatriots of Newcastle industrialists who moved to the southern coastal regions of China. Newcastle knitwear producers claimed that their counterparts in China could produce essentially the same commodities at prices below the costs of production in Newcastle. In my book (Hart, 2002), I draw on You-Tien Hsing's (1998) study of a comparable group of Taiwanese industrialists who moved to Fujian province in China. What this comparative exercise makes clear are not only sharply different practices of labour discipline, but also the way redistributive reforms dating from the socialist era were underwriting accumulation.

The retention of peasant property – along with other state-sponsored subsidies securing the reproduction of the workforce – have been both underappreciated and absolutely central in defining the conditions of 'global competition' emanating from both Taiwan and China. What is distinctive about both China and Taiwan – and dramatically different from South Africa – are the redistributive land reforms beginning in the late 1940s that effectively broke the power of the landlord class. The political forces that drove agrarian reforms in China and Taiwan were closely linked and precisely opposite. Yet in both socialist and post-socialist China, and in 'capitalist' Taiwan, the redistributive reforms that defined agrarian transformations were marked by rapid, decentralized industrial accumulation *without* dispossession from the land.

To the extent that the relationship between the conditions of reproduction of labour power and industrial accumulation in East Asia has been recognized, it has focused on housing in the city states. In *The Shek Kip Mei Syndrome* (1990), Manuel Castells and his colleagues pointed out that state-subsidized public housing in Hong Kong and Singapore operated to lower the money wage while maintaining the social wage, and contributed substantially to industrial competitiveness. These are, however, are two small city states. In societies with large, and largely impoverished rural populations, urban housing cannot perform this function without tight restrictions on access. This is precisely what happened in socialist China, where restrictions on movement were necessary to guarantee urban dwellers' access to housing and other forms of social security. Beyond the city states and urban China, connections between industrial production and the conditions of labour reproduction have been forged in the countryside.

These direct connections between production and the conditions of reproduction of labour in Taiwan and China compel attention to the significance of agrarian dispossession in South Africa. When Taiwanese industrialists moved to places like Newcastle and other decentralized regions of South Africa, they encountered a workforce expropriated from the land and thrust into radically commodified forms of livelihood. The intensity of labour conflict unleashed by these forms of production derives, I suggest, not only from the inability of the majority of Taiwanese industrialists to deploy gendered forms of negotiation on the factory floor, but also from the absence of the sort of social wage subsidy that characterized Taiwanese and Chinese industrial trajectories. One rough indication of this point that I discuss more fully elsewhere (Hart, 1995) is that in 1995, when cheap knitwear produced by Taiwanese industrialists in China began flowing into South Africa, wages in Taiwanese knitwear factories in Newcastle were nearly double those in Fujian when calculated in terms of prevailing exchange rates. Yet real wages – calculated in terms of Purchasing Power Parity – were 30–40 per cent lower. In comparing their situation with those of their compatriots who had moved to China, Taiwanese industrialists in Newcastle consistently complained not only about low worker productivity, but also how much higher wages were in South Africa. What was missing, of course, was any sort of recognition of the radical inadequacy of these wages – or of how they themselves were the product of East Asian agrarian reforms.

This misrecognition is particularly ironic, since part of what attracted Taiwanese industrialists to South Africa in the 1980s was precisely the availability of cheap luxury housing, as well as access to the appurtenances of white privilege – including educational, health and other facilities. As one industrialist put it, 'you can live like a king in South Africa!' In addition, the English education that their children receive in South African schools enables them to become far more globally mobile than if they had been raised in Taiwan. There is, in fact, a double irony since it was precisely the converse of these racialized subsidies – namely dispossession – that has, at least in part, undermined the accumulative capacities of Taiwanese industrialists.

These claims have some important continuities with earlier debates, but with some new twists. A key argument in the race–class debate that raged during the 1970s was the reserve subsidy thesis, which posited that, at least until the first half of the twentieth century, capital latched on to women's labour in subsistence agriculture in the former reserves to subsidize low wages of male migrant workers. The functionalist tendencies in this argument came under attack from those who pointed out that the deeply gendered migrant labour system, at least in part, reflected a degree of agency by patriarchal societies resisting full proletarianization.

Despite this and other critiques, there is no question that mining capital, in particular, derived huge benefits from workers' access to land in the reserves particularly in the earlier phases of capitalist expansion. Essentially what I am doing is turning the reserve subsidy thesis on its head, and arguing that one of the defining features of South Africa in the post-Second World War period is the depth and extent of racialized dispossession under apartheid that severely eroded the social wage – and that formed a key element of the terrain on which post-apartheid neoliberalism took hold. Since the mid-1990s, the erosion of the social wage has, if anything, accelerated for many South Africans.

Post-apartheid dynamics: neo-liberal contradictions

One of the great ironies of the post-apartheid era is the ANC's embrace of fairly orthodox neo-liberalism. This shift to the right was not simply a consequence of top-down imposition of structural adjustment by the World Bank and the IMF. On the contrary, Fine and Padayachee (2000: 5) note acerbically that 'South Africa is in the remarkable situation of having adopted and persisted with the policies of the Washington consensus when it was under no obligation to do so and, most ironically, after its nostrums had already been rejected by the most ardent exponents.' The neo-liberal turn is most usefully understood in terms of complex political struggles within and beyond the ANC, in the course of which alternatives to neo-liberalism were sidelined (Marais, 1998). Chief among these were the comprehensive neo-Keynesian proposals set forth by the Macro-Economic Research Group (MERG) in its report entitled *Making Democracy Work*. Powerful figures within the ANC and the business community summarily dismissed the MERG report almost immediately upon its publication at the end of 1993.

South African neo-liberalism marches under the banner of GEAR, an acronym for Growth, Employment, and Redistribution announced in June 1996. Many observers regard GEAR as a sudden retreat from the redistributive commitments of the Reconstruction and Development Program (RDP). The RDP formed the basis of the ANC's electoral platform in the 1994 elections, promising a 'people-driven' fulfilment of basic needs. In practice, soon after the new government assumed power, strategically placed groups modified the RDP in a neo-liberal direction. In addition, as Harold Wolpe noted in an incisive article written shortly before his death in 1995, the RDP was riddled with tensions: 'firstly, while the RDP operates on a deeply contested terrain, in crucial respects it eradicates sources of contradiction and probably contestation and conflict by asserting harmony; secondly, on this basis it constructs a consensual model of society which is the premise for the accomplishments and goals of the RDP; and thirdly, on the basis of this premise, it also conceptualises the state as the unproblematic instrument of the RDP' (Wolpe, 1995: 91). Proponents of GEAR briskly dismissed the populist discourse of the RDP. In presenting GEAR as a *fait accompli*, ANC Finance Minister Trevor Manuel made clear that it was non-negotiable.

The central premise of GEAR is that a conventional neo-liberal package – tight fiscal austerity, monetary discipline, wage restraints, reducing corporate taxes, privatization, trade liberalization and phasing out exchange controls – will lure private investment (both domestic and foreign), unleash rapid export-led growth, tighten labour markets and drive up wages. In an apparent departure from orthodox neo-liberalism, several pieces of post-apartheid legislation provide for some degree of protection of workers in formal employment: these include the Labour Relations Act (LRA) of 1995 which entrenches rights of organized workers; the Basic Conditions of Employment Act of 1997 which establishes minimum standards for those not subject to collective bargaining, including working time and the rights of pregnant women; and the Employment Equity Act of 1998 which prohibits unfair discrimination. Designed to appease Cosatu (the Congress of South African Trade Unions), labour legislation is currently under threat.

Defenders of GEAR often point out that social spending forms a relatively large proportion of the budget. On one level, this is certainly the case. Between 1994/95 and 1997/98, for example, the share of social services (including health, education, social security and welfare and housing) in government spending rose from 45 to 46.9 per cent – a figure significantly higher than the average for East Asia (33.5 per cent), South Asia (26.5 per cent), other parts of sub-Saharan Africa (26.1 per cent), Latin America (31.3 per cent) and the Middle East/North Africa (28.6 per cent) (Mokate, 2000: 66–7). Yet things are not as bright as they appear at first glance. First, if one looks at social spending as a proportion of GDP the picture changes, since fiscal austerity has meant that total government spending as a proportion of GDP is relatively low. Second, not all budgeted expenditures are actually spent; the Department of Welfare, for example, was able to disburse only 1 per cent of the R204 million (approximately US$29 million) it received for poverty relief programmes in the 1998/99 financial year, and there is a similar pattern across other ministries.

While these spending logjams may well be temporary problems that will be ironed out in time, there is a third dimension of fiscal austerity with profound long-term implications – namely, the proportion of the South African budget going to 'economic services' (about 10 per cent) is extremely small, and dramatically lower than averages in other parts of Africa, Asia and Latin America. This includes, very importantly, land reform, which has thus far received a miniscule proportion of the limited budget – a large chunk of which had also not been spent by the late 1990s. There is a further irony. Just as the backlogs in spending on land programmes were beginning to move through the pipeline, the Ministry of Land Affairs put a stop to what was probably the most effective of the land reform programmes in terms of redistribution on the grounds that policy will henceforth focus on developing a capitalist farmer class. Cherryl Walker (2000) provides a detailed account of these policy shifts in her superb study of land reform and its relationship to gender in post-apartheid South Africa. I will return later to suggest some important connections between the history of dispossession and the conditions of reproduction of labour, and how these in turn are linked with the rising costs and privatization of urban services.

Before doing so, I want to sketch the broad contours of trends in growth, employment and redistribution in the era of post-apartheid neo-liberalism (Table 7.1). To say that economic performance has fallen short of GEAR targets is an extreme understatement. Direct foreign investment has been negligible, particularly in industry; domestic capital has continued to flow out of the country; and formal sector employment seems to be contracting at an accelerating rate:

All indications are that employment has continued its precipitous decline not only in non-agricultural sectors, but in agriculture as well. In a study conducted in 1996 for the ILO, Bell and Cataneo predicted that import liberalization was likely to have large negative effects on manufacturing employment, including employment in relatively low wage sectors and regions where women workers are concentrated. They also maintained that South Africa's comparative advantage in international

Table 7.1 Trends in growth and employment

	1994	1995	1996	1997	1998	1999
Growth	3.2	3.1	4.2	2.5	0.6	0.9*
Employment	−0.4	−1.1	−0.7	−1.7	−3.7	na

Notes: *Growth* is defined as per cent change in GDP at constant 1995 prices. *Employment* is defined as per cent change in employment in the non-agricultural formal sector.
* The growth figure for 1999 is an estimate.

Source: South African Reserve Bank *Quarterly Bulletin*, December 1999.

trade lies in capital-intensive manufactures and not, as is traditionally argued, in labour-intensive sectors. Drawing on a growing body of more recent research, Imraan Valodia endorses these arguments. Trade and industrial policy in the post-1994 period have, he argues, brought about extremely rapid exposure to global competition, and are beginning to shift the economy onto a path of capital intensification – with sharply differential implications for men and women workers:

> First, the employment effects [of trade liberalization] are impacting most negatively on those sectors of the economy that employ large numbers of women. The restructuring processes in these labour-intensive industries have resulted in massive job losses in sectors that have traditionally employed large numbers of women. A recent ILO study ... estimated an 18% fall in clothing and textile industries between 1994 and 1997. The negative employment effects are being generated primarily through processes of rationalisation and downsizing in industrial enterprises, processes which, a number of case studies have shown ... are increasingly leading to informalisation and flexibilisation of women's work. Second, the longer-term trajectory of the South African economy is being shifted to capital-intensive production, thereby favouring the employment of men in the formal sector of the economy. The pattern that seems to be emerging is therefore that the short-term costs of trade liberalisation are being borne disproportionately by women, whilst the potential longer-term employment benefits of the liberalisation process are likely to favour men. (Valodia, 2000: 6)

In addition to growing unemployment, a number of recent studies document a rapid rise in sub-contracting and other 'flexible' labour practices, particularly in the clothing industry. The Confederation of Employers of South Africa (COFESA), for example, advises employers on how to convert employment contracts into service contracts, thereby transforming workers into 'independent contractors' and bypassing minimum standards labour legislation and collective bargaining agreements (Valodia, 2000). At the same time, growing numbers of women are ending up in the survivalist segment of the informal economy where, despite official commitment to 'small and medium enterprises', access to state support is virtually nil (Lund *et al.*, 2000).

The most recently available evidence on trends in income distribution and poverty deals with the period 1991–96. In a report entitled 'Winners and Losers: South Africa's Changing Income Distribution in the 1990s', Whiteford and van Seventer (1999) estimated that, while racial inequalities persist – white per capita income was almost nine times higher than Africans' in 1996 – black South Africans' share of income rose from 29.9 to 35.7 per cent between 1991 and 1996. Yet almost all of this increase was concentrated in the top 10 per cent of black households, while the poorest 40 per cent of black households suffered a fall in income of around 21 per cent. All indications are that these tendencies accelerated after 1996 in the context of massive increases in unemployment, declining private sector investment and strict fiscal austerity. In addition, HIV/AIDS is taking a terrible toll.

If one turns from these bleak and depressing macro indicators to the dynamics at work in particular places, a more varied picture emerges that is suggestive of both possibilities and constraints. Beginning in mid-1996, the second phase of my research focused on detailed historical and ethnographic research in Newcastle as well as in Ladysmith. The starting point of this second phase was significant, because it marked not only the advent of GEAR, but also local government elections in KwaZulu-Natal. The first phase of local government restructuring (1995–2000) entailed former white towns and black townships joining together as single administrative entities. It has also been accompanied by the increasing importance of the local state as the key site of both redistribution and accumulation.

The rising importance of the local state in the context of neo-liberal 'globalization' is of course an extremely widespread phenomenon, occurring in many different parts of the world. Yet in post-apartheid South Africa, it has appeared in a particularly stark and intense form. As part of the political compromises in the constitutional negotiations, the first phase of local government restructuring (1995–2000) reinscribed apartheid geographies, with former white areas garnering a disproportionate share of power. Over this period, some of the key contradictions inherent in the post-apartheid order have been deflected to what has come to be termed in official parlance 'the developmental local state'. With only 10 per cent of municipal budgets coming from the central fiscus, local authorities are responsible for raising 90 per cent of their revenues locally (mainly from property taxes and service fees). At the same time, both central authorities and local constituents are placing growing demands on the local state. A statement by Crispin Olver, Deputy Director-General of the Local Government section of the Department of Constitutional Development in 1998, lays out the situation with stunning clarity:

> South Africa is currently undergoing a major change within its public sector, in which government functions, virtually across the board, are

being decentralized to the local level. District health services, municipal police forces, local housing programs, child care – name the department and there will be some or other function on its way down. Two forces are driving this decentralisation: a fiscal squeeze at national and provincial level, leading to the shedding of functions (and hence to what we call 'unfunded mandates' being dropped on local government); and a realisation that many functions can be provided more efficiently at local level.

Tensions provoked by this unfunded devolution of functions became powerfully apparent in the first phase of local government restructuring. Local politicians and bureaucrats have found themselves perched precariously on seismic fault lines, confronted with direct and urgent demands for redistribution in the face of fierce fiscal austerity and, simultaneously, with helping to promote 'local economic development' – a process that frequently pits different groups and classes against one another, and places local authorities under intense pressure to attract foreign investment.

Since 1996, I have been engaged in trying to follow how these processes are playing out in Ladysmith and Newcastle, and their adjacent townships. From a comparative perspective, the two places are particularly interesting. Only 100 km apart, both exemplify apartheid era dispossession and industrial decentralization described earlier – including close connections with Taiwan and, more recently, with Mainland China. Each is comprised of a former white town separated by a 'buffer zone' from black townships formed through forced removals in the 1960s and 1970s. Newcastle is somewhat larger than Ladysmith, but in most other respects they are structurally very similar. Yet local political dynamics are dramatically different. Not only is the ANC far stronger in Ladysmith than in Newcastle; in addition, the labour movement is far better organized, and local councillors are held far more accountable to their constituents.

In my book, I trace out the overlapping struggles in multiple arenas, both local and trans-local, that have produced these sharply divergent trajectories (Hart, 2002). I also show how race, ethnicity and gender articulated with class processes in distinctively different ways in the two places. For purposes of the present chapter, I want to draw on sharply divergent local political dynamics in Ladysmith and Newcastle in the second half of the 1990s to explore the tension between so-called LED (local economic development) strategies on the one hand and key social policies – those having to do with service charges in the townships – on the other.

Since 1996, the central government has made clear that local economic development – including, very importantly, attracting foreign direct investment – is a primary responsibility of local government. In towns like Ladysmith and Newcastle, white local government officials have long been engaged in strategies to pull in investment. What is new is that councillors representing township constituents are now charged not only with attracting investment, but also with 'linking LED to poverty alleviation' and securing the conditions of accumulation by maintaining labour discipline.

A set of ten case studies in different parts of South Africa commissioned by the Department of Constitutional Development in 1998 concluded that 'hardly any of the municipalities reviewed in this project have made any formal attempt to explicitly link economic development with poverty alleviation' (DCD, 1998: 5) and that 'the essential policy direction appears to be a reliance upon market forces to allow the benefits of trickle-down to poor communities' (DCD, 1998: 31). Efforts to draw more general lessons from the case studies politely avoid any reference to GEAR, although one contributor notes that 'SA local governments on their own cannot solve the complex problems of poverty and erase the legacies of apartheid planning' (DCD, 1998: 32). Yet this point is flatly contradicted by the coordinator of the study who blithely asserts that 'Local initiatives and *relative autonomy from national resources* are key elements to ensure robust local partnerships and collaborative strategies' (DCD, 1998: 52, emphasis added).

The ironies inherent in such claims become clear when one considers how active LED strategies have played out in practice in Ladysmith and Newcastle. In the late 1980s and early 1990s, Newcastle was probably one of the largest recipients of industrial foreign direct investment (FDI) relative to its size in South Africa; since the mid-1990s, Ladysmith has taken over that position with the influx of industrial investment from Mainland China. Both places are deeply connected with transnational centres of accumulation, and represent precisely the pattern of export-oriented FDI upon which GEAR is predicated. In both places these FDI-led local growth strategies have proven socially explosive. As in the past, the intensity of struggles on the factory floor derives not only from relatively low wages and poor working conditions, but also the way racial, ethnic and gendered forms of difference are produced along with material commodities.

These conflicts at the point of production in turn are deeply inter-twined with struggles over the conditions of reproduction of labour, albeit in locally specific and varied ways. To appreciate the larger significance of these local divergences, one must focus on how the costs and provision of urban services have changed in the post-apartheid era. Particularly in large urban townships like Soweto formerly run by so-called Black Local Authorities, boycotts of rents and service payments became a key weapon in the struggle against apartheid in the 1980s (Swilling *et al.*, 1991). In 1995, the new government launched a lavishly funded national campaign entitled Masakhane (an Nguni word meaning 'let's build together'), ostensibly aimed at building popular confidence in local government and reconfiguring understandings of citizens' rights and responsibilities. In practice, Masakhane quickly became associated with an effort to reverse the 'culture of non-payment'. Yet the following year payment levels fell still further, and the amount owed to local authorities has continued to increase. At the same time, the costs of service provision have been rising, and municipal services are increasingly being privatized. By 1997 there were widespread service disconnections, accompanied by public protests against municipalities that, in some areas, became extremely violent. These in turn underscore the contradictory imperatives embodied in the local state in the post-apartheid era. In addition to securing the conditions of accumulation, newly elected local councillors have confronted the local fallout from fiscal austerity, as well as often fierce opposition from former white areas to any sort of cross-subsidization of services. In former bantustan townships like Madadeni (Newcastle) and Ezakheni (Ladysmith), post-apartheid austerity has hit particularly hard. During the apartheid era, these townships received relatively high levels of state subsidies, and township households paid relatively low, flat service charges that were in fact well below the costs of service provision. Under the new dispensation, local authorities are under intense pressure to raise service charges.

In Newcastle, struggles over rising service charges have been extremely chaotic. The crisis erupted shortly after the local government elections in mid-1996, when the ANC unexpectedly won the election. Historically, the Newcastle townships had been a stronghold of the Zulu nationalist Inkatha Freedom Party (IFP). One of the most unpopular Taiwanese industrialists joined the IFP, paying huge amounts of money into party coffers on the understanding that he would become mayor. As he explained to Alison Todes and me in 1995, his plan was to turn Newcastle into a free trade zone, build an airport and ban all union activity! What in fact happened was that IFP failed to win a majority of seats in the council – largely because numbers of registered IFP supporters stayed away from the polls. In July 1996, when Phelele Tengeni and

I spent some time in Madadeni talking to people about the election results, their response was consistent: they expressed considerable resentment about the money he spent trying to buy votes. Why, they asked, if he is so rich does he not pay decent wages? Soon after the local government elections in 1996, white municipal bureaucrats – who retained considerable power – pushed through a budget that increased service charges from R16 to R84 a month. ANC councillors claimed that the increased service charges took them totally by surprise; they were not given a chance to go through the budget document, and were railroaded into approving it. Escalating service charges provoked an explosion of resentment in the townships, resulting in an almost total boycott of service payments. Despite a costly public relations campaign to 'win hearts and minds' of township residents, the boycott has continued and conditions in Madadeni and the adjacent township of Osizweni have deteriorated sharply.

The contrast with what has happened in the Ladysmith and the adjacent township of Ezakheni is dramatic. The ANC won a major victory in the 1996 election, prompting the resignation of six senior white municipal officials and enabling the ANC councillors to appoint a new top echelon of bureaucrats. Instead of simply hiking up service charges as in Newcastle, municipal bureaucrats and councillors representing the townships worked out a strategy to maintain service charges at a relatively low level while increasing payment rates and local revenues. They also instituted an extraordinary system of open budget meetings, consulting with constituents about their priorities. Although operating within a tightly constrained budget, local government has brought about some quite significant improvements in the townships, and has been extremely successful in gaining access to provincial-level sources of revenue for social services. Yet councillors and township residents recognize that the low, flat service charges are not sustainable. In the absence of large increases in state subsidies a system of metering will have to be put in place – at which point, costs of living are likely to escalate.

Although councillors and local bureaucrats in Ladysmith have managed for the time being to stave off the devastating effects of fiscal austerity, their efforts to attract investment have generated profound tension. On one level they have been extraordinarily successful, pulling in some 20 factories from Mainland China since 1996. Over the same period the flow of Taiwanese investment into Newcastle has slowed dramatically. This contraction reflects both the South African government's recognition of Mainland China instead of Taiwan in November 1996, and perhaps more importantly, the sharp contraction in the knitwear industry in Newcastle as a consequence of cheap imports from Mainland China. As we saw earlier, the commodities (mostly brightly coloured jerseys) are identical to those made in Newcastle and are produced, ironically, by relatives of Taiwanese industrialists who moved to Southern coastal provinces of China. Not surprisingly, a number of Taiwanese who have remained in Newcastle have switched from industry to commerce, selling imported knitwear mainly to street traders. The Mainland Chinese industries that have moved into Ladysmith include not only clothing but also various forms of metal-working, stationery, pots and pans and the like. They are all linked to the Shanghai local government, and are using Ladysmith as a point from which to break into African markets and, in the case of clothing, to take advantage of South African quotas under the Multi Fibre Agreement. Employing mainly women, their wages and labour practices are very similar to those of small-scale Taiwanese producers in Newcastle.

The influx of Mainland Chinese investment has generated deep conflict between ANC councillors on the one hand, and key industrial unions on the other. This is all the more ironic, as many of the councillors are former members of the militant youth movement in the 1980s that received strong support from the unions; others, particularly women, are former shop stewards. Union officials claim that councillors fail to inform investors about the Labour Relations Act; that employers systematically violate workers' rights and that unions are constantly being called upon by dissatisfied workers to intervene on their behalf. For ANC councillors, Chinese investment presents an intense dilemma: while clearly aware of poor wages and working conditions, they point to the need to generate employment – yet they also confront their constituents' resentment over wages and working conditions in Chinese factories, as well as direct challenges from erstwhile allies in Cosatu.

The intractable dilemmas inherent in these conditions became powerfully evident in the open budget meetings in the Ladysmith township of Ezakheni. Following a particularly hostile challenge from a group of township residents over conditions in Chinese factories, the mayor made the following speech:

This community is aware that I am the representative sent overseas to invite industrialists to locate here. The issue of bringing industrialists is a real headache. Industrialists are looking for a particular type of workforce. If we go overseas we go kneeling to beg. It is difficult to beg a person and put conditions. Yes, we have government by the people for the people. But the industrialists are not on our side. What happened was that the only indus-trialists prepared to come are Chinese. The Europeans are not interested. Once abroad, we asked why are you paying such low wages? What they told us was that the products are cheap. When sold, they don't bring much profits. These industries are just feelers. If conditions are good, they say they will bring bigger industrialists. In this situation we are in difficulties. If we demand more, they will go – we will send them away. We need to take this seriously. When they say they will leave, they will do it. In Maritzburg, 600 workers recently lost their jobs. I also give an example of an article I read. We have countries around us that are poorer – like Zimbabwe. There was a government employee there who worked for more than two months before he received his salary. He was given two million in Zimbabwean money. But if we convert to rands, he only got R48. As the situation is, when indus-trialists are threatening to leave they really mean it. [In other places] they are paying less than in our country. People should be able to differentiate these issues [i.e. those that we can do something about from that we can-not]. Roads, sewerage, and water – these are issues for this municipality and we will see to it. I thank the community, even if they are shouting at us. They are hard on us so we will be able to work better in the future. (Closing speech by the Mayor of Ladysmith-Emnambithi at an open budget meeting held in C Section of Ezakheni, 6 July 1997, translated from isiZulu to English by one of the councillors)

This vivid statement of the vagaries of transnational capitalism, articu-lated through official discourses of neo-liberal globalization, underscores the embattled position in which ANC councillors found themselves.

Conclusions

A key tenet of neo-liberal orthodoxy is a sort of economic Darwinism in which export-oriented, low wage production forms the lowest set of rungs on a predetermined evolutionary ladder. In this model of universal con-vergence, economically 'backward' societies – or segments within them – must ascend the ladder in an orderly fashion, biting the bullet of low wages and oppressive labour conditions. The ladder itself is constituted through FDI, supposedly lured in by restraints on government spending, high interest rates and favourable exchange rates. In practice, as a number of critics have pointed out, foreign capital drawn in by these measures is far more likely to be volatile portfolio investment than directly productive investment. In addition, as the Brazilian activist and intellectual Roberto Unger observes, the neo-liberal project is unsustainable on its own terms, particularly in the context of profound inequalities:

> Carried to the hilt, it produces massive unemployment ... and
> accelerates internal dualism: the division of the country between a
> minority of beneficiaries and a majority of victims. More generally, it
> leaves government without the resources and capabilities with which
> to invest in either people or infrastructure. As social needs go unat-
> tended, bottlenecks in the production system begin to build up.
> Moreover, the draconian policy may prove self-defeating by sapping
> the very confidence it was designed to inspire, as domestic and for-
> eign investors begin to expect future political trouble from present
> social unrest. (Unger, 1998: 57)

One response has been a form of conservative social democracy that
argues for some degree of redistribution to contain social unrest and
enable neo-liberal project to move forward. Precisely this sort of revisionist neo-liberalism is now ascendant in the World Bank, in the guise
of 'social development' and 'social capital' (Hart, 2001).

The far greater challenge, posed with particular force and clarity by
Unger, is to refuse the Thatcherite dictum that 'there is no alternative' to
neo-liberalism in either its orthodox or revisionist form. In opposing the
economism that underpins neo-liberal discourses of globalization, a key
imperative – one that Gramsci (1971) made clear in his prison writings –
is to avoid swinging to the opposite extreme of voluntarist notions of
radical contingency and endlessly open possibilities.

By focusing on the relationship between production and the conditions of reproduction of labour power, I have called attention to the historically specific – and deeply gendered as well as racialized – processes
and practices that have shaped what are, in effect, sharply divergent
trajectories of labour-intensive forms of industrialization. I have also
shown how the East Asian 'cases' that neo-liberal proponents invoke in
support of their evolutionary claims are sharply at odds with the evolutionary model. Instead, they represent distinctively non-Western forms
of accumulation, effectively underwritten by massive redistributive
reforms driven originally by Mao's mobilization of the Chinese peas-
antry in the first part of the twentieth century. The broad significance of
these East Asian trajectories for contemporary South African debates is
that they force the history of racialized dispossession to the forefront of
attention, and illuminate its deep connections with the erosion of the
social wage across a wide swathe of South African society.

In the post-apartheid era, the social and spatial legacy of dispossession
is clearly evident in the profound tensions between production and the

conditions of reproduction of labour. These tensions, in turn, have become condensed within the so-called 'developmental local state'. At the same time, I have outlined how structural constraints inherited from the past are being reworked in significantly different ways in seemingly similar places. On one level, the participatory budget process that emerged in Ladysmith in the first phase of local government restructuring represents an example of precisely the sort of institutional innovation to which Unger calls attention. Yet we have also seen how broader configurations of political–economic forces imposed sharp constraints on these creative democratic impulses.

Pressures on the local state have intensified with the latest round of local government restructuring set in place at the end of 2000 that slashed the number of local authorities and vastly increased their size. These new demarcations effectively dissolve rural–urban boundaries, and create a space for desperately poor residents of rural ghettoes to lay claims on the severely limited resources of towns and small cities like Ladysmith and Newcastle. Whether or not their political inclusion in reformed local state structures translates into concrete material benefits that expand their life chances, and the forms of power relations – including gender – through which this does or does not happen, will define the character of South African society for generations to come.

The dissolution of rural–urban boundaries brought about by this latest round of local government restructuring underscores the salience and urgency of agrarian questions in this era of neo-liberal 'globalization'. There is now a large and growing body of literature that documents in compelling detail the limited and halting character of agrarian reform in the post-apartheid era, including the sharp disjuncture between a formal commitment to gender equality and the actual practices of land redistribution and tenure reform (e.g. Cousins, 2000; Walker, 2000).

Through a comparative focus on the connections between production and the conditions of reproduction of labour power, I have tried in this chapter to shed some new light on agrarian questions. The point of drawing on East Asian connections to dramatize the history of dispossession is *not* to propose a technocratic redistributive 'solution' to the evident limits of low wage export production in post-apartheid South Africa. Instead, these connections provide a means for delinking the land question from agriculture narrowly defined, and re-articulating it in terms of the social wage and broader livelihood imperatives.

At least in principle, a broadly based and historically grounded redefinition of the social wage holds open the possibility for organized labour to shift from a rearguard defence of diminishing, relatively well-paid, and predominantly male jobs to forging broader alliances and coalitions with other social forces – including those pressing for agrarian reform, as well as other movements such as those taking shape around HIV-AIDS – to engage both with macro-economic policy, and with locally and regionally specific conditions. As Hein Marais (1998) has pointed out, a strategy of connecting struggles in multiple arenas is not simply a matter of pitting 'civil society' against 'the state', but of recognizing how they define one another through constantly shifting engagements. Whether and how a strategy of linking what are commonly seen as separate rural and urban struggles under the rubric of the social wage could work in practice is likely to hinge crucially on understandings of gender not simply as 'women' but as defining elements in the exercise of power, deeply entwined with race, ethnicity and other dimensions of difference, as well as with the material conditions in which people find themselves.

Note

* Revised version of a paper prepared for the UNRISD Conference on Globalization, Export-Oriented Employment for Women and Social Policy, Bangkok, 27–28 October 2000. Revised November 2001.

References

Altman, M. (1995) 'Labour Regulation and Enterprise Strategies in the South African Clothing Industry', *Regional Studies*, 30(4): 387–99.

Ardington, L. (1984) 'Decentralized Industry, Poverty and Development in Rural KwaZulu', paper presented to the Carnegie Conference, Cape Town: University of Cape Town.

Bell, T. (1983) *The Growth and Structure of Manufacturing Employment in Natal*, Durban: Institute for Social and Economic Research, University of Durban-Westville, occasional paper no. 7.

Bell, T. (1986) 'The Role of Regional Policy in South Africa', *Journal of Southern African Studies*, 12(2): 276–92.

Bell, T. and N. Cataneo (1996) *Foreign Trade and Employment in South African Manufacturing*, Geneva: International Labour Office, occasional report no. 4, Employment and Training Department.

Bonnin, D., S. Hassim, M. Friedman, A. Todes and A. Vaughan (1991) 'State, Gender and Restructuring in South Africa in the 1980s', paper presented to the Conference on Women and Gender in Southern Africa, Durban: University of Natal.

Castells, M., Lee Goh and R. Y. Kwok (1990) *The Shek Kip Mei Syndrome: Economic Development and Public Housing in Hong Kong and Singapore*, London: Pion.

Cousins, B. (ed.) (2000) *At the Crossroads: Land and Agrarian Reform in South Africa in the 21st Century*, Bellville: University of the Western Cape, Programme on Land and Agrarian Studies.

Department of Constitutional Development (1998) *Case Studies on Local Economic Development and Poverty*, Pretoria: Government Printer.

Elson, D. and R. Pearson (1981) 'The Subordination of Women and the Internationalisation of Factory Production', in K. Young, C. Wolkowitz and R. McCullagh (eds) *Of Marriage and the Market: Women's Subordination Internationally and its Lessons*, London: Routledge, 18–40.

Fine, B. and Z. Rustomjee (1996) *The Political Economy of South Africa: From Minerals-Energy Complex to Industrialisation*, London: C. Hurst & Co.

Fine, B. and V. Padayachee (2000) 'A Sustainable Growth Path', in J. Coetzee, J. Graaff, F. Hendricks and G. Wood (eds) *Development: Theory, Policy, and Practice*, 269–281, Cape Town: Oxford.

Gramsci, A. (1971) *Selections from the Prison Notebooks*. Edited and translated by Q. Hoare and G. Nowell Smith, London: Lawrence & Wishart.

Harrison, P. and A. Todes (1996) 'Evaluation of the Regional Industrial Development Programme in KwaZulu-Natal', report to the Board for Regional Industrial Development, Durban: University of Natal.

Hart, G. (1995) ' "Clothes for Next to Nothing": Rethinking Global Competition', *South African Labour Bulletin*, 19(6): 41–7.

Hart, G. (1996a) *Global Connections: The Rise and Fall of a Taiwanese Production Network on the South African Periphery*, Working Paper, Institute of International Studies, Berkeley, CA: University of California.

Hart, G. (1996b) 'The Agrarian Question and Industrial Dispersal in South Africa: Agro Industrial Linkages Through Asian Lenses', *Journal of Peasant Studies*, 23(2/3): 245–77.

Hart, G. (1998) 'Multiple Trajectories: A Critique of Industrial Restructuring and the New Institutionalism', *Antipode*, 30(4): 333–56.

Hart, G. (2001) 'Development Debates in the 1990s: Promising Paths and Culs de Sac, *Progress in Human Geography*, 25(4): 605–14.

Hart, G. (2002) *Disabling Globalization: Places of Power in Post-Apartheid South Africa*. Berkeley: University of California Press; Pietermaritzburg: University of Natal Press.

Hart, G. and A. Todes (1997) 'Industrial Decentralisation Revisited', *Transformation*, 32: 31–53.

Hsing, Y. (1998) *Making Capitalism in China*, New York: Oxford University Press.

Hsiung, P. C. (1991) 'Class, Gender, and the Satellite Factory System in Taiwan', PhD dissertation, Los Angeles, CA: University of California.

Hsiung P. (1996) *Living Rooms as Factories: Class, Gender, and the Satellite Factory System in Taiwan*, Philadelphia: Temple University Press.

Jaffe, G. (1988) 'Commuter Labour: Changing Women's Lives, Changing Households', *Agenda*, 3: 3–9.

Jaffe, G. (1991) 'Female Commuters: A Study of their Position in the Workforce and the Effects of Household Work on Industrial Structures', paper presented at the Conference on Women and Gender in Southern Africa, Durban: University of Natal.

Joffe, A., D. Kaplan, R. Kaplinsky and D. Lewis (1995) *Improving Manufacturing Performance in South Africa: Report of the Industrial Strategy Project*, Cape Town: UCT Press.

Lee, C. K. (1995) 'Engendering the Worlds of Labor: Women Workers, Labor Markets, and Production Politics in the South China Economic Miracle', *American Sociological Review*, 60(3): 378–97.

Lund, F., J. Nicholson and C. Skinner (2000) *Street Trading*, Durban: School of Development Studies, University of Natal.

Macro-Economic Research Group (MERG) (1993) *Making Democracy Work: A Framework for Macro-Economic Policy in South Africa*, Cape Town: Centre for Development Studies, University of the Western Cape.

Marais, H. (1998) *South Africa: Limits to Change*, New York: McMillan.

Mokate, R. (2000) 'Macro-Economic Context', in J. May (ed.) *Poverty and Inequality in South Africa: Meeting the Challenge*, Cape Town: David Philip, 51–71.

Murray, C. (1988) 'Displaced Urbanization', in J. Lonsdale (ed). *South Africa in Question*, Chapter 3, London: James Currey.

Olver, C. (1998) 'Metropolitan Government for the 21st Century', *Development Southern Africa*, 15(2): 289–91.

Ong, A. (1987) *Spirits of Resistance and Capitalist Discipline: Factory Women in Malaysia*, Albany: State University of New York Press.

Ong, A. (1991) 'The Gender and Labor Politics of Postmodernity', *Annual Review of Anthropology*, 20: 279–309.

Pickles, J. (1991) 'Industrial Restructuring, Peripheral Industrialization, and Rural Development in South Africa', *Antipode*, 23(1): 68–91.

Pickles, J. and J. Wood (1989) 'Taiwanese Investment in South Africa', *African Affairs*, 88: 507–28.

Platzky, L. and C. Walker (1985) *The Surplus People: Forced Removals in South Africa*, Johannesburg: Ravan Press.

Platzky, L. (1995) 'The Development Impact of South Africa's Industrial Location Policies: An Unforeseen Legacy', PhD dissertation, The Hague: Institute of Social Studies.

Posel, D. and A. Todes (1995) 'The Shift to Female Labour in KwaZulu-Natal', *South African Journal of Economics*, 63(2): 225–46.

Posel, D., M. Friedman and A. Todes (1993) 'The Unrecorded Categories: Women and Gender in the Economy of Region E', report prepared for 'Economic Development for Region E', Durban: Natal Regional Advisory Committee.

Pudifin, C. and S. Ward (1986) 'Gender and Decentralisation in Isithebe', Masters thesis in Town and Regional Planning, Durban: University of Natal.

Simkins, C. (1983) *Four Essays on the Past, Present, and Possible Future Distribution of the Black Population of South Africa*, Cape Town: Southern Africa Labour and Development Research Unit, University of Cape Town.

Swilling, M., W. Cobbett and R. Hunter (1991) 'Finance, Electricity Costs, and the Rent Boycott', in M. Swilling, R. Humphries and K. Shubane (eds) *Apartheid City in Transition*, Oxford: Oxford University Press, 174–96.

Tomlinson, R. and M. Addleson (eds) (1987) *Regional Restructuring under Apartheid: Urban and Regional Policies in Contemporary South Africa*, Johannesburg: Ravan Press.

Todes, A. (1997) 'Restructuring, Migration and Regional Policy in South Africa: The Case of Newcastle', PhD dissertation, University of Natal, Durban.

Unger, R. M. (1998) *Democracy Realized: The Progressive Alternative*, London: Verso Press.

Urban Foundation (1990) *Regional Development Reconsidered*, Johannesburg: Policies for New Urban Futures Series, no. 2.

Valodia, I. (2000) 'Economic Policy and Women's Work in South Africa', paper presented to the Conference of the International Association for Feminist Economics, Istanbul.

Walker, C. (2000) 'Agrarian Change, Gender, and Land Reform: South African Case Study', Geneva: UNRISD.

Whiteford, A. and D. van Seventer (1999) *Winners and Losers: South Africa's Changing Income Distribution in the 1990s*, Menlo Park: WEFA Southern Africa.

Wolpe, H. (1995) 'The Uneven Transition from Apartheid in South Africa', *Transformation* 27: 88–101.

Index

accidents, 49, 80, 88n2, 100, 131, 170
accountability, 119
Africa Growth and Opportunity
    Act, 188
African National Congress (ANC), 22,
    195, 212, 217, 219–20, 221, 222
agriculture
    China, 71–2, 76, 210
    Korea, 35, 36
    Mauritius, 176
    South Africa, 211, 214, 224
    Taiwan, 210
Altman, M., 199
Anand, Harjit S., 108
anarcho-syndicalism, 134
ANC see African National Congress
apartheid, 193, 194, 195–6, 199–200,
    204, 212, 219
Asian financial crisis
    cause of, 57n5
    China, 87
    financial liberalization, 57n5, n7
    Korea, 8, 10, 23, 31, 33, 34–5,
        41–5, 47
    manufacturing employment
        trends, 97
assembly line work
    China, 73, 75–6, 77–81, 82
    feminization of work, 93
    maquiladoras, 4, 16, 133, 135–7,
        140–50, 152n17, n20
    see also factory work; manufacturing

Bangladesh
    migrant workers in Mauritius,
        18, 173
    women's wages, 99
bantustans, 193, 195–6, 197, 200,
    202, 219
Battersby Report (1998), 172
beedi industry, 109
Bell, Trevor, 200, 202, 214
Berenger, Paul, 169

border industrialization policies
    Mexico, 135
    South Africa, 196
Botha, P. W., 196, 199
Brachet-Márquez, Viviane, 14–17,
    126–58
Bunwaree, Sheila, 17–19, 159–92

capital, 121–2
capital goods, 144, 145–8, 149, 150,
    152n24, 153n27
'care' work, 7
    Korea, 53
    Mexico, 16, 140
    see also unpaid family/household
        work
Carrillo, Jorge, 147
Castells, Manuel, 210
casual work
    India, 105
    Philippines, 101
    see also daily-based workers;
        informal employment;
        temporary work
Cataneo, N., 214
chaebols, 8, 10, 32, 33, 42, 47, 58n9
Chang, Ha-joon, 4, 26n6, 33
child support, 132
child-care provision
    burden falling on girl children, 93
    Korea, 47, 53
    Mauritius, 179
    Mexico, 16, 132–3, 140, 141,
        147–8, 150
Chile, home-based work, 102
China, 7–8, 12–14, 23, 24, 67–90
    agrarian reforms, 210
    competition with Taiwanese
        industrialists in South Africa,
        210, 211
    currency and banking, 26n10
    economic reforms, 13, 69, 70, 71,
        72, 84, 87

229